Jeri Woon.

7: II : 59:

THE IRISH WRITERS

THE
IRISH WRITERS

1880–1940

★

LITERATURE UNDER PARNELL'S STAR

by

Herbert Howarth

SALISBURY SQUARE · LONDON

MADE AND PRINTED IN GREAT BRITAIN
BY C. TINLING AND COMPANY LIMITED,
LIVERPOOL, LONDON AND PRESCOT.

CONTENTS

WITH THANKS TO

H. A.

and

A. B. J. P.

AT FIVE O'CLOCK IN THE AFTERNOON

ACKNOWLEDGMENTS

THIS book is meant primarily for the general reader of literature, though I hope it will have some interest for the specialist in Anglo-Irish literature too. It is concerned with the six writers, Moore, Lady Gregory, Yeats, AE, Synge, and Joyce, in relation to the quick advance of Irish nationalism during their time and its political and social accomplishment. In particular, it considers how they reacted to Parnell's fall, and how they modified and developed the legend of Parnell in their work.

The importance of Parnell in Joyce's picture of his country has long been known. His early books declared it; and a number of American scholars, probing beneath his explicit statements, have illuminated his feelings for the dead "Chief". I am only following in their wake (the right word in this context) and feel indebted to them, especially to Richard Kain and Marvin Magalaner, whose *Joyce: the Man, the Work, the Reputation* luckily came into my hands at an early stage of the drafting. (I elatedly read the galleys of their book one night in the Joycean setting of the Victorian parlour of a Bristol railway hotel). But I have tried to go further than other critics—with the exception of Richard Ellmann —have yet done, by examining the writers preceding Joyce, the men and women of the central literary movement, to see whether they were as decisively affected as he was by the crisis of 1890-1 and as interested in the mythology which smoked from it.

During four years of work I have incurred many obligations, and there may be friends or institutions whose help I omit to acknowledge in this paragraph or elsewhere in these pages, and whose pardon I ask. I owe most to four American universities: Michigan, Pittsburgh, Montana State, and Minnesota. The Chairmen and members of their Departments of English have been the best of hosts, and their Librarians have helped a troublesome enquirer with books and microfilm. And I would like to thank : Mr. Charles Abbott for hospitality at his home and at the Lockwood Memorial Library, University of Buffalo; Dr.

ix

ACKNOWLEDGMENTS

Chandler B. Beall, editor of *Comparative Literature*, University of Oregon, for his interest and encouragement; Dr. Malcolm Brown of the University of Washington, Seattle, for criticism of the chapter on Moore; Mr. Alan Denson, who sent me literally thousands of words of correspondence on the book and whose researches on AE, which he made available before their publication, I envy; Mrs. Mary B. Clapp of Missoula, Montana, for suggestions and information; Dr. Filippo Donini and the Cultural Division of the Italian Embassy in New York for microfilm of Joyce's *Piccolo della Sera* articles; Mrs. Jean Frampton who typed a chaotic manuscript with wonderful skill; my daughter Lorenka for newspaper research at Colindale; Dr. J. Mitchell Morse of Pennsylvania State University, who welcomed three of my family to a memorable week-end of Joycean conversation and who criticised Chapters V, VI, and VII; Dr. Lawrence Clark Powell of the University of California, Los Angeles, for a Yeats–Olivia talk (will he remember it?) as he drove along the coast, and for access next day to the Nineties shelves of the William Andrews Clark Memorial Library; Dr. Joseph Prescott of Wayne State University, whose devotion to Joyce taught me much, who first pointed me to the reading of Magalaner and Kain, and who criticised Chapters I and II, (and who brought three fellow-experts on Irish literature—Kain, Harry Campbell, and Vivien Mercier—to see us at Madison, Wisconsin, and we talked Yeats and Joyce till the early morning); Mr. Geoffrey Robinson of the Rockliff Publishing Corporation for his gentle and judicious editorial guidance; Dr. Robert Stange of the University of Minnesota for his criticism of Chapters II and III; Dr. Simon Yudkin for a kind communication on a medical point; the secretarial staff of the Department of Economics at the University of Wisconsin, who showed me the Irish pictures in their care; and my wife for much coffee and some curious erudition.

HERBERT HOWARTH

CHAPTER I

A MYTH AND A MOVEMENT

CAPTAIN O'SHEA filed divorce proceedings against his wife, citing Parnell as co-respondent, on December 24th, 1889. The case came into court on November 15th, 1890, and the divorce was granted on November 17th. In Dublin on November 18th the National League pledged itself to stand by Parnell. On November 25th the Irish Parliamentary Party gave him its vote of confidence. But a day later the Party met again, gravely disturbed, more than half the members ready to change their minds. A debate raged until December 6th, when Parnell was left with twenty-six followers while forty-four opponents moved to another room and declared his chairmanship terminated.

What caused the change of heart of November 26th? It is curious to correlate the historical record with the legend of Parnell's fall as it developed among the Irish—a legend of an Irish disgrace, which coloured their literature for fifty years. To an English reader the record spells an English disgrace, only a little less striking than the hounding of Oscar Wilde a few years later. When Parnell's association with Mrs. O'Shea was made public in the divorce court, the dominant nonconformist section of the English Liberal Party raised a clamour against him. The National Liberal Federation, meeting at Sheffield, decided that "if Parnell is allowed to remain as a leader of the Irish party, all further co-operation between them and the English Liberals must be at an end". Mr. Gladstone, whose private opinion on the moral question may have been more individual, acted in accordance with his party's wishes, and drew up a letter notifying the Irish that they could not rely on him to pursue his programme for Irish Home Rule if Mr. Parnell continued to be their chief.

Now begins the Irish participation in the ignominy of the affair. Gladstone's notification had not been received when the Irish members met on November 25th. They had cast their vote for Parnell before it was communicated. They heard of it almost as soon as they left the Committee-Room; and, published in the Press by Cabinet decision, it precipitated the renewed meeting next day. Many of his party now urged Parnell to withdraw. They judged that step to be a political necessity. For Home Rule seemed, with Gladstone's support, to be a certainty in the reasonably near future. Without Gladstone's support Home Rule might be postponed indefinitely. Parnell's retort, elaborated in a manifesto to the Irish people, was that Gladstonian Home Rule was a degree of autonomy so pared down as to be almost worthless. Beneath this correct but somewhat rationalising argument lay two deeper considerations determining his refusal to capitulate. Temperamentally it was impossible for him to bow to collective opinion; he conducted politics despotically; in his dealings with his country, his Parliamentary group, and his sweetheart alike, he insisted on being a king; he lived what Yeats, writing with his example in view, later recommended to every leader, a Shakespearian contempt for the crowd. Politically he saw that if the Irish accepted England's dictation of their choice of leader, they were foreswearing the independence they claimed, and that if Gladstone judged it fitting to dictate that choice he did not really honour or understand the independence for which he pretended concern. In bowing to the Liberal Party's threat, the forty-four Seceders affronted the dictum of O'Leary, that there are some things a man may not do to save a nation.

At least there *were* arguments of national interest, however insufficient, prompting the men in the Committee-Room. The same thing cannot be said in defence of the violent agitation against Parnell that swept Ireland during the next nine months. A moral frenzy was fomented not in the interests of the nation, but in the interests of the structure of society and the preservation of orthodoxy. Cardinal Manning had been shocked by the terms of Parnell's public manifesto. He deemed him carried away by arrogance. "If Parnell goes to Ireland", he wrote to Gladstone, "the issue will be between dangerous politics and the faith of Ireland." He had heard the voice of a man who was prepared to wreck every authority in order to establish his own. It was not because Parnell was Protestant that he feared his success, but because he was autocratic and personalist. On December 3rd he published a directive against him. That may have finally determined the outcome of the struggle in the Westminster Committee-Room; it certainly determined the character of the revulsion against Parnell and his candidates in the Irish country districts; and the interpretation of the directive by many local clergy intensified the bitterness and violence. There were devoted Catholics who resisted the collective feelings of their faith, and remained loyal to the Chief. Katharine Tynan was one of them, so was her father; in *Twenty-Five Years* she had given a glimpse of the problems and the integrity of the Catholic Parnellites. By and large the townships of Ireland, where there was sophistication and intellect, stood by Parnell. But the countryside manifested an anger typical of the hostility of the common man for his own fleshly sins, a hostility which he can indulge when they are disclosed in others; the name of Kitty O'Shea was bandied in abuse and obscene verse to destroy the dignity of Parnell; the "mud-cabin vote" swung against his candidates; physical violence was offered to his supporters. Parnell had appealed to his followers: "Do not throw me to the wolves." "They did not throw him to the English wolves," commented James Joyce in the *Piccolo della Sera* twenty years later, "they tore him to pieces themselves."

★

Parnell was dead at the end of ten months' campaigning against the determination to oust him. His body was brought from Brighton to Dublin for burial on October 10th, 1891. When the coffin reached Westland Row before dawn thousands of men and women were already waiting for it. It was taken from a deal case—"which was thrown aside", writes St. John Ervine, "but, as it fell, crowds seized it and tore it into fragments that they might have even that as a relic of him"—and carried to City Hall. It lay there under O'Connell's statue through a wet and stormy morning and noon, while 30,000 people filed past and plucked an ivy-leaf from it.

The procession moved to the cemetery in the afternoon. The storm was declining. Katharine Tynan has described the scene. She says that the sky over the grave had cleared, and that the stars were looking out of a quiet green and gold space. When the coffin was lowered into the pit, a woman shrieked and there was a second's confusion. As it touched earth, a meteor sailed across the clearing and fell. "He had omens and portents to the end", she wrote.

Many spectators saw, or as time passed believed they had seen, the portents. Standish O'Grady said: "I state a fact—it was witnessed by thousands. While his followers were committing Charles Parnell's remains to the earth, the sky was bright with strange lights and flames. . . . Those flames recall to my memory what is told of similar phenomena, said to have been witnessed when tidings of the death of St. Columba overran the northwest of Europe."

★

Irish writers slowly recognised Parnell's death as the source of the creation of the Irish Republic. Out of the public passions and the ignominy that caused his death a myth flared up that produced the Rising of 1916 and the quick subsequent events: revolution, civil war, and the Republic. There had been a superiority in Parnell that is not easy to grasp when, so many years later, one reads the biographies. His aloofness, his very despotism, had made men ready to worship him. His followers invested him with the status of a prophet. Those who hated him most after the divorce proceedings hated him because they could not bear their prophet to be less than immaculate. The Irish committed the

4

crucial act of killing their prophet, and the guilt, the desire to purify the guilt, the belief that his sacrifice sanctified, the belief that sacrifice assures rebirth, gave them irresistible vigour in the next generation.

The Irish Parliamentary Party which had thrown him over in order to survive, survived pointlessly when it had thrown him over. It ceased to matter, because it no longer had a man of stature directing it, because it despised itself for having abandoned him, because the ardent young despised it. The young gradually integrated his memory into their hopes of an ancient, powerfully imaginative, physically powerful and audacious Ireland. A literary movement found symbols and a language for their dream. The literary movement thereby inflamed—half-consciously, for it doubted the value of dynamite—the militant movement. Events proved, as always, that, much as one might wish otherwise, militancy prevails and obtains what words and wisdom alone do not. Parnell was reborn in the intransigent underground from which he had, by class, temperament, and policy, stood apart.

MESSIANISM

Yeats had published the *Wanderings of Oisin*, in which the Fenians are contrasted with the priests, in 1889. Celtic legend, and a challengingly militant voice, are present in it. The new literary movement pre-dated the Parnell crash. Yeats and his friends, poets and painters and sculptors of his own age, were conscious in the 'eighties that an earlier generation of Irish writers had made it their business to support the Irish nationalist movement with poetry and with a social and political philosophy. By 1889 they had already set out to continue the work of Davies, Mangan, and Ferguson—to continue and to deepen it, for they felt that, Mangan's best poetry apart, it had been too superficial a reflection of the political movement, and that it must establish more subtle values and humanise the political movement. What Parnell's death immediately did for the writers and artists, besides raising their passions, was to raise their sense of responsibility, indicate emphatically the necessity for Irish self-criticism; and because there were men and women looking for guidance in the perplexity that followed the 1891 schism, it multiplied their audience.

The beliefs and the myths that consolidated in Irish imagining and Irish writing after Parnell's death, were not new. They had been eddying among the people for at least a century. But the fall and death and portentous burial of the Chief pulled them to a focus. They had been filtering into literature as something attractive but scarcely understood. Now the poets seized on them deliberately.

The essence of these beliefs was Messianic. Among the oppressed, Messianism is always strong. Ireland had been an occupied land, a land exploited, for 700 years. Its peasants were among the poorest in Western Europe. For a point of comparison we have to think of Portugal and Spain, perhaps of Morocco or pre-Kemalist Turkey, or Egypt. In these countries the poor had long been enfolded within the close organisation of Catholicism or Islam. They were faithfully orthodox, but beneath the orthodoxy they moved to the rhythm of more primitive convictions, which lived in their stories, proverbs and parables, and songs. The oppressed wait for a Messiah to come to redeem them—literally to bring them food and raiment and consolation. The Irish oppressed were more than once ready to identify a political leader with Him. How quickly they gave the nineteenth-century leaders such names as the Counsellor, the Agitator, the Liberator.

There was a period when they seemed to recognise Him in O'Connell. While compiling *Mr. Gregory's Letter-Box*, Lady Gregory met an old peasant on a mountain pass, fell into talk with him about politics. He told her this story, which she included in the book, about O'Connell's father:

> O'Connell was a grand man, and whatever cause he took in hand it was as good as won. But what wonder. He was the gift of God.
> His father was a rich man, and one day he was out walking he took notice of a house that was being built. Well, a week

later he passed by the same place, and he saw the walls of the house were no higher than before. So he asked the reason, and he was told it was a priest that was building it, and he hadn't the money to go on with.

So a few days after, he went to the priest's house, and he asked was this true, and the priest said it was. So, says O'Connell, "Would you pay the money back to the man that 'ud lend it to you?" "I would", said the priest. So with that O'Connell gave him the money that was wanting, 500 *l.*, for it was a very grand house.

Well, after some time the priest came to O'Connell's house, and he found only the wife at home. So, says he, "I have some money that Himself lent me". But he never had told his wife of what he had done, so she knew nothing about it; and says she, "Don't be troubling yourself about it, he'll bestow it on you." "Well", says the priest, "I'll go away now, and I'll come back again."

So when O'Connell came in, the wife told him all that had happened, and how a priest had come, saying he owed him money, and how she said he'd bestow it on him. "Well," said O'Connell, "if you said I'd bestow it, I'll bestow it." And so he did. Then the priest said "Have you any children?" "Ne'er a child", said O'Connell. "Well, then, you'll have one", said he, and that day nine months their young son was born. So what wonder if he was inspired, being as he was the gift of God."

As a young Catholic lawyer defending the poor, O'Connell worked with inspiration and inspired the watching public. The hopes that he attracted were never wholly forgotten, not even after his failure of 1843. In that year it seemed to the younger men that he declined the opportunity to lead a rebellion against England—declined, that means, the violence which must precede the millennium. After that his power ebbed away from him. New leaders were sought, new Messianic candidates; but even a false Messiah is never forgotten, if his moment has been radiant. Half a century after O'Connell's best days, Yeats read of him, as we shall see, and responded to the story with emulation. More than half a century later Lady Gregory transcribed the legend of his birth from the old peasant.

Only a few years after that she was transcribing evidence of the incorporation of Parnell into the popular mythology. At Spiddal on Galway Bay she listened to an old man addressing a crowd with urgent gestures. " 'Tha se beo, tha se beo'—'he is living, he is living', I heard him say over and over again. I asked what he was saying and was told: 'He says that Parnell is alive yet'." The Irish imagination was hungry for a leader like Christ or Charlemagne or Barbarossa—a hero whose death is only similitude, who rises again, who will come, a Golem, from his covert when his people need him. Joyce, objectively recording the mind of Dublin, said as much:

> Somewhere imperceptibly he would hear and somehow reluctantly, suncompelled, obey the summons of recall. Whence, disappearing from the constellation of the Northern Crown he would somehow reappear reborn above delta in the constellation of Cassiopeia and after incalculable eons of peregrination return an estranged avenger, a wreaker of justice on malefactors, a dark crusader, a sleeper awakened, with financial resources (by supposition) surpassing those of Rothschild or of the silver king.

The hopes and torments of Ireland, and the legends that promised a metamorphosis, belonged to the poor. They took effect, were translated into action, when they seeped to the better-off and the educated. They filtered into sheltered homes through the servants, with whom the education of the children lay. The nurses had the greatest advantage. Perhaps no single influence ate so deep into the minds of the politicians and writers of Ireland as the stories of their nurses, told them at the most impressionable age. Lady Gregory's old Catholic nurse, Mary Sheridan, brought the traditions of '98 and the anecdotes and language of the people, their passion and insight, to the Protestant home at Roxborough. Bernard Shaw had an old nurse, who equally stimulated his sense of justice though not equally successfully his national sentiment. At Parnell's home, Avondale, Ireland's history penetrated through the housekeeper and her husband who served at the gate. Katharine Tynan writes:

> Old Gaffney at the gate lodge at Avondale was old enough to remember the Rebellion. He used to tell how a rebel named Byrne was flogged from the mill to the old sentry-box in Rathdrum by the orders of a savage named Colonel Yeo. How this gallant gentleman ordered the lashes to be inflicted on the front part of the body instead of the back; how the bowels protruded as the man ran stumbling and shrieking, "For the love of God have mercy on me, Colonel Yeo"; how the savagery was not abated till he died.
>
> In this story told by old Gaffney, the gatekeeper at Avondale, to the growing boy—Mr. Parnell used to tell it without apparent emotion—lay the genesis of a great Irish rebel.

These atrocious or hungry memories ferment with the antique underground religion of the peasants, and the result is, obviously, hatred of the oppressor, but also a readiness to endure the chaos of revolution, and a sharp vision of a sheer Utopia that the revolution supposedly will confer. While it is recognised that a military struggle will be destructive, the temper with which it is faced is sanguine. The Messiah seems to walk ahead: on him the agony centres, through him the obstacles drop apart. By a natural development the most urgently-dedicated men and women have hours when they dream that they may be chosen for the Messianic sacrifice.

As they listened to their nurses, those mid-nineteenth-century children glimpsed, through the window or between the bars of a gate or peering from a swaying carriage, certain typical characters and scenes, which, printed on their minds, became inseparable from their sense of their land and its problems and destiny. Such was the image of the duelling landlords, that craggy and violent image shared by Yeats and Moore. A man who has killed all his

9

opponents, whose appetite for fighting is still insatiable, gallops down a road. The country-folk are shocked by his history and are determined to have no more of it. They block his passage with the priest at their head. It seems they have him coralled, but he knows their passions better than the Father, and with a rough joke he topples their patriotism on to his side—"Now lads, which will ye choose, the Mayo cock or the Galway cock?" and they break ranks with a cheer and he rides past to the kill. Such, again, is the image of the Irish tinkers and their promiscuous marriages. Lady Gregory was struck by the reminiscence of an old lady who, years earlier, had sat on a wall at Kilkenny and had seen the tinkers at their annual rally bartering wives with one another—"yes, they did so, it was their custom . . . and the children went away with the women."

The minds that made the Irish literary movement, the Irish Risorgimento, were shaped at the earliest age by the tradition of the rebellion and the hopes of a Messiah and interpenetrated by images like these. When they grew older, they consciously acquired cognate material and grafted it on to the original stem. At first they gathered it because they undertook activities that brought them into touch with the people, like Lady Gregory undertaking her charitable round among her tenantry. Then, beginning with Yeats, they acquired it by deliberate seeking.

LITERARY MESSIANISM

The outburst of theosophical discussion among the Dublin art students in 1885 has become a commonplace of literary history. Enquiring into esoterica as part of their search for a differentiating power, Yeats and AE learned to connect the legends of rural Ireland with a central body of underground tradition.

It seemed to AE in retrospect that one of the most influential books they met in their explorations of the next five years was Madame Blavatsky's *Secret Doctrine*. However crude the presentation, they found there that the drifting hopes of Ireland were part of a widespread faith. The promise of a Messiah; the revolutionary context of His coming; the belief, which Fenians like John

Mitchel and James Stephens had held, that oppressed peoples become free during an international conflagration—these hopes of the Irish could be traced in esoteric literature. Let us see Yeats making the discovery in one among the curious books he opened. George Rodway of London was publishing titles concerned with theosophy and the antiquarianism which was the forerunner of anthropology. His 1887 list included *The Real History of the Rosicrucians* by Arthur Edward Waite. The trend of the book was not particularly favourable to the devotees of secret cults, but Yeats' eye picked out the passages that suited his inclinations. At the beginning of Chapter II he found a short account of the expectation of a Messiah early in the seventeenth century and of the earlier prophecies of Paracelsus, notably his declaration that the comet of 1572 was "the sign and harbinger of the approaching revolution", and his promise in his *Treatise of Metals* that a discovery would be opened to the world by "a marvellous being . . . who as yet lives not". These passages stimulated his memories of childhood hearsay and traditional patter noted during his wanderings or when gathering folk-lore in libraries.

At the same date AE was saying in correspondence with Carrie Rea: "I think the world is striding greatly into the light, let us go with it".* It is a theosophical transcription of the nine-teenth-century belief in progress, but it is more, a first vague translation of the peasant legends of the Messiah into the inter-national prophecy of the millennium.

By 1889 Yeats was studying Blake with Edwin Ellis in prepara-tion for their work of 1893. In the Prophetic Books he found the New Jerusalem, the dramatic image which the Reformation adepts, whom he had already met in Waite, had handed down from the Middle Ages, and which Blake, on receiving it from them, had transformed. Writing from the excitement of the American war of liberation and the French tumult, Blake had sharpened religious prophecy with the accents of the revolution-ary; on the ancient tradition that the Messiah or Golem will walk

*See *Letters from AE*, edited by Alan Denson, Abelard-Schumann, London and New York.

to accomplishment through ruin he had impressed the interpretation of freedom through militant insurrection. So satisfied with this doctrine and its poetry that he convinced himself Blake was Irish, Yeats began to think of Ireland's freedom coming as part of the rebirth of all the nations in a violent conflict. He hastened his study of Irish folk-lore with an enhanced sensitivity to the Messianic suggestions in it. He came across a prediction ("all over Ireland", he says in his unreliable, blarneying way) "of a coming rout of the enemies of Ireland, in a certain Valley of the Black Pig". This he understood both as a promise for Ireland—she will scatter her enemies and be free—and as a promise to the world—the battle will be the world conflagration anciently foretold.

The rational and humane side of the Irish thinkers sometimes blenched at the Armageddon image, but they overcame their doubts by reminding themselves of the sufferings of Ireland unliberated. When John Mitchel, a generation earlier, had been rebuked by his Doppelgänger:* "And, for the *chance* of getting Ireland severed from Britain in the dreadful *melée*, do you desire to see all Europe and America plunged in desperate war?" he had replied that he would rather war than a repetition of the Irish famine of the 'forties and had cited an Armageddon image from the Old Testament. Richard Ellmann has shown in *Yeats: the Man and the Masks* that between 1893 and 1896 Yeats was talking a great deal about the war in which the world would fall apart. The first reference in the *Letters*, edited by Allan Wade, shows a tinge of the ambivalence of Mitchel's inner colloquy. Dated December 1895, it is an enquiry to the actress Florence Farr—in her capacity as a higher member of the Order of the Golden Dawn—whether the Venezuelan crisis, over which the Press speculated that America might go to war, means that "the magical armageddon has begun at last". If so, he goes on, "The war would fulfil the prophets and especially the prophetic vision I had long ago with the Mathers's, and so would be for the glory of God,

*John Mitchel, *Jail Journal. Original edition with a continuation* . . . Gill, Dublin, and Unwin, London, 1913, p.80.

but what a dusk of the nations it would be!" He assimilated the problem into a poem, *The Valley of the Black Pig*, published in the *Savoy*, April, 1896:

> The dews drop slowly and dreams gather: unknown spears
> Suddenly hurtle before my dream awakened eyes,
> And then the clash of fallen horsemen and the cries
> Of unknown perishing armies beat about my ears. . . .

Yeats was less sure than AE that the outcome of the conflagration must be light and a universal settlement. Sometimes he was content to see the final battle as the consecration of darkness. In 1902 he was talking to a poor woman of Sligo, a soldier's widow: "And presently our talk of war shifted, as it had a way of doing, to the battle of the Black Pig, which seems to her a battle between Ireland and England, but to me an Armageddon which shall quench all things in the Ancestral Darkness again."

Ellmann has shown how the expectation of the Messiah flared up in 1896. In June that year AE wrote to Yeats: "You remember my writing to you about the awakening of the ancient fires which I knew about. Well it has been confirmed and we are told to publish it. *The Gods have returned to Eri* and have centred themselves in the sacred mountains and blow the fires through the Country. They have been seen by several in a vision . . . I believe profoundly that a new Avatar is about to appear and in all spheres the forerunners go before him to prepare. . . ." Undeterred by the cacophonous prose of this announcement, Yeats, who received it in London, was enthusiastic. It became a matter of urgency for him to share the revelation. He travelled to Ireland with Arthur Symons that summer. One night at Edward Martyn's estate, Tillyra, he had a vision. Having invoked the spirits of the moon, he saw, between sleeping and waking, "a beautiful woman firing an arrow among the stars". The same woman, a "symbolic Diana", appeared that same night to Symons, his fellow-guest. William Sharp, a letter soon told him, had also about that time seen an arrow shot into the sky, piercing a faun's heart. Also, a stranger's child had dreamed of a man shooting at a star with a gun and bringing it down, whereupon it lay in a cradle.

The barb transfixed Yeats' imagination and remained embedded there for the rest of his life. He published the evidence of the coincidental visions and dreams a generation later in *The Trembling of the Veil*. By then he was conscious of what he wanted to prove by it. Certain modifications crept in, as compared with the above account (which is based on a letter to William Sharp, August 1896). He no longer said that the woman fired her arrow "among the stars", but at a star, and reported the presence of a galloping centaur: "I saw between sleeping and waking, as in a kinemato-graph, a galloping centaur, and a moment later a naked woman of incredible beauty, standing upon a pedestal and shooting an arrow at a star." Of the centaur I shall write in the chapter on Yeats. The immediate point is that three elements are configured with it in the vision: the star of Bethlehem; the comet of 1572 on which Paracelsus had hinged his prophecy of a modern Messiah; the lights that flamed over Parnell's grave. We know that this last element is involved, because Yeats says so in a poem of the 'thirties, *Parnell's Funeral*, using there the vision of 1896 and the comparative material as presented in *The Trembling of the Veil*:

> Under the Great Comedian's tomb the crowd.
> A bundle of tempestuous cloud is blown
> About the sky; where that is clear of cloud
> Brightness remains; a brighter star shoots down;
> What shudders run through all that animal blood?
> What is this sacrifice? Can someone there
> Recall the Cretan barb that pierced a star?
>
> Rich foliage that the starlight glittered through,
> A frenzied crowd, and where the branches sprang
> A beautiful seated boy; a sacred bow;
> A woman, and an arrow on a string;
> A pierced boy, image of a star laid low.
> That woman, the Great Mother imaging,
> Cut out his heart. Some master of design
> Stamped boy and tree upon Sicilian coin.

The imagery and the matted anthropological references of the second stanza are clarified by the notes to *The Trembling of the Veil*. There we find that, advised by "a man learned in East-Mediterranean Antiquities" (whose name he, typically, can no longer remember or trace), Yeats understands the salient images of his vision as follows: the shot star is the sun with its annual death and rebirth (and we know from other work of his that he regards the sun as symbol of the kingly mind); it is also Balder "who is shot to death that is life by means of a sprig or arrow of mistletoe"; the woman who shot the arrow is "the Mother-Goddess, whose representative priestess shot the arrow at the child whose sacrificial death symbolised the death and resurrection of the Tree-spirit, or Apollo"; the heart is taken, in an ancient festival, from the body of the sacrificed child and placed in the chest-cavity of the figure that is to be the child reborn; the arrow is "a sign of Initiation and Rebirth".

This is Yeats' reading in old age of the lights in the Dublin sky in the fall of 1891. The dropping meteor over Parnell's grave had been shot down by the Mother-Goddess. The third stanza of the poem unequivocally identifies Parnell's fate in Ireland with the archetypal situation. The Irish political martyrs of a century earlier, Emmet, Fitzgerald, Wolfe Tone, had been murdered by "strangers", the occupying British—

> But popular rage,
> *Hysterica passio* dragged this quarry down.
> None shared our guilt; nor did we play a part
> Upon a painted stage when we devoured his heart.

Three statements are hurled by Irish poet at Irish reader (that is the meaning of "we"): the death of Parnell was an Irish act, an all-impassioned Irish act; it was the sacrifice of the leader in his role as Balder the beautiful; the sacrifice postulates rebirth, or in the Irish context a national rejuvenation, when the heart of the sacrificed hero is eaten. Then comes a terrible last verse disowning these very statements. That last verse, drenched with bitterness after a lifetime's struggle, need not concern us yet.

The immediate point is this: enquiry into Irish history and legend and into analogues, endless spiritual exercises, endless involvement in the rough fury of Irish living, led Yeats to collate the scattered drifting prophecies of a Messiah and believe that they could be, or should have been, fulfilled in a birth linked with the national sacrifice of Parnell. He had worked slowly—it is striking how very slowly—to that conclusion. But it was clear to him in old age that the thinking of his early and middle years had already pre-supposed it.

WRITERS AS FORERUNNERS—THE SACRED BOOK

Ellmann and Jeffares have described how Yeats set himself, after the exchange with AE in 1896, to inaugurate a cult and a ritual for the "forerunners". The Irish writers were to be evangelists. In fact, the image of John the Baptist became a favourite among all the writers. George Moore had a natural bent to the imitation of the Evangelist. At the warmest point of his relations with Yeats, after they had collaborated for only a short time, he professed himself unworthy to unlatch his shoes. Later his view modified, and for him, as for each of the writers in turn, there came a moment when he wondered whether Parnell's spirit had passed into his own person. There is, in fact, a double character to the prophesying (the endless prophesying that makes the record of Irish nationalism in these years as hectic as the Old Testament). Sometimes literature and journalism prophesy a leader of the State, and often enough writers seem willing to take on this practical role. Sometimes they more modestly write as if an unknown man will appear as leader, and they, favoured scribes who prepared the way for him, will recognise him, interpret him, and write his scriptures. The chapters that follow will document these conflicting claims. For the moment it may be useful to show how the writers talked about the writing of a sacred book. A conversation recorded by Moore in *Hail and Farewell* allows us to hear some of them speculating. The occasion is one of their evening gatherings in Dublin in the first years of this century:

Then we began to talk, as all Irishmen do, of what Ireland was, what she is, and what she is becoming.

There is no becoming in Ireland, I answered; she is always the same—a great inert mass of superstition.

Home Rule, said AE, will set free a flood of intelligence.

And perhaps the parish priest will drown in this flood.

AE did not think this necessary.

Do you think the flood of intelligence will penetrate into the convents and release the poor women wasting their lives?

I'm not thinking of nuns, John Eglinton said; those who have gone into the convents had better remain in them; and Home Rule will be of no avail unless somebody comes with it, like Fox or like Bunyan, bringing the Bible or writing a book like the *Pilgrim's Progress*. . . .

These sentences are to be accepted, not perhaps as a replica of a conversation but at least as a condensation of sayings in vogue, and it is significant that the decisive pronouncement on the need for the Bible of the independent nation is put into the mouth of Eglinton. He is the man of taste, the non-fanatic, prejudiced if anything against Gaelism and separation from England. If he says that the task of the literary movement is to produce a sacred book, he says it soberly.

Yeats expected to be the author of that book. He defined it to himself originally as an exposition of psychic lore, familiar to the country people of Ireland. In the preface to the new edition of *The Celtic Twilight*, 1902, he promised: "I shall publish in a little while a big book about the commonwealth of faery, and shall try to make it systematical and learned enough to buy pardon for this handful of dreams." He and Lady Gregory busied themselves with that system for the next fourteen years and more. Then, as will be described more fully in the later chapters, Yeats recognised that the book was her work—recognised it because he also recognised that it was not the sacred book he had dreamed of. The sacred book would still be his occupation; it would be a philosophy of history. With the help of the spirits who communicated with him through his wife's automatic writing he began the slow preparation of *A Vision*. While engaged on that he reminded the public of the imminence of a sacred book, by choosing as title of his autobiographical essays *The Trembling of the Veil*, the preface to which narrates how he had discovered in an "old diary"—the kind of source he loves to quote, because it implies that he had already divined as a young man what maturity confirmed—his note of a saying of Mallarmé: "Is it true", he asks, "that our air is disturbed, as Mallarmé said, by 'the trembling of the veil of the Temple', or 'that our whole age is seeking to bring forth a sacred book'?"

Towards the end of his life he ceased to insist that *A Vision* was a holy book, or that any Irish writer had written one. His thoughts blackened by the angry view that all that had been said in Ireland was a lie, he conjectured that the scriptures of the age were probably not of Irish provenance, but had been written earlier in continental Europe. Perhaps they consisted of the quadrivium: *Faust, Louis Lambert, Seraphita, Axel.*

Lady Gregory, an admirer of Shaw, who was after all nearly her own age, thought *he* might be both the sacred writer and the political, Messianic leader, and this though he had largely kept apart from Irish affairs. When she was meditating *The Jester*, Shaw was in her mind, and in her note to the play she comments: "looking now at the story of that Great Jester, in the history of the ancient gods, I see that for all his quips and mischief and 'tricks and wonders', he came when he was needed to the help of Finn and the Fianna, and gave good teaching to the boy-hero, Cuchulain." She liked Shaw and trusted him, perhaps hoped with these remarks to coax him; but although he occasionally made a gesture for Ireland, his bent, ambition, hatred of childhood memories, were too much against a full response. Yet though he wrote neither in Ireland nor for Ireland, the Irish pattern of thinking was engrained in him. The Irish passion for a sacred book drove him. He attempted three: *Man and Superman; Back to Methuselah;* and *Saint Joan.* The second was his most serious offer, the primitive scriptures of "Creative Evolution . . . the religion of the twentieth century". The third was less a sacred book than an Irishman reporting, in the light of his country's experience, on the nature and techniques of a nationalist Messiah, and how a Messiah is thrown to the wolves.

Although delighted with himself, delighted with his success in seizing the international pulpit and mesmerising world attention, Shaw knew that his art was defective and its durability uncertain. In 1912 he added to the current predictions of a greater writer coming: "I am", he said to an interviewer, "only one of the first attempts of the new Ireland. She will do better—probably has done better already—though the product is not yet grown up enough to be interviewed".* A decade later he thought he had found the younger man, the half-Irish T. E. Lawrence, and made a protegé of him. Lawrence transposed the dream of freeing a people from Ireland to the Near East, and wrote the story of his struggle in a book to which he gave a title which seemed to promise a sacred book. Many Englishmen who have not had time to open *Seven Pillars of Wisdom* think it is a key to the supreme oriental knowledge. Whereas it is a study of political aspirations and political cynicism which perhaps only a man with mixed Anglo-Irish blood could have written. Discontented with it, he tried again, with the documentary compiled in the light of Joyce's achievement, *The Mint;* and by willing a long delay before its publication he invested it with an apocryphal aura, so that again, as with *Seven Pillars*, the book radiates a legend which its text cannot match. Lawrence had an instinct for all the devices which impress the public with the sacred status of a book, but he never succeeded in making a book which could live up to the impression. Yet his books have their minor merit, and a place on the margin of the Irish achievement—and also on the margin of the English romantic achievement.

Of all the prophets of the Messiah AE was the most persistent. He can be heard foretelling the man of destiny again and again.

*See the quotation from the New York *Evening Sun*, in Lady Gregory's *Our Irish Theatre*.

Here he is, for example, in 1917, advising John Quinn about young Irish poets:* "if they are not great, like Yeats, still they all have contributed genuine poetry, and I feel that this confluence of poets means that a great man is going to arise and that we are forerunners or disciples or torch-bearers. I am convinced that in the next few years you will hear of a very big man in Ireland doing great things".

Joyce's *Ulysses* was almost immediately heard of, but AE did not see Joyce as the man he had promised. The Irish were always talking about each other—but jealously and captiously. They jostled each other, all candidates for the role of Messiah or evangelist or leading organiser, whatever exactly it was to be. It has been said that Yeats showed his transcendence from the outset: Katharine Tynan remembered so in 1913; and there is an essay of AE dated 1896 that calls him great. Yet in the 'nineties Yeats was apprehensive that AE might outstrip him. In 1894 the publication of *Homeward* established that poet's claim to equality or near-equality. Lady Gregory summoned both men to take a look at them before making her decision that Yeats was the right candidate for the national laureate and adopting him and devising a programme of special nourishment to power him for the work. It took some years before Yeats was sure that he was safely ahead. After the turn of the century a coldness came between the two poets diminishing what had been their helpfulness to one another. Yeats had by then, it is true, reasons to assail the nature of AE's influence on the younger poets, but that was not the sole condition of his attitude. He was jealous of any near rival. Of a talent at the opposite pole to AE's he was equally jealous and critical: of Shaw's. He was jealous of Moore, and Moore was jealous of him.

ANTI-MATERIALISM

The rivalries in the Irish movement are worth noting, because they illustrate how the men concerned felt they were doing more than writing verse: they were prescribing a course for Ireland,

*See *Letters from AE*, edited by Alan Denson.

perhaps for the world. So they elevated the jealousies of any literary coterie into the nailing of each other's heresies. But the views they shared, the common stock of thinking from which they developed their different results, are as important as their differences.

It would have been sufficient justification of the Irish struggle for political freedom from England simply to say "We want to be free". The literary movement was curiously uncontent with that. It elaborated a social case as well: England stood for commerce and "materialism", whereas Ireland stood for "imagination and spirituality". The world must support Ireland's freedom-movement, and the Irish must fight the harder for it, because the purity of the imagination, its preservation from the world's slow stain— visibly symbolised in the creeping of industry over the once pretty English rural Midlands—was at stake.

Yeats and AE inherited this argument from the Young Ireland group of the mid-nineteenth century. Davis had been its exponent, and his version of it Yeats and his contemporaries found in Charles Gavan Duffy's *Young Ireland*. That book is a piece of Irish nationalist history remembered and reported after nearly thirty years (thirty years of absence which the extraordinary author had spent in rising to the premiership of Victoria and a British knighthood). "When I was twenty years old", Yeats said, "we all read Gavan Duffy's *Young Ireland*, and then read the Young Ireland poets it had introduced to us." The book had appeared in London in 1880, and in Ireland in 1883. Duffy quoted lengthy passages from Davis, the burthen of which was that Ireland, physically and politically oppressed by Britain, would be finally and irrevocably conquered if she gave up her imaginative integrity by imitating British commercialism.

It is clear that Davis emphasised this thesis as a last stand. He might save the last shred of Irish individuality that way—to save political freedom seemed a remote prospect. When Yeats and AE read him in the 'eighties and took up the cry, they altered its character. They made it a weapon in a renewed Irish drive for liberation. Conditions were propitious to it. First Matthew

Arnold and then William Morris had been criticising British materialism from within, had demanded a new scrutiny of the purposes of living and accordingly of the proper way of living, and had detected in the Celtic ethos a principle of spiritual health akin to what they were recommending. Yeats and AE began their work under the immediate influence of Arnold and Morris. AE regarded Arnold as a fount of "vitality and wisdom". Yeats had met Morris in Dublin when he was a boy (Morris had come there to lecture on the Celtic legends, but was disturbed at the unpreparedness of the Irish audience), then gravitated towards him in London. Their authority, and authoritative phrasing, assisted the restatement of the Young Ireland doctrine. Professor John V. Kelleher, who has dealt brilliantly* with this subject, has argued that the whole Irish literary mythos is mainly a borrowing from Arnold's intuitive presentation of the Celtic mind; but in fact, as the material in *Young Ireland* shows, the foundations of the mythos had been laid in the 'forties; the importance of the work of Arnold was to give the young Irishmen the courage to build on them and to make the non-Irish world appreciative of the developments.

It became a convention of the Irish movement that Ireland had kept her spirituality, her contact with the soil and thus her contact with the archetypes, because she had been spared the Roman invasion. There is a typical passage in AE's introduction to *The Wild Bird's Nest, Poems from the Irish*, by Frank O'Connor. He argues that the Romans were great builders, but also great destroyers: in England, France, and Spain they obliterated "almost all traces" of the culture which preceded their own; but in Ireland, which they never made part of their empire, "there are rich survivals of . . . the primaeval culture of the imagination". AE wrote that passage as late as 1932, still using the ideas and language of 1900. Their currency in Dublin in 1904 gave Joyce one of his serio-farcical rollicks: measuring the Romans and the English, materialist manufacturers of water-closets, against the Jews and the Irish, builders of altars to Jehovah. Joyce hooted derisively at

*In *Perspectives of Criticism*, edited by Harry Levin, Harvard University Press, 1950.

the Irish claim to spirituality, and yet shared it too. In the early pages of *Ulysses* there is a hint that, before he thought of carrying Europe into Irish literature for the purpose of civilising Ireland, he had imagined himself as carrying Ireland into Europe. He had seen himself as a new St. Columba. Every Irish writer had felt like that. While the French neo-classicists were developing the thesis, later to be taken up by T. S. Eliot, that the tradition which had grown from Attica through Rome into Western Europe was the world's highest achievement and that its continuation was the world's best hope, the Irish were claiming that that tradition was limited and barren, and could only be fertilised by the uncontaminated Irish fancy.

The problem about claims as lofty as the Irish made is that they have to be at least within beckoning distance of reality. Real Ireland contrasted sharply with the spiritual Ireland of the nationalist thesis. It is part of the merit of Anglo-Irish literature, seen as a whole, that it takes account of the contrast and includes a refutation of the "spirituality" claims as well as a statement of them. Side by side with the early imagination-praising pages of Yeats, there are the realistic pages of George Moore describing the peasants brutalised by insecurity and starvation, and Joyce's mockery of the much-vaunted chastity of Ireland, and Sean O'Casey's tenement scenes. These acts of self-criticism were essential, or the Irish would have died of complacency. But there had been, it should be added, a kernel of truth in the myth of spirituality and in the consequent attack on English materialism (an attack which never gave credit to the forces in English literature fighting that materialism). Rural Ireland *did* secrete energy under its filth, for race memories are kept alive by contact with the soil. Literary nationalism got hold of this energy and activated it.

AREAS OF ANALOGY

There is another source of political energy, drawn on by all the nationalist movements in Europe in the nineteenth century: analogies with other freedom-movements and imitation of their heroes. The analogies might be taken from early history, as from

C

the extinguished Spartans at Thermopylae, or from recent experiences, as Blake quickly made an energising myth of America's independence. As nationalist adventures flared up here and there, a fresh stock of images of inspiration and comfort accumulated. It is interesting, for example, to watch the rapid crystallisation of the most notable of them: the Garibaldi image. The Italianists in England turned Garibaldi's Sicilian exploit into song and story almost instantaneously. Miss M. E. Braddon rushed out *Garibaldi and Other Poems*, prefacing it "The wonderful Sicilian campaign, which has made this departing year of 1860 one epic poem, has suggested the brief record here offered to the reader". In 1880 Duffy thought of Garibaldi and Kossuth when he described the contrasting failure of O'Connell to lead armed rebellion against England in 1843. In 1916 the Irish underground remembered Duffy's comment and Garibaldi's success and seized the Dublin Post Office. In the subsequent four years when it still hung in doubt whether their enterprise would lead to Irish freedom or not, or whether the Black and Tans would stifle terror with terror, Lady Gregory propped her mind with the thought of Garibaldi. At that date in India Nehru, who had conceived himself as a national leader when he read the history of Garibaldi in his teens at Harrow, kept his eyes on Ireland's emulation of the Thousand and planned India's way of doing it.

But the area of analogy which the Irish tapped for the profoundest encouragement was neither modern nor European. They thought of themselves in terms of Israel. They thought of England as Pharaonic Egypt. They dreamed of an Irish Passover, the march of the nation from the house of bondage. Half the effect of *Ulysses* depends on this analogy. Bloom is Jewish not only because Joyce, an exile, was fascinated by the Jewish experiences in exile, but primarily because Joyce desired to elaborate on the current Dublin identification of Ireland with Israel. In the Aeolus chapter he quotes John F. Taylor's speech comparing the Irish and the Jews and promising, in virtue of the comparison, that Ireland will produce a new Moses and a new

Law. The same speech had stayed in Yeats' memory, and is recalled in *Autobiographies*. Yeats in an early essay drew a comparison of his own between Ireland and Judea at the time of Christ's birth. Shaw, his ear to the ground as usual, made an epigram for Larry Doyle out of the Irish-Jewish comparisons current in 1904. Lady Gregory wrote a play, *The Deliverer*, produced at the Abbey in 1911, identifying Moses with Parnell. The habit of analogising Ireland and Israel criss-crosses Anglo-Irish literature for half a century. And in the upshot a striking likeness between Ireland and Israel that emerges from this literature is that the Irish writers longed to be "a light to the Gentiles". Yeats wrote that the Irish race, transformed by a national art, would become "a chosen race, one of the pillars that uphold the world".

Concurrently the Irish had the sense of an analogy with a Homeric people, which gradually became an analogy with Odysseus, and so gave Joyce the other half of his characterisation of Bloom. In the early poems of Yeats there is some confusion: they look at Helen—Maud Gonne—from the Trojan as much as from the Greek standpoint. But the Greek prevailed, the habit being rooted in older Irish tales. There is an Odyssean pattern to some of the early Irish stories, which were being rehabilitated and published in the 'eighties and 'nineties. The oratory of the John Taylor period uses allusions to the Odyssey and Ithaca as well as to Israel. In the early years of this century the analogy was in active circulation. We know, from the striking dream of Yeats which Professor Jeffares has published,* that the Odyssey image penetrated the dream-life of the writers before Joyce had begun work on his summation of it.

A third area of analogy tapped by the Irish was Germany. When Yeats went back from Ireland to London in 1887 he fell among Wagnerians, such as W. Ashton Ellis, already author of No. 11 in the Transactions of the London Lodge of the Theosophical Society, *Theosophy in the Works of Richard Wagner*, and next year, 1888, appointed editor of the new periodical, *The*

*See p.307 below.

Meister. His friend, Arthur Symons, added to his knowledge of Wagner, and then Martyn and Moore. He saw how Wagner had represented and consolidated the unification of Germany by making his art out of the early national epics: Bayreuth was a shrine at which his nation became more conscious of itself and the whole world more German-minded. It seemed possible to him that he and his movement could do as much for Ireland through a drama rooted in the old Irish cycles. In fact, it is probable that when Miss Horniman gave her financial support to the Abbey Theatre she did so because, a passionate Wagnerite, she saw in Celtic drama a new *Ring.* She gave because of Yeats, to be sure, but also because he promised her an Irish equal to Wagner. When Eglinton fired the first shot of the lively Dublin *Daily Express* controversy of 1899,* by doubting whether the ancient legends offered suitable subjects for an Irish national drama, Yeats retaliated by pointing to *Peer Gynt* and Wagner's *Ring.* The most prominent Irish journalist in London, Shaw, had meanwhile published *The Perfect Wagnerite;* and though Wagner's music was not the kind to which Dublin was temperamentally addicted (for we know from Joyce how its real love centred on the more charming vocal graces offered by drawing-room ballads or light opera), Ireland was conscious of the significance of the German master. In the next ten years Irish literature practised the use of him as a point of reference, and Joyce took up the work and continued it through *Ulysses* and *Finnegans Wake.*

THE IRISH SIEGFRIED—CUCHULAIN

The German hero, Siegfried, is a projection of the ideal of joyous power. The Irish hoped to create a hero-model with something of the same qualities. Yet they chose Cuchulain—a "dark sad man", as AE confesses in *The National Being.* A foreigner is bound to wonder at the choice. Tragedies stalked this violent figure. He offended the war-goddess, the Mor-rigu, and she fought against him. He fought his own son, and, as they did not

*The contributions to the debate were reprinted by the *Daily Express* as *Literary Ideals in Ireland*, Dublin, May 1899.

know one another, being both governed by a tabu not to tell their genealogy, killed him by the use of his weapon of last resource, the invincible thirty-barbed Gae-Bulg. He fought for three days against his friend Ferdiad and killed him with the Gae-Bulg. He died at an early age with no child to follow him. These seem gloomy auspices for a national movement. On the other hand, he had a total loyalty to his obligations, and an un-limited capacity for sacrifice. His most celebrated feat was to hold the ford against the host of the enemies of Ireland—a Garibaldian feat such as Ireland needed if she was to overthrow an empire. So (although Yeats first used him in poetry for specific personal reasons, haunted by his killing of his son), the literary movement, working from Standish O'Grady's account of him, began to make him a national symbol. The fall of Parnell helped in that determination. Cuchulain's loyalty to land and clan and tabus was counterpointed by his marital infidelity, and that fact chimed with the Parnell associations. Parnell's spirit survived as Cuchulain of the poems and dramas. When Lady Gregory applied her gift for the Kiltartan idiom to the purposes of the national movement, her first step was to translate the Cuchulain stories. AE in his writing at the outset of this century urged every Irish boy to read the legends and take Cuchulain into his soul as a revelation of his own potential. "Cuchulain", he wrote, "represents, as much as Prometheus the heroic spirit, the redeemer in man." Even the gentle AE felt, like his colleagues, that the heroic energy of Cuchulain was no less a gift to the world than the fire Prome-theus brought or Christ's mission of pacific love.

There is one play of Yeats in which he relieves the tragic aura that usually invests Cuchulain. In the "heroic farce", *The Green Helmet*, Laeghaire says of him:

> He was born to luck in the cradle, his good luck may amend
> The bad luck we were born to. . . .

The whole play has positive implications: Cuchulain trying to quell the jealous quarrels between Conall and Laeghaire (cf. the quarrels of the sects in Ireland); Cuchulain offering his head as a sacrifice, while his wife, Emer, tries to prevent him with the cry "Live and be faithless still"; Cuchulain's head not smitten off but crowned with the green helmet by the Red Man, who praises him for his cheer and Irish fantasy:

> And I choose the laughing lip
> That shall not turn from laughing, whatever rise or fall;
> The heart that grows no bitterer although betrayed by all.

In that play of 1910 Yeats sets out to make a Cuchulain who is debonair and gay as well as strong.

But before that date and after, in almost every other work, Yeats uses him for a dark confrontation of suffering. This was the complexion he took as a national image. As a revolutionary model he offered tragic sacrifice to his adepts. They expected to hold the ford by living as violently and dying as darkly.

It is ironic that the non-Irish world knows the figure of Deirdre better than Cuchulain. Presumably the tragedy of a beautiful woman is easier to like than the tragedy of a violent, rampant man. Yeats once observed to Ricketts: "You paint the tragedy of Man, most people only understand the tragedy of Woman, or the pitifulness of their tragedy." I can imagine Yeats and Synge arguing in the shades: "A pity it is we made Deirdre so fine a figure. The English—yes, and the Americans even—are pleased to think of Ireland as a melancholy beauty. She is in some manner vulgarised in their reading, and Cuchulain is forgotten, being but an unpronounceable name." Yet three dramatists attempted the Deirdre story. It may be that the story fascinated Ireland because it involved a breach of the chastity that meant so much to her, and a punishment of the breach; certainly the emphasis is thrown on to this point by Standish O'Grady, who was horrified when AE made a play honouring Deirdre. Or it may simply be that in Dublin as well as abroad there was a temptation to delight in the figuring of Ireland as a sad and suicidal beauty. Certainly that figuring was the most effective single move in the literary campaign to capture the world's sympathy for the independence drive. It mobilised the support of all "souls" for Ireland at the most critical juncture. The trouble was the figuring omitted the violence and those other masculine features of Cuchulain which better square with her politics and the conduct of her people.

SUCCESS AND ITS CONSEQUENCES

The boys did read of Cuchulain and reflect on him, as AE had wished. The youth-leaders reflected on him and taught his code of sacrifice. It is said that one of the leaders of the 1916 Rising, Pearse, had been a lover of the Abbey and the new Irish poetry. Yeats claimed that Cuchulain had fought in the Post Office that Easter when the Garibaldian handful, perhaps 2,000 of them, seized it and held it for a week. Ireland confirmed his claim when, rebuilding the Post Office, they had Oliver Sheppard cut a statue of Cuchulain for the interior.

The Easter Rising surprised the mass of Irishmen and the act of violence at first shocked them. Then when its leaders were shot, the hush of martyrdom fell. Everywhere young people desired to make an equal sacrifice. What had been an underground plot conducted by a very few became a national revolution. It was pressed forward by a terrorist spearhead using the weapon of assassination. The British Government retaliated with equal terrorism. In 1922 the Government at Westminster accepted the situation and offered independence, whereupon the Irish fought among themselves as to the degree of freedom they judged necessary: freedom with Dominion status or as a totally autonomous republic. It had been assumed throughout the nineteenth century that Ireland would get her freedom by Parliamentary action, and in the early years of this century, right up to the eve of 1916, Bernard Shaw was saying that violence could not move Britain and that the statutory way was the only way. But the politically-expert Shaw was wrong, and the schoolteacher Patrick Pearse was right, and so was the a-political Joyce, who, although his hero Bloom was to grow into a pacifist, recorded clearly, in his early Italian newspaper articles, his view that only Irish force had ever exacted concessions from England. There was, in fact, aid from a vital streak of liberalism in England, but mainly Irish violence at last separated Ireland from Britain after 700 years.

Yeats was convinced that this result, after so many failures, was due to the literary movement. He was right. He and his friends had released a long-blocked energy out of the past. They had done it by rearing the heroic model of Cuchulain, their Golem. That by itself might not have been enough. But they had gathered the shreds of a Messianic myth into one and infused it into Cuchulain, and they had created the legendary conditions for the emergence of a Messiah. A condition of salvation is the descent into hell, and this is often construed as a descent into filth—sometimes the filth of sex, sometimes the filth of poverty, sometimes both. Parnell's fall had involved sexual passions; prompted by that the Irish writers made sex one of their subjects. The facts of Irish peasant life provided them with filth in the other sense, and they made literature of tinkers and beggars and lice in the beggars' rags. So they produced a printed simulacrum of the Messianic conditions, and political Ireland then produced the equally necessary conditions of bloodshed and chaos, the stamping of Og, Gog, and Magog. All the conditions were fulfilled, and eventually there was an Irish Republic.

That is not the end. All national movements encounter their greatest problems in the aftermath of their crises. The political explosion brings a sense of extraordinary purity. The sacrifice of human life for an ideal seems to sanctify. If the political attempt fails, the purity remains intact: it stays in the minds of those who survive, is passed to their children, communicated abroad through books and writing. Other movements may be formed by virtue of it. But if the political attempt succeeds, those who have fought feel with regret, with desolation even, that the moment of purity is dissolving, that they will never be as fine again as they were at the hour of sacrifice. They almost wish they had not succeeded so that the fineness of feeling might be preserved. They long for an opportunity to keep the struggle in being so that they may recover it.

The centre of any study of Yeats, Lady Gregory, and AE must

be how they viewed the Irish freedom-movement while they nourished it towards its crisis, but the essential coda of the study must be how they responded to its success and how they commented on this inevitable final problem of nationalism. In the case of the last great Anglo-Irish writer, Joyce, the circumstances change: the coda comes forward to the very centre of the story. It was his fate to see from the outset the negative properties of the Irish cause and to foretaste the bitterness of success, and in his tragi-comedies he tries to display the worst of the facts and so to offer in advance the possibility of correcting them or accepting them—but which?

CHAPTER II

GEORGE AUGUSTUS MOORE

1852-1933

MOORE was born in 1852 at his family's home, Moore Hall, by Lough Carra in County Mayo. His father, a landlord with a considerable estate, had in his early days been a traveller in the Levant and down the Nile; had had a passion for horse-racing, which he resumed with success in later life; from 1847 had given himself to Parliamentary work as Independent member for Mayo. The family was Catholic, but with Protestant antecedents on the father's side.

George Moore grew up an outstanding example of the legendary "backward boy", negligent and idle, exhibiting no promise. At Oscott, a Catholic public school in the English Midlands, where his father had once been a brilliant pupil, he declined to interest himself in the curriculum, preoccupied with his fantasies. "I would lean over my desk," he recollects, "a Latin grammar in front of me, my head clasped between my hands, and abandon myself to my imagination." He was developing the process to which many references in his mature work point, a process in which fancy builds and unbuilds possible patterns while intellect watches and then seizes one and makes something of it. Yeats and AE preached the significance of reverie from the 'nineties onwards. Moore was working through reverie twenty years earlier, though he invented no mystique of it, and in fact it led him to a knowledge of the material world which the Irish literary movement of the 'nineties despised.

Inheriting his father's estates and revenue, Moore left for Paris

in the spring of 1873 and stayed seven years. Yeats, Synge, and
Joyce were later to make their way home through Paris; Moore
set the example. Excited by Parisian painting, poetry, and theatre,
he tried his hand at each of these arts in turn. He published a
volume of Baudelairesque poems, *Flowers of Passion*, in 1878, and
another, *Pagan Poems*, in 1881. (These now rare volumes, and his
concurrent theatrical experimentation, are admirably described
by Professor Malcolm Brown in his *George Moore: a Recon-
sideration*.) What decided him to be a novelist was an economic
shock: he was called home from Paris when his tenants ceased to pay
rent, Michael Davitt having formed the Land League with its
policy of collective resistance to the landlords. He mended his
affairs by, very practically, selling his timber, then decided to
bolster his income by writing, and deliberately sat down and
produced in 1883 a three-decker novel, *A Modern Lover*. It was
successful enough to justify him in continuing; he thereupon
decided to write an English version of Zola, and, documenting
the scenery of the Midlands and the lives of travelling actors,
made *A Mummer's Wife*. Published in 1885, that was so sweeping
a success that it confirmed him in the career of novelist. He settled
down to regular composition, consistently bringing out new
work, both novels and a genre in which he developed a distinct
voice, autobiographical memoirs (beginning with *Confessions of
a Young Man* in 1888). The decadence of his themes between
1887 and 1891 having disappointed some of his readers, he
regained the public esteem through *Esther Waters* (1894) written
in the central British tradition of the philanthropic novel. He then
became aware, partly through contact with W. B. Yeats, of the
post-Parnell events stirring in Ireland: he found that the nation
expected a leader, and that the writers believed they would provide him or would have the task of announcing him and writing
his policy. After a quarter of a century's absence he resettled in
Ireland, expecting to be acclaimed as leader or spokesman of the
national conscience. He expressed himself in favour of the revival
of Gaelic; began to write on Irish subjects; and, when insufficient
attention resulted from these steps, demonstratively demanded it

by announcing his conversion from the Catholic to the Protestant Church. He then wrote the neatly-organised *The Lake*, published in 1905, offering, through the drama of Father Oliver who gives up his parish for a new life in America, secularisation as the key to Ireland's problems. But he knew that that concise, contrapuntal novel was not vigorous enough to be the sacred book that he felt himself destined to write for Ireland. He decided to cast that book in the form of a record of his own relationship with his country, and he began the trilogy, *Hail and Farewell*. When the first part was ready for the press, he slipped away from Dublin, and watched the results from the shelter of London. *Ave* came out in 1911, *Salve* in 1912, *Vale* in 1914.

In the course of revising his religious position in Dublin, Moore had read the Bible. The reading had confirmed a long-standing interest in the personality of Jesus and the contrasting personality of Paul. He sketched a play *The Apostle,* and published it to secure copyright in 1911, and elaborated the material as the novel *The Brook Kerith* in 1915.

Lastly came a period of story-telling—story-telling in the sense of the traditional story-teller's art, which, stimulated by what he had seen the younger Irish making of the folk-idiom of their country, he decided to show he could handle more persuasively than Yeats—and historical romances. A *Story-Teller's Holiday* is dated 1918. The most famous and successful of the romances, *Héloïse and Abélard,* follows in 1921. Then come *Peronnik the Fool* (1924); the translation of *Daphnis and Chloë* (1924); *Ulick and Sóracha* (1926—in the Nonesuch Edition, handsomely designed by Francis Meynell); *Aphrodite in Aulis* (1930).

Like Yeats, in whom he deplored the practice, Moore devoted endless time to rewriting his early works. He did not like to leave traces of innocence or early clumsiness in his texts, and some texts he suppressed from his collected works. To see the real Moore, and to follow the history of the novel, and the history of ideas reflected in the novel, we nowadays need reprints of the original versions of all his books. Many libraries lack copies of *A Modern Lover*, and their readers cannot weigh up the pioneer qualities of that book. Many lack the original *Drama in Muslin*. Many lack *Mike Fletcher*, a repudiated novel which is both amusing and sociologically interesting. In the case of such books as *Evelyn Innes* and *Sister Teresa* we need reprints which will give us the various versions which Moore wrote.

Moore's prestige stood high in the 'twenties. An ardent coterie of young men regarded him as the supreme stylist. By the 'forties he dropped into reputation's midnight, and young men in the universities today have often read nothing of his. The fall can be measured by John Crowe Ransom's experience, as described in a letter to me: "I used to read everything I could get of Moore's which was at all stylized, I found the style so delicious. I never could take him very seriously as a force or a thinker. And now no one hears any more about him, so far as I can see." However, Malcolm Brown's book, published by the University of Washington Press in 1955, marked the beginning of a revaluation, which should establish Moore's right level: not as lofty as the public once expected, but high none the less, for if styles grow old, intelligence does not; and Moore had intelligence, and he had a resilient sympathy.

PAINTING: THE NEW SUBJECT-MATTER

As a young man Moore had a passion to create. It began as a drive to re-create whatever he saw with pleasure: to re-create it, and to add something from himself in the process. Painting was the first art to awaken him. He at once wanted to become a painter. It was his temperament to plunge into enthusiasms, but to be capable of a rapid and sane disenchantment, and in the disenchantment to salvage valuable material. That happened in Paris. He found that he could not paint creatively, but that certain paintings sparked a fire in him, and that he could borrow suggestions from them and transfer them to literature.

In 1875 the Impressionists held their first exhibition at the Hôtel Drouot. Moore has told in *The Confessions of a Young Man* how he attended: he went to mock, but became a convert. Douglas Cooper, writing in *Horizon*, has given reasons for believing that Moore was not, in fact, converted as suddenly as that. Mr. Cooper thinks that Moore remained a sceptic for a decade (until the movement had carried the intelligentsia of England and France), that he then changed sides just in time, and thereafter postured as an aboriginal convert and thus won an undeserved reputation for artistic perspicacity. Personally, although willing to believe anything of Moore, whose impudence is one of his charms, I doubt whether Mr. Cooper is right. What is certain is this: when Moore sat down very early in the 'eighties to write his first novel and looked inside himself for material, he saw that his knowledge of the Impressionist painters and their objectives, and recollections of their pictures, provided something of central interest to him, on which he could write meaningfully, and new to the reader.

That first novel, *A Modern Lover*, has not received the attention it deserves. Moore handles three themes: (1) the reactions of women in love, (2) the character of the 'modern lover'—that is, the feminine man, (3) the subject-matter of art, discussed in terms of the Impressionists' discovery of new subjects. Moore's modern lover is a young painter who after various affairs marries for advantage, and after early contacts with experimental painters separates from them to paint a pseudo-classical *Cytherea*, a money-making success. The story of this double treason enables Moore to describe, with eager detail, the work of a group of experimental painters. He makes them a British group, led by a Scot, Thompson, but the pictures they paint resemble the canvases of the Hôtel Drouot Exhibition as later described by Moore in *The Confessions of a Young Man* and in his critical essays *Modern Painting*.

His experimentalists are "striving to formulate a new art. Bar girls, railway trains, and tennis players flared in the gayest of colours." "They declared that a new aestheticism was to be discovered; that the materials were everywhere around them; and that only the form had to be found . . . to render modern life in all its poignancy and fulness." Thompson's revolutionary Academy picture shows "a pretty but dirty girl whitening the steps of a house. Red geraniums flared in the window, where a large card announced that there were lodgings to let. The girl sat on her heels, with one red hand resting on her bucket, talking to the milkman, who had put down his cans." The artists associated with Thompson have followed this lead: "Stanley had a picture of two washerwomen, one ironing and the other yawning; Crossley, a picnic party, a flare up of blue and red dresses; Frazer, a railway junction; and as for Holt, his picture was neither more nor less than a group of peasant women bathing."

Two kinds of excitement show in Moore's account of the pictures. First, he is quickened by the Impressionist treatment of colour; he several times uses the verb "flared" to catch the colours; he points out the effect of such strokes as the whisk of cadmium yellow in Monet's railwayscape. Secondly, he sees that the Impressionists have opened up an area of subject-matter that art has ignored as if it did not exist or did not matter. Whatever was workaday, seedy, and depressing becomes worthy of the eye of the artist: in fact, once examined and its colours and point described, it seems the more apocalyptic just because it has been previously ignored. In Thompson's picture of the servant-girl whitening the steps, his friends find "the positivism of art", an art in concord with the age, "purely material and experimental". It is in fact the Parisian art that follows 1875. In London it emerges more slowly. Moore's account of it in *A Modern Lover* invites it to emerge, and Moore works thirteen years to produce a literary equivalent of it. There are half a dozen winsome pages in *A Modern Lover* that show Moore attempting verbal Impressionist paintings, especially his Thames scenes. He attempts it differently and more harshly in *A Mummer's Wife*, describing, with Zola as his model, the towns of the Midlands and the lives of struggling actors. Even amid the exoticisms of *The Confessions of a Young Man* he both discusses it and actually attempts it—in his account of his lodgings and the servant-girl. Then he writes *Esther Waters*, the story of a servant-girl. With that he feels that he has made a contribution perfect within its range. He has entered and reported the life of a girl like that girl who whitened the steps. The possibility that he glimpsed in the new painting of 1875 he has developed as far as he knows how, and he loses interest and turns to different objectives.

His thirteen years' struggle for the new subject-matter, the discovery of colour and meaning in the seedy, was pioneer. In 1883 nobody else in England had seen the possibilities. There is the seediness but not the significant colours in such contemporary work as John Law's *A City Girl*, which appeared with Moore's realistic novels on Vizetelly's list in 1887. By 1900 there was a growing sense of them. In the 'eighties and 'nineties young men out of the universities began to go down to the poor districts of the East End of London to do "social work". And in addition to going for reasons of social conscience, they sometimes went for the attraction the darkness and drabness offered: that was the case with Roger Fry, for example, as described by Virginia Woolf in her biography. Flecker tried to write poetry made of the dingier parts of Camden Town. J. D. Innes has a painting, *Camden Town*, dated 1908. It may be that this movement would have developed without Moore; strong impulses were making for it; but the fact is that Moore first saw the opportunities and adventured with them, and his full-scale attempt of 1894, *Esther Waters*, was his greatest public success and every young man in the next twenty years would necessarily be aware of it.

In *The Confessions of a Young Man* Moore had thrown out a promise that when the realists brought new subjects to English literature from France, the new matter would breed new forms. In English poetry the problem was that the new subject-matter, though it attracted young poets like Flecker, did not immediately give them new forms. They tried to accommodate it to the late-nineteenth-century singing forms. These were inadequate. That is why Flecker's *Camden Town* ballad discourages even the sympathetic reader. Some poet had to bring new, appropriate forms for these subjects. Eliot brought them. Thompson's girl whitening the steps, with a red geranium in the window above her, is essentially the subject of that early Eliot intuition of

> the damp souls of housemaids
> Sprouting despondently at area gates.

38

The *Rhapsody on a Windy Night*, the half-deserted streets of *The Love-Song of Alfred J. Prufrock* and some of the London scenes of *The Waste Land*, have a family connection with the paintings Moore described in *A Modern Lover*. But Moore was not a progenitor of Eliot's art. In fact, Eliot has always ignored Moore's existence, as far as I know. Moore had found these subjects in Paris, and Eliot went there in 1910 to find them for himself. He then did something similar to what Moore had done nearly thirty years earlier. He carried the French themes into his own English literature. He was more fecundative than Moore, being a poet and adapting French forms as well as French subject-matter to English poetry. Through him they became the common possession of our English-speaking world in the first half of the twentieth century. (It is just possible, as Alan Goddard at Montana State University suggested to me, that Eliot was helped in this process by the Ash-Can school of American painters, who shortly after 1900 began to seek and paint squalor in the eastern cities of the States. I have looked, and am still looking, for evidence on this question; so far all I can offer is a coincidence of date, that at the turn of the century Maurice Prendergast was working in Boston, using Impressionist techniques that he had learned in Paris from 1886–9, and that from 1900 he was making excursions to New York City to paint scenes in Central Park and on the waterfronts.* It would be interesting to know whether Eliot saw the Exhibition of the Eight ("Apostles of Ugliness") at the Macbeth Gallery in New York in 1908, or the Armory Exhibition of 1913. If there is anything in Mr. Goddard's suggestion, it will, taken with the impact of the Impressionists on Moore a generation earlier, strikingly illustrate the way in which modern painting has pioneered for modern literature.)

SOME CONTRADICTIONS, IRISH AND EUROPEAN

Moore's concern with Esther Waters' world is paradoxical. In *The Confessions of a Young Man* he had surrounded himself with

---

*See Homer Saint-Gaudens, Introduction to *A Survey of American Painting*, Carnegie Institute, Pittsburgh, 1948.

D

exotica, borrowed from the Continentals, especially Huysmans, and warranted by Pater, that were to become the distinctive belongings of the "aesthetic" group in the 'nineties. Similarly he had denounced considerations of pity and the social justice preached by "the pale socialist of Galilee". Now, in his servant-girl novel, he deprived himself of the exotic pleasures, and the insight with which he described Esther's struggle to bring up her baby touched the public conscience and actually led to practical reforms to alleviate the difficulties of unmarried mothers.

These contradictions are not peculiar to Moore. They run through the artistic history of the 'nineties. The very movement that led to a heightened sensibility to the appeal of the drab working-world also led to Axel and his rejection of living, which his servant could do for him. In London in the 'nineties the exponent of French literature, as Moore was the protagonist of French painting, was Arthur Symons. It was Symons who took Yeats to Paris to see *Axel* and interpreted the play to him. At the same period Symons was also investigating the music-hall. He haunted the music-halls, studied their techniques, made poems out of what he saw. This was his avenue of entry into the popular and seedy; and it will be noticed that T. S. Eliot, who first saw the value of the French symbolist poets through Symons' book on them, has also interested himself in the music-hall and its modern equivalents, and imitated their techniques as part of his exploration of means to bring poetry before an audience as wide as the Elizabethan dramatists' audience. In general, it can be said of the 'nineties that the men who were most fascinated by the conception of the artist's marriage with extraordinary beauty were also fascinated by the discovery of vitality—and therefore of beauty—at the most humdrum levels of existence.

There was a special reason in Moore's Irish landlord background for his servant-girl sensitivity. In his writings about his father and that old generation of landlords he has remarked on their habit of making love to girls among their servants or their tenantry. He did not practise the habit; his predilections, in rebellion against it, took him to wealthy and perfumed women; but the image of it was a barb in his imagination, productively irritant. It made him the more responsive to the new subject-matter which the canvases of the Hôtel Drouot had opened up; and it conditioned him to choose, of the subjects the Impressionist example offered him, the study of a servant-girl for his master-piece in the style.

So there is that faint reminiscence of Irish instinct in *Esther Waters*, which Moore always said was written by the Englishman in him. Yeats and AE, coming into their strength at the date of its appearance, saw the book, and all that Moore had produced before it, as predominantly English, because concerned not with spiritual issues but with "social habits and customs" and therefore "materialistic". The new Irish literary movement leant on the preaching of Thomas Davis, summarised in the first chapter, that England served Mammon, and that Ireland would finally succumb to England if she too became interested in successful commerce and industry. AE, in pursuit of that thesis, constantly wrote against the industrialisation of the English Midlands, cursing their "ghastly life". But AE had not seen the English Midlands. Moore had been at school there, and later he renewed his know-ledge by repeated travel through them and visits to friends. He was familiar with the English industrial pattern of drabness of town and freshness of field, checkerworked. He often speaks, at once justly and devotedly, of the golden spaces between the Midland towns. When he went to Hanley to record the industrial environment behind the plot of *A Mummer's Wife*, he accurately caught the mixed light and shadow:

> At the bottom of the valley, right before her eyes, the white gables of Bucknell Rectory, hidden amid masses of trees, glittered now and then in an entangled beam that flickered between chimneys, across brick-banked squares of water darkened by brick walls.
>
> Behind Bucknell were more desolate plains full of pits, brick, and smoke; and beyond Bucknell an endless tide of hills rolled upwards and onwards.

The American tariff had not yet come into operation, and every wheel was turning, every oven baking; and through a drifting veil of smoke the sloping sides of the hills with all their fields could be seen sleeping under great shadows, or basking in the light. . . .

Moore makes literature, later to be imitated by Arnold Bennett and intensified and heightened by D. H. Lawrence, out of the Midlands which epitomise for Younger Ireland the most undesirable and contaminating side of English civilisation. Similarly when he describes the agglomeration of London in *Esther Waters*: he has learned from Zola enough to summarise the London scene realistically, and from the Impressionist painters enough to quicken the description:

A true London of the water's edge—a London of theatres, music-halls, wine-shops, public-houses—the walls painted various colours, nailed over with huge gold lettering; the pale air woven with delicate wire, a gossamer web underneath which the crowd moved like lazy flies, one half watching the perforated spire of St. Mary's, and all the City spires behind it now growing cold in the east; the other half seeing the spire of St. Martin's above the chimney-pots aloft in a sky of cream pink. Stalwart policemen urged along groups of slattern boys and girls; and after vulgar remonstrances these took the hint and disappeared down strange passages. . . .

The Irish nationalists might call the light that he throws on to that scene "vulgar", but so he meant it to be, and did not think it any the less suitable as literature for that.

A fascinatingly contradictory aspect of the *Esther Waters* descriptions of popular England is that they are not only lit by the flaring torches of the Impressionists—making a combined music-hall-Impressionist literature—but, in some cases, designed after the example of a painter who was anti-Impressionist. William Powell Frith was an angry Academic critic of the Impressionists, and completely represented the ideals of solid middle-class England, which Moore as an individual and the Irish as a group abhorred. Yet Moore took him at least twice as a model—and the younger Irish were continually conscious of him. Born in Yorkshire in 1819, Frith had worked for some years in London as a conventional "costume-painter". In 1851 on his summer holiday in Ramsgate he had suddenly decided "to try my hand on modern life", had painted the beach scene with the people documented in their holiday activities, and, showing that at the Academy of 1854, had experienced—despite some censure of "vulgar Cockney business"—an immense success, winning the approval, particularly, of the Prince Consort, who immediately understood what he was attempting. He then sought for another opportunity to show the nineteenth-century crowd with its *kaleidoscopic** display of common life. At a race-meeting at Hampton he realised that the mixed racing crowd in its holiday mood offered what he wanted; he resolved on the theme of "Derby Day", and went to see the Derby at Epsom in 1856 with that as his objective. *Derby Day* was exhibited at the Academy in 1858. "Never was such a crowd round a picture", says his diary for the opening day, May 3rd. A policeman was summoned to keep order as the over-enthusiastic viewers pressed forward. On May 5th Jacob Bell wrote that he had "found the people smelling the picture like bloodhounds". By special decision the picture was then railed off to protect it, a decision for which the only precedent in ninety years had been the protection of Wilkie's *The Chelsea Pensioners reading the Gazette of the Battle of Waterloo* in 1822. The public, the Prince Consort, the Villa, were satisfied that *Derby Day* was "the picture of the age". Only the world of art had its doubts. Frith's technical skill, especially his control of the groupings, was recognised, but, as a lady of pre-Raphaelite

---

Kaleidoscopic is a key word for what the artists attempt from Frith's *Derby Day* to Eliot's *Waste Land*. See Frith's *Autobiography*, vol. I, p. 272. The autobiography was published in 1887 and had run into eight editions by 1891, an indication of the extent to which Frith was accepted as the man of his time. See also Jonathan Mayne's valuable account of Frith in the catalogue of the Festival of Britain Exhibition of his works at Harrogate, 1951.

Joyce in *Ulysses* and *Finnegans Wake* is the final development of Moore's response to two schools of painting. His books combine the naturalism of Frith with French Impressionism: and they are Kaleidoscopes in Frith's sense.

tendencies told Frith (not knowing his identity): "the 'Derby Day' is in a very low style of art—it is vulgar". The higher art thought little of Frith, and he honestly thought little of the higher art and attacked Impressionism. Moore, apologist of the Impressionists, accordingly refers in *The Confessions* to "the meanness of Frith". Yet what Frith did in his Ramsgate beach scene Moore did in a rapid sketch of Brighton at the end of *A Mere Accident;* and what Frith did in *Derby Day* Moore does in *Esther Waters.* All the jargon and circumstances concerning race-horses and races Moore understood well from his father's interest, and he contrived the plot of his novel so that he could take advantage of this ready knowledge. But when he came to describe Derby Day he ignored horses and racing. As in Frith's picture, horse and jockey can be glimpsed in the distance: the crowd in its variety is the subject. Just as Frith rejoiced in the technical achievement of "composing great numbers of figures into a more or less harmonious whole", Moore rejoiced in the triumph of his "30 or 40 pages: no racing, only the sweat and boom of the crowd—the great Cockney holiday".

The Cockney crowd, the Cockney character became an attractive ingredient of the early writing of H. G. Wells in the decade following *Esther Waters.* As with Moore's Midland industrial scene, subsequent usage by others entails a bifurcation, the upward growth which results in *The Waste Land*, the downward diffusion through Wells and outwards. If it is curious that a painter seized the theme so long a time before literature could use it, it is even more curious that an Irish writer had to carry it into English literature. But Frith had that powerful fascination for the Irish to whom he was so antipathetic. As a small boy in London in 1875 W. B. Yeats had often been sent by his quasi-pre-Raphaelite painter father to the National Gallery, and there, says Hone, "Willie always went straight to Frith's 'Derby Day', although he had heard at home of better things". It is certain that he also knew Frith's subsequent and almost equally famous kaleidoscopic painting of Paddington Station; it is a matter for speculation whether he knew the late picture in which Frith returned to his old "costume" work and did Swift and Vanessa, and whether, having read the paragraphs in Frith's *Autobiography* where Frith discusses the scene and concludes: "... it required a more powerful pencil than mine to portray the crushed heart and mind of Vanessa, or the lightening fury of Swift . . ." he remembered, overleaped, and went beyond them in *The Words upon the Windowpane*. Hating English materialism the Irish were yet entangled with it: nothing discloses that more strikingly than their compulsive interest in Frith, their disdain of his art and ideas, their assimilation of his into their art.

Particularly unacceptable in Frith's art was its Victorian spirit of all's well. There may be sad perceptions in his crowd-scenes, but over all the feeling is of warm complacency, the interest and rightness of life as it is. By a feat of virtuosity Moore incorporated into *Esther Waters* the warmth of *Derby Day*, the "sweat and boom" as he calls it, without the complacency. *Esther Waters* is not a complacent book; it deals with the issue of the acceptability of life, and decides against. The Derby Day scene, a summer day spent when Esther's prosperity was at its highest, nowhere suggests, as perhaps Frith's art does, that life is entirely summer. It is an interesting part of life, but it does not make life right. By rotating the interest of *Derby Day* into an art which is a criticism of life, Moore prepared for the usage of a similar interest by Eliot in a much more profound criticism.

NIHILISM: AN UN-IRISH IRISH THEME

Is *Esther Waters* a criticism of life? Does it decide that life is unacceptable? It is usually regarded as a statement of courage. The servant-girl Esther bears her illegitimate child, fights to save the boy and bring him up, by tenacity and sacrifice sees him grow up. One might be tempted to say, and perhaps the success of the book lay in the public readiness to say, that the last paragraphs of the book justify her, and make the narrative a narrative of success:

He took his mother in his arms, kissed her, and they

walked towards Mrs. Barfield together. All was forgotten in
the happiness of the moment—the long fight for his life, and
the possibility that any moment might declare him to be
mere food for powder and shot. She was only conscious that
she had accomplished her woman's work—she had brought
him up to man's estate; and that was her sufficient reward.
What a fine fellow he was! She did not know he was so
handsome, and blushing with pleasure and pride she glanced
shyly at him out of the corners of her eyes as she introduced
him to her mistress.

But amid the delicate balances of the last four chapters a note
of doubt sounds repeatedly: a note of warning; a refrain of decay,
loneliness, inconclusiveness; a note that says that anxiety for a
child never ceases even when he grows beyond his majority; that
care is never rewarded; that separation, alienation, the disappear-
ance of mates, is the common lot. That is the purpose of Mrs.
Barfield's constant references to her son, Arthur, living away
from her in the north, hating his birthplace, refusing to marry;
she reads the sporting-press for her news of him, always expecting
to learn that he has been injured or killed racing. That is the
purpose of the realist, unsentimental recording of Esther's own
son's lack of success in his jobs and his recourse to soldiering.
That is the purpose of the near-symbolist treatment of the wild,
dismantling weather and the decrepit Barfield lands:

The women walked on in silence, passing by long ruins of
stables, coach-houses, granaries, rick-yards—all in ruin and
decay. The women paused and went towards the garden;
and removing some pieces of the broken gate they entered
a miniature wilderness. The espalier apple-trees had disappeared beneath climbing weeds, and long briars had shot
out from the bushes, leaving few traces of the former walks—
a damp, dismal place that the birds seemed to have abandoned.
Of the greenhouse only some broken glass and a black
broken chimney remained. A great elm had carried away a

large portion of the southern wall, and under the dripping trees an aged peacock screamed for his lost mate.*

At the best Esther's sacrifice has only done what Swift in the *Words upon the Windowpane* shouts that he will not do: "Am I to add another to the healthy rascaldom and knavery of the world?" At the worst, and inevitably in the end, it has added to the crookedness, pain, and consumption of the world. The story of *Esther Waters* is, in fact, a story of pointless courage and devotion.

Although Yeats was to use the same theme *à l'outrance* in his Swift play, he had, I fancy, missed the final significance of *Esther Waters* when he ranked it as evidence of what he felt to be Moore's incurable attachment to "the root facts" of existence. It is rather a gesture of disattachment. If we doubt this, arguing perhaps that the balance of the book is so delicate that the conclusions are left open, we can settle the matter by looking at the tendencies of Moore's work in the six or seven years preceding *Esther* and the six or seven subsequent years. On the one hand, much of it bubbles with a delightful zest. Fortune has provided Moore with income, leisure, access to the arts and people he desires, and the sensibility to enjoy them. He repeatedly observes how the human race longs to continue itself, and so it should if living is as flavourful as his style betokens. On the other hand, he repeatedly states, in precept or fable, the uselessness of living. In *The Confessions* he transcribes, and again in *The Story-Teller's Holiday*, the Balzac fable of the Spanish nobleman on whom fell the lot of executing his parents at their request, since on that condition their enemies would spare him and he would continue their line—but he

*Forty years later Charles Madge published the following fragment made from this chapter of Moore's;

> A howling wind . . . peaches and grapes
> Behind the battlements . . . an ailing child.
> The elm that fell and broke the garden wall.
> The aged peacock screamed for his lost mate.

That was in his first volume of verse, *The Disappearing Castle*, 1937, put together at the time when he was developing the social study known as Mass-Observation, with its concentration on the importance of recording "social habits and customs" at the levels which Zola and Frith had in their different ways indicated to Moore, which Moore had explored in *Esther Waters*, which Eliot explored more keenly later.

remained solitary and celibate. The slight story, *A Mere Accident*, 1887, is a first study in celibacy as Moore sees it actually operative in his cousin Edward Martyn. His hero says: "Bad enough that I should exist! Why precipitate another into the gulf of being?" When his fiancée, Kitty, is dead, he remarks that he could not have consummated the marriage—it would have been a new Abélard, a new Héloïse (Moore often foreshadows his late books in the early ones).

In *Mike Fletcher* Moore presses the study further. "Let the world be my monastery," says John Norton at the outset of the book. Then Mike himself, a portrait apparently drawn from Frank Harris, takes this up: although given to self-indulgence, he has learned from Schopenhauer that "not to create is the only good; the creation of life is the only evil". He conceived "an astonishingly beautiful poem" on the theme: man has abnegated the power of procreation and accepted oblivion, and eventually the last human being is walking the earth, and in the empty landscape "A broken wall that a great elm tears and rends startles the silence".

Moore was later ashamed of *Mike Fletcher* and suppressed it. But his grounds were technical, he was not revoking the view of life on which those passages turn. One proof is that that image of the falling elm and the broken wall passed into the landscape at the end of *Esther Waters*.

Mike concludes that we should hate our parents: "Why were we born? Why are we taught to love our parents? It is they whom we should hate, for it was they who, careless of our sufferings, inflicted upon us the evil of life."

After he had finished *Esther*, Moore returned to the exploration of celibacy, with the collection of stories, *Celibates*, and with *Sister Teresa*, his record of Evelyn Innes' retirement to a convent and her struggle there to overcome the longing for the world. In these works he is attempting clinical histories, rather than passing a judgment: in fact, perhaps the ultimate result is to draw the reader back towards acceptance of life, for the celibate condition is shown as harsh. But the bias of Moore's thinking is nonetheless still against procreation. In 1904 he interpolates into a revised edition of *The Confessions of a Young Man* this sentence: "That I may die childless—that when my hour comes I may turn my face to the wall saying, I have not increased the great evil of human life—then, though I were a murderer, fornicator, thief, and liar, my sins shall melt even as a cloud". When Moore added this, something had recently happened. He had settled in Ireland and been joined there by his English friend "Stella". When she wanted marriage and children, he had left her. Thus he had confirmed by his conduct the thought he had been juggling with as literature for over a decade.

His words sound a twentieth-century motif. Here is another Irishman uttering it: "I think the planet is in a damnable condition, which no change of party, or social reform, will do more than palliate insignificantly. What is wanted is a new master species— birth control for us, to end the human race in 50 years—and then a clear field for some cleaner mammal. I suppose it must be a mammal?" This is T. E. Lawrence writing to the Socialist M.P. Ernest Thurtle in 1929. He writes like a man who believes what he says, and we know that he lived as if he believed it. Yeats, without sharing the belief, uses it powerfully in two of his epitaphs on the Irish nation-making ecstasy: *The Words upon the Windowpane* and *Purgatory*. One of the paradoxes of Anglo-Irish literature is to have included these documents of nihilism. The Irish national movement insisted on *vitality*. Yeats looks back at the end and seems to say "Whether there was value in it or not, at least what we did was vital. Everybody in Europe when we were young mouthed about vitalism. We in Ireland lived it." All this is true; and yet it is equally true that, within it, this Manichaean theme of the undesirability of life is heard. Only Joyce, as we shall see when we look at *Ulysses*, deliberately repudiates it and speaks for the continuance of life.

SUBVERSION VIA SEX

But Moore is a ball of contradictions, and though his nihilism is (outside the artificially Paterian version of it in *Mike Fletcher*) striking and oppressive, it is offset by that ebullience already noted, and by his interest in sex, at once impish and intelligent. From his first novel he made the conduct of women in love his subject. *A Modern Lover* showed ladies of all classes abandoning prudence in favour of a self-centred artist, who manages them with an astutely parasitical effeminacy. The twentieth-century reader finds Moore's account written with penetration and with the eighteenth-century pointedness (so much better retained in Ireland than in England), but also with considerable restraint. For the middle-class readers in the circulating libraries, on which the British publishers of the three-decker novels depended for their sales, Moore's penetration, however civilly expressed, was an offence. The circulating libraries acted on their subscribers' complaints, whereupon Moore launched a lifelong campaign, brilliantly conducted, to preserve his freedom to publish what he wrote, and decided that he could scarcely employ himself more satisfactorily than in shocking "the Villa". In the early editions of *The Confessions of a Young Man* he wrote: "We have a surplus population of more than two million women, the tradition that chastity is woman's only virtue still survives, the tavern and its adjunct Bohemianism have been suppressed, and the Villa is omni-potent and omni-present".

The same problem excited the concern of English-born writers in the next generation, beginning with a protest by E. M. Forster in his novels of 1905 and 1907. When Forster searched the problem he found that the way to oppose the Villa was to discover the Earth. In 1883, and still in 1888, that discovery was not yet within Moore's capacity: he reached it, in fact, when he wrote *The Lake* in Ireland; and *The Lake* was published in the same year as Forster's first novel, *Where Angels Fear to Tread*. Even in *The Lake* and afterwards the intimations of earth that come to him are glancing, the lights thrown back by the surface, not the depths as Forster and D. H. Lawrence divine them. His instincts were not powerful enough to carry him far. But they took him to the preliminary act of raising sexual issues, and of doing it exasperatingly, with a pagan, Pannish mischievousness. The exploration of sexuality by modern writers is related to the rediscovery of the earth and its primal rhythms.

Moore's second novel, *A Mummer's Wife*, made a further step into the area of sexual exploration and thus of subversion of the Villa. Susan Mitchell wrote of it: "as an artist and an Irishman he could not be sentimental, and he degraded the runaway wife as if he had learned his doctrine of retribution in the plain black and white it would have been taught him by any parish priest in Connaught." But to its readers in the 'eighties the frankness of the presentation of Kate's behaviour outweighed the sense of retribution. They thought it indecent—and then bought it. By 1887 the publisher, Vizetelly, was claiming ten editions. "All London has read *A Mummer's Wife*", Moore wrote to his mother on July 17th, 1885. But did male London forbid female London to read it? One definite case is on record, and that not in a Philistine villa. In the pre-Raphaelite artists' colony, Bedford Park, where the Yeats's were again living from 1888, the young poet, who in his old age was to write of sex nakedly, forbade his sisters to read the novel.* Susan Mitchell was a lodger in the house at that time, and apparently was for moral purposes *in statu sororis*, so the ban on the book extended to her. In bed at night she "gulped guilty pages" of it. We can see from her account of the book that by its entry into Kate's mind it was in fact a frightening revelation of a shuttered part of herself to the contemporary woman reader. "I shrank from it," continues Susan Mitchell, "as the periwinkle from the pin . . . it is a powerful novel; I was impaled on the point of it and I know I have not the courage to read it again."

For a reader of the calibre of Susan Mitchell the importance of Moore's writing on sex lay in its truthfulness or penetration, and in the constant play of intelligence through it. There is sense in this reaction. Every observer who came across Moore from John Eglinton to Virginia Woolf found him, for all his frequent jumps into absurdity, lit by intelligence. But his motive was subversion.

*How does this square with Yeats' claim, in *Dramatis Personae*, to have read nothing of Moore's before 1897 or later? Did he impose a ban on a book he had not even read? I do not know, but take Susan Mitchell to be a reliable witness. She tells the story in her book on Moore.

From beginning to end of his life his conduct was prompted by the desire to shock, to cause an explosion. The sexual method was the surest: in England, as we have seen; and even more so, in Ireland. Katharine Tynan has reported that prior to the Parnell divorce no one in Ireland discussed sex. George Moore was an Irishman ahead of his nation in that respect. The English environment in which he was living in the 'eighties and 'nineties provoked him; intent to shock, he found he could disconcert English complacency that way. Thus he had a reputation and a technique ready to bring with him into Ireland and to use as a blast against the prudery and the purdah of his own folk; and in that he was, as in a number of other things, a pioneer, opening up the literature of sexuality in which Joyce and the late Yeats were to work more thoroughly and significantly.

A FIRST LOOK AT IRELAND

Even during the French and English periods of his life, Moore was consciously an Irishman. In *The Confessions* he gives his narrator the name "Edmund Dayne". Dayne means "Irishman". So in *Evelyn Innes* he calls Yeats Ulick Dean—Dean being pronounced Dayne just as Yeats is pronounced Yates.

His first novel had considered, apart from an excursion to Paris, English scenes but examined them from a Gallic angle (for he saw that it would be effective to set himself up as *le plus Parisien des Anglais*). His second novel had explored the English provinces. For his third, *A Drama in Muslin*, he took recourse to his own country; and concurrently he worked on a small volume of Irish sketches, published in French in 1886 as *Terre d'Irlande* and in English in 1887 as *Parnell and his Island*, which are an exposure of the shaggy poverty of the peasants and the ignorance of the landlords. "I am an Irish landlord," he says, "but that doesn't prevent me from recognising that it is a worn-out system. . . ."

A Drama in Muslin handles two themes: the clash between a mother and the daughters she puts on the marriage-market; the presentation of Ireland torn between landlord and tenant. Moore tries by a sleight of hand to intertwine the two, to show the first as if it *were* specifically Irish and in fact the obverse of the second:

> The history of a nation as often lies hidden in social wrongs and domestic griefs as in the story of revolution, and if it be for the historian to narrate the one, it is for the novelist to dissect and explain the other; and who could say which is of the most vital importance—the thunder of the public against the oppression of the Castle, or the unnatural sterility, the cruel idleness of mind and body of the muslin martyrs who cover with their white skirts the shames of Cork Hill?

It is a clever, wilful passage, written to cause rage in upper-class Ireland. There was a problem of the purdah in Ireland, a problem of importance, related to the nation's capacity to evolve.★ In a review of *Ave* a quarter of a century later Susan Mitchell said "Moore has tilted at the purdah . . . it is a form of tourney in which he excels." But the tilting in *A Drama in Muslin* is in fact not against a specifically Irish version of the purdah. It is against the constraints on women and the family bondage common at this date and for two generations to come, throughout the British Isles, whether in Celt, Anglo-Saxon, or Jewish society. In 1879 Meredith had built his best novel, *The Egoist*, out of the problem. Yet *A Drama in Muslin* is, as far as the muslin theme is concerned, a simpler, thinner *Egoist:* thinner, yet fairly taut, and here and there lit by a flash—"Had fate favoured Mrs. Barton she might have been a royal courtezan".

For the working-out of the Irish political theme Moore appeals

★I have sometimes wondered whether the word "purdah" is fair, especially when thinking of the pages of Synge in which he tells of the girls walking across the fields or down the roads and calling badinage at him. But Susan Mitchell uses the word. Moore describes conditions that deserve it. Mary Colum reports how the men-students tried to drive her out of the Abbey during the debate—to preserve her modesty (see page 228). Yeats tells how a Dublin typist broke down and refused to copy *Leda and the Swan* (I have known an Arab girl refuse to type words she thought unsuitable for her sex).

A passage in AE's letters (in Alan Denson's volume) adds information. Writing to Weekes on April 21st, 1910, he says that he would like the women on the farms to have more colourful lives; "I want dances and amusements in the country and pretty girls conscious of their looks; and a number of other things which are only to be got by agitation. On the small farms the women have a wretched time. The Protestant girls are all right, the Catholic girls are kept under by the clergy. The Protestant girls have all kinds of social entertainments. The priests don't like the sexes meeting before marriage, and I want to stir up some thought on the matter."

to his Zola training. But he is not a visiting stranger as he was when he took his notebook to the Potteries. He is writing of a situation he knows intimately; has known from boyhood; in which as proprietor he plays a part, though the artist in him disowns the landed man. Being personally involved, he seems at moments to make a melodramatic music out of the Irish scene rather than to report it. As the revolutionary anger spreads and the assassinations begin, he writes with a feverish rhetoric, contrasting directly with the near-eighteenth-century satirical writing in parts of the muslin chapters. Nevertheless, if there are passages of rhetoric and melodrama, there are others sharp with authentic detail: the poverty-stricken crowd watching the carriages arrive for the Castle Ball; and the following paragraph in which the Zola method* and Moore's ingrained knowledge of his country mate:

> Through the streaming glass they could see the inevitable strip of bog; and the half-naked woman, her soaked petticoat clinging about her red legs, piling the wet peat into the baskets thrown across the meagre back of a starveling ass. . . . And further on there are low-lying swampy fields, and between them and the roadside a few miserable poplars with cabins sunk below the dung-heaps, and the meagre potato-plots lying about them; and then, as these are passed, there are green enclosures full of fattening kine, and here and there a dismantled cottage, one wall still black with the chimney's smoke, uttering to those who know the country a tale of eviction and the consequent horrors: despair, hunger, revenge, and death. And above all these, sweeping along the crests of the hills, are long lines of beautiful plantations, and, looking past the great gateways and the outlying fir-woods, between the masses of the beeches you can see the white Martello-tower-like houses of the landlords.

*To do justice to Moore's rural writing here it is worth remembering that Zola's *La Terre*, intended "faire pour le paysan . . . ce que j'ai fait dans *L'Assommoir* pour le peuple des faubourgs de Paris", was begun in February 1886, published in 1887. *A Drama in Muslin* appeared in January 1886. As regards the chapters on the faubourgs of Dublin, however, Moore knew *L'Assommoir* well, and had proposed translating it.

Moore is to report the problem of tenant and landlord again in *Vale* when he is writing at the height of his powers, when all the nostalgia, all the significance that a theme can carry is at the command of his pen; he then produces richer paragraphs, but not one so forceful as this, where from reportage he moves organically to the imaging of the opposing classes: the "Martello towers" of the landlords are associated with English power and resistance to the ragged insurgents who "throw that long dim line against the shore".

Joseph Hone has called the book "a document that the historian should not disregard". And it displays Moore as the only famous writer of his time to show the old Ireland. Bernard Shaw used to complain that the writers of the Irish literary movement and of the Abbey Theatre presented an ideal Ireland, the nation they thought should exist instead of the one that did. That complaint could not be applied to *A Drama in Muslin*. Moore is writing of the contemporary, real, ugly, sad Ireland, which, to borrow a phrase from the novel itself, is part of the texture of his habitual thought.

Moore's work of the 'eighties includes a remark on Irish politicians. In the first edition of *The Confessions* he included, as a running judgment on books and writers, a comment on Mabel Robinson's *Disenchantment*. He wrote:

> . . . the figure of the Irish politician I accept without reserve. It seems to me grand and mighty in its sorrowfulness. The tall, dark-eyed, beautiful Celt, attainted in blood and brain by generations of famine and drink, alternating with the fervid sensuousness of the girl, her Saxon sense of right alternating with the Celt's hereditary sense of revenge, his dreamy patriotism, his facile platitudes, his acceptance of literature as a sort of bread basket, his knowledge that he is not great or strong, and can do nothing in the world but love his country. . . .

It is a tantalising picture, drawn at the date when Parnell's reputation is at the peak, but describing a pre-Parnell politician.

Moore's father, whom he adored, had been an Irish Parliamentarian; Moore's portraits of him usually emphasise his Byronic vigour; but those lively traits strike him as so inappropriate to an Irish politician, that he here lets them go and acknowledges this melancholy portrait of Miss Robinson's as symbolically the fitter.

When the next edition of *The Confessions* appeared, the strong, anti-platitudinous, resolute Parnell had fallen and been buried, but his myth had begun to rise, a new "figure of the Irish politician" was forming, and Moore deleted this passage.

A FIRST LOOK AT WAGNER

Deriving the practice from Zola and the French rather than English predecessors, Moore had trained himself to write the novel of "social habits and customs". In depending on these for *Esther Waters* he had, as in *A Mummer's Wife*, denied himself his natural pleasures, which were, in conversation and reverie: painting; the stage; music; religion; sport. In *Esther Waters* he had drawn on sport, but abstemiously; and he had touched on the sensuous delight of religion, but in the most austere possible form of the meetings of Plymouth Brethren. Symons and Yeats, to whom he dedicated his next novel, *Evelyn Innes*, published in 1898, evidently influenced him to abandon the self-denying disciplines. *Evelyn Innes* is the work of a man released to self-indulgence. There is scarcely a sentence but takes him among the arts, antiques, the questions of religion, in which he is at home.

The result is a pointed commentary on the Irish criticism of the materialist bias of nineteenth-century English literature. In freeing himself from the objectives that Ulick Dean considered materialist and turning to sources of exaltation, Moore wrote a more obviously commerce-bound book than anything he had yet done: a book in which all conduct related to wealth.

What Moore gained from his self-indulgence was not spirituality nor exaltation, nor significance nor purpose, but a pleasure in writing and a delighted experiment in literary architecture. It is an experiment based on Wagner. In Chapter I something has been said regarding the Irish awareness of Wagner. Moore had become a devotee of Wagner under the stimulus of his cousin, Edward Martyn, and his French friend, Edouard Dujardin, editor of *La Revue Wagnérienne*. He planned *Evelyn Innes* in terms of a parallel between Evelyn's emotional growth and the destinies of Wagner's heroines. The technique of parallelism, of illuminating the significance of a story by counterpointing it with a systematic series of allusions to a masterpiece which is part of the common cultural heritage, was not new. The Augustans for their special satirical purposes had practised it: Dryden in *Absalom and Achitophel;* Pope in *The Dunciad;* then Fielding in *Tom Jones* and *Jonathan Wild* had shown how athletically and effectively it could be used in the novel. Moore in *Evelyn Innes* and the sequel, *Sister Teresa,* renewed the technique for the modern age. He came upon it for himself by his addiction to art, by his capacity to understand himself as one of those persons for whom art is a closer reality than their primitive instincts. He reinstituted it, and since 1898 the most important works in English have depended on it: Eliot's *Waste Land* with its use of the Grail legend (also involving Wagnerian material) and his *Four Quartets* with their Beethoven framework; Joyce's *Ulysses* with its Homeric framework and *Finnegans Wake* where the complex use of parallelisms includes a Tristan and Isolde motif.* And having made a first elated essay in *Evelyn Innes,* Moore kept the possibilities of Wagnerian parallelisms in mind, to use them on a larger scale in *Hail and Farewell.*

All the signs of the later Moore appear together for the first time in *Evelyn Innes* and *Sister Teresa.* The oddest thing is, that although *Evelyn Innes* practises the technique of parallelism—one of the particular attractions of which is to the artist, and certainly to the taste of our age, that it invites a taut inter-relating of every detail in the book—it also introduces, or its continuation, *Sister Teresa,* introduces, Moore's later habit of anecdote which is not closely related to the theme. In *Héloïse and Abélard* and *Ulick and Sóracha* there are many digressive anecdotes, sometimes

*And Joyce may have taken his cue for this parallelism from the sequence in the 1901 edition of *Evelyn Innes* where Evelyn and Ulick go to Chapelizod, that she may the better play her role for having seen the landscape of Isolde's childhood.

colourful and attractive, but always, it seems, pure digressions: the author seems to say that he is a story-teller, and that story-tellers traditionally meander into sub-stories. Perhaps the fact that these digressions make their first appearance in *Sister Teresa*, written when Moore is back in Ireland and interested in the literary revival with its emphasis on "folk", shows that they do stem from a conviction that it is folk to digress from the main course of a story. A time may come when readers will again welcome these traditional excursions. At present it is, for most of us, more stimulating when the details of a story are knit into an integral structure like a nineteenth-century musical composition, which early twentieth-century literature is so often intent to emulate. Yeats noticed the two conflicting potentialities in Moore: "he would have been a master of construction, but that his practice as a novelist made him long for descriptions and reminiscences". For "practice as a novelist", which is off the track, read "his conception of a story-teller".

A SECOND LOOK AT IRELAND

In 1893 Moore talked of hating Ireland: "I have no wish to hear anything about Ireland." Within a short time a meeting with Yeats changed that. The appearance of Ulick-Yeats in *Evelyn Innes* marks the beginning of a new view of Ireland.

Ireland as it enters *Evelyn Innes* through the personality of Ulick is no longer the real Ireland of landlord and tenant, as Moore had known it and previously described it, but the neo-ancient Ireland of the young poets, where there is direct access to the spirit world, for the soil is no longer the filth of a peasant's cabin but a sign of the primal instincts. From Yeats and Martyn, and, in the light of the interpretation their talk shed, from the columns of Dublin's *Daily Express* which was regularly mailed to his London rooms, Moore had become aware of the new literary movement and its ideals and promises. Moreover, a visit to Ireland in May 1895 had impressed the landscape on his memory with a new meaning: he had gone to his mother's death-bed on "a bridal-like day . . . the most beautiful day I had ever seen, the most winsome, the most white, the most wanton, as full of love as a girl in a lane who stops to gather a spray of hawthorn."

In *Hail and Farewell* he has made a seductive narrative of the change of mind which decided him to resettle in Dublin. He walked through Edward Martyn's estates thinking of the Boer War and his hope for a British victory—thinking

> . . . that to raise an army of seventy thousand blacks would be a fine trick to play upon the Boers, I often returned through the park full of contempt for my countrymen, my meditations interrupted occasionally by some natural sight—the beauty of the golden bracken through which the path twisted, a crimson beech at the end of it, or the purple beauty of a line of hills over against the rocky plain freckled with the thatched cabins of the peasantry. Nor do I remember more beautiful evenings than these were; and, as the days drew in, the humble hawthorns shaped themselves into lovely silhouettes, and a meaning seemed to gather round the low, mossy wall out of which they grew, until one day the pictorial idea which had hitherto stayed my steps melted away, and I became possessed by a sentimental craving for the country itself. . . .

"It would be strange", he goes on in his satiric, impish way, his way of theatrically pretending nakedness to cover his nakedness, "it would be strange if Cathleen ni Houlihan were to get me after all." Ten pages later he lies awake all night worrying about a Boer retreat, and thinking of the Irish past mirrored in the swords in the Dublin Museum, the splendid bits that the ancient Irish put into their horses' jaws, the Book of Kells, the Cross of Cong:

> After that I must have fallen into a deep lethargy. On awakening, I remembered the autumn evening in Edward's park, when Cathleen ni Houlihan rose out of the plain that lies at the foot of the Burran Mountains, and came, foot-sore

and weary, up through the beech-grove to me. I had not the heart to repulse her, so hapless did she seem. . . .

The morning paper reports that 500 British troops have been captured by the Boers:

> The morning paper was picked up from the hearthrug, and the news of the capture of our troops read again and again, the same thrill of joy coming into my heart. The Englishman that was in me (he that wrote *Esther Waters*) had been overtaken and captured by the Irishman.

Instead of "a warm heart, a beautiful imagination, firmness and quiet purpose", which he had previously discerned in England and knew still to be there and could not forget, he was now aware of—this time he borrows his language from AE—"a shameful and vulgar materialism from which I turned with horror".

This shapely story is, like all *Hail and Farewell*, absurd and winsome, posed and genuine, comic and meaningful. Some of the best expositors of the Irish literary movement tell the students in their lecture-rooms to disregard Moore as a witness of what happened in Ireland. But he cannot be disregarded without loss. He is not a plain, sane, honest witness, but if we read him properly he has an enormous amount to tell us. What is behind this story? What really induced Moore to settle in Ireland? We know from the climax of *Hail and Farewell*—which I shall later quote—that he knew of the expectation that a god-given successor to Parnell would emerge and save Ireland. I believe that when he caught the first hint of this legend from Yeats he was fascinated. His early writings show that he had a latent susceptibility to Messianism. In *The Confessions of a Young Man*, when he speaks, in language meant to shock the Villa, of "the pale socialist of Galilee", the Swinburnian phrase includes a nervous response to the Christian image as well as a blast at it. (Besides, Galilee was, like many places of the Near East, associated with his father's travels, and to name Christ "of Galilee" was to excite a penumbral image of Christ as "my father, the young explorer whom I love".)

The bias of Moore's mind was to be Christ's evangelist and so always to be watching for his appearance. He evangelised in turn for the Impressionists, Zola, Pater, Huysmans. In the mid-nineties when he recognised the genius of Yeats, he played, for a short time, John the Baptist to Yeats' Christ. Captivated by the Irish expectations on the eve of 1900, he recognised that the scene was made for him. The only doubt was whether his role would be the Messiah or the evangelist. *Hail and Farewell* describes, in addition to the tale of conversion just quoted, how three times in the King's Road, Chelsea, a voice from the sky told him "Go to Ireland". So he went to settle in Ireland under this Pauline omen. But *Hail and Farewell* also records Moore's claim to the Messianic role itself.

CONTRIBUTIONS TO IRELAND

His first contribution to Ireland was the interpolation into the cheap double-column edition of *Evelyn Innes* in 1901 of chapters describing Evelyn in Ireland. Ulick, now somewhat reshaped in the image of AE, takes her to see the sacred places of Ireland, partly on the same itinerary that Moore pursues with him in *Salve*, and expounds the revival of the Irish identity. Thus Moore makes *Evelyn Innes* at this point a novel of information, of propaganda, to announce the new Ireland to Britain and the world.

Then came *The Untilled Field*, a set of stories written so that they might be translated into Gaelic (for Moore was offering an enthusiasm for the revival of Gaelic as his badge of admission into the nationalist movement). In the late 'eighties Moore had read Turgenev, and noted, like other Irish writers such as Lady Gregory, the relevance of his kind of country flavour and his kind of national sense to the Irish scene. But these Moore stories that began as an oblation ended as a criticism of Ireland. Moving about the Irish countryside to bring his acquaintance up to date, he reports conditions not greatly different from those of *A Drama in Muslin*. His narrative is simpler, easy and confident, gay when gaiety is possible; but the facts of a story like *A Playhouse in the*

West are as painful as ever. Despite the Yeatsian talk of *Evelyn Innes* and then the vision of the Burran Hills, Moore, when he looks at Ireland in 1902, again sees the troubled old Ireland; he does not see with the transforming vision of his new allies of the revival; he remains realist and, except perhaps in *The Wedding Gown*, a critic who admits no vitality in his land. The story *In the Clay* returns for its material to the opening chapter of *A Modern Lover:* a sculptor needs a model; how can he overcome the scruples of the Dublin girl whom he has in mind for his statue? Note that when William Powell Frith asked an Albany Street orange-girl to be his model in 1853, he had the greatest difficulty in persuading her: she was Irish and Catholic; her confessor would not give her his sanction; eventually she was the subject of *The Sleepy Model*. In Moore's story nearly half a century later the girl is more easily persuaded, but her brothers smash the statue. The story ends: "This is no place to live. It is no country for an educated man. It won't be fit for a man to live in for another hundred years. It is an unwashed country." In a writer for whom art is the currency of his life this is a devastating denunciation. Another story, *Julia Cahill's Curse*, finishes " 'When', I said, 'will a ray from the antique sun break forth and light up this country again'." He finds only one word of mitigation: there is something "dear" in her people. They are, then, worth redeeming; but this man who came to Ireland with the fancy that he would be welcomed as a redeemer is too truthful a writer, and too subversive in his approach, to pretend to see signs of redemption.

In 1903 Moore asked to be received into the Irish Protestant Church and notified the Press of his conversion. The explanation that he tendered to himself, as described in *Hail and Farewell*, is that, seeing Ireland as a country without light, a country that had never benefited, despite all the eighteenth century had given her, from an *Aufklärung*, he traced the responsibility to the influence of the Roman Catholic Church. Following this line of thought—an old one with him, perhaps facilitated by the years spent in France with her rift between clericalism and anti-clericalism—he argued that Catholicism must always be hostile to art and thus to civilisation. Had Catholicism produced even one great book? He persuaded himself that the answer was no. Then Ireland under Catholicism could not be reborn and civilised. So he must set an example of withdrawal from Catholicism. Such were his arguments. They had little to do with his real motives. Moore's acquaintances in Dublin regarded his step as a typical spoof on a public scale. Susan Mitchell in a calypso in *Aids to the Immortality of Certain Persons in Ireland* said:

No more in pagan carelessness I skip down Ely Place, .
Softly I glide through Dublin with the convert's
  timid grace—
The lamp of Protestant reform lights up my bashful
  face.

Ye pretty little Papist maids, whatever your degree,
Come hither fearlessly and sit on my converted knee,
Bid me to live and I will live your Protestant to be.

It's all the fun I'm like to get out of my little joke—

Moore's gestures were never without a whiff of the public joke. But this was not just a leg-pull. It was the severest possible attack on his brother, Colonel Maurice Moore, as the living representative of his Catholic antecedents. We know from some pages of *Salve* that before making an open declaration of Protestantism Moore told himself that it would be "dastardly" to his brother. He flew into it willy-nilly. It was iconoclasm, the smashing of the Lares and Penates. Not by chance was parricide an issue in Irish literature and drama. Again and again writers turn to smash their hearth. Moore, the eldest of them, does it most persistently and perhaps with an extra viciousness because he wears the mask of absurdity. Only, he shifts the attack away from his father, who is apart as his personal hero, to the other members of his family.

His mother's death, his new sensitivity to the beauty of Ireland, his response to the traditions of mediaeval Ireland and the pathos of the present, had not modified his fundamental inner revolt.

They had overlaid it with accretions, below which it was violent as ever. To attack his family on the religious issue was also to subvert that Irish nationalism in whose interest he had come to Dublin, in whose interest he claimed to protest against the restricting influence of Catholicism. Essential to the nationalist movement was the closing-up of sectarian differences. Otherwise England would find it too easy to divide and rule. Moore was tampering at a vulnerable point. He must have known this, but the spirit of revolt was stronger than any other in him.

The wilful conduct of 1903 becomes the literature of 1905, in his next novel, *The Lake*. When he transposes the problem into a novel, his wilfulness, the destructivity of his revolt conjoin with and are modified by tact, sensitivity, understanding. He tells of a priest, living by a lough, who, having driven Rose, a young girl, from his parish, comes to recognise that he did not so much deplore her moral fall as envy it, being in love with her. Through letters from her as she crosses Europe and penetrates the East with her scholar-employer he is sensitised to the land-scape around him, and through the landscape to the value of life. In a moment of natural perfection (such as Moore had known when he looked at the Burran Hills from Martyn's park) he responds to a "pagan enchantment", discovers that mind and body are one, and feels "like an instrument that had been tuned". He swims the lough, where his parishioners will think he has been drowned, and from the opposite shore tramps towards the coast, America, the turmoil of a new lay life. In fact Moore takes up that last sentence of *Julia Cahill's Curse*. *The Lake* is an extension of the metaphor of "the antique sun" as used there. Rose Leicester, so Moore wrote to his brother, is the animating Springtide. She brings back the sun that shall warm Ireland again. That warmth comes not from the lamp of Protestant reform, but from a pagan relationship with the natural world.

The Lake is a balanced, humanistic work. It allows, as humanism must, that where two viewpoints clash, both may be valid, though one must ultimately be preferred. While the Moore who is a resident of Ely Place, Dublin, is cracking squibs at Catholicism for the discomfiture of his family, the Moore of *The Lake* writes the priest's letters with sincerity and gives quiet credence to the miracle that saves Father Moran. One might compare the credence lent by Gide, tinging it with an allowance for the operations of voluntary belief, to the miracle in *Les Caves du Vatican*.

Like *Les Caves du Vatican* this Irish study of religious and lay faiths is worked out by a contrapuntal technique. A Catholic theme is played against a pagan, the faith and works of a religious life against the labour and ideals of a scholar. There is the image of early Christian Ireland, an Ireland of which Moore loved to think, when the architect, the metal-worker, the jeweller, the teacher flourished, and when the poet-mystic, Marban, inhabited his cell on the island in the lough; and this is set against the image of early oriental history, the history of the Hebrews and of civilisations in the interior of Asia and their contributions to the Christian system. In relation to Moore's future work this last image is fascinating to the critic. It is as if he is in mind already leaping ahead to his own Palestine journey of 1914 in pursuit of *The Brook Kerith;* on the way to that his scholar and Rose traverse the art-galleries and museums of Europe, thus tracing the route of Moore's spiritual pilgrimage through the arts to the study of the prophets; and the journey through Egypt into the Middle East also retraces the journeys Moore's father had made in his 1830 hey-day. But Moore keeps in check the personal factors which might have tempted him to accentuate the appeal of eastern exploration as compared with the "sympathetic history" of Ireland. These two themes are played against each other and at last inverted, when the priest writes to Rose: "You, who began by living in your instincts, are now wandering beyond Palestine in search of scrolls; and I, who began my life in scrolls, am now going to try to pick up the lost thread of my instincts in some great commercial town." It will be seen that Moore, having joined the literary-nationalist movement, is rebelling against it from within. Ireland's country priest goes away to a commercial town! This is defiance of the policies of Moore's literary colleagues in Ireland. A lapse into the ways of commerce was precisely what

AE feared for his country. The priest's discovery that body and mind are one is equally against the grain of the thinking of the Irish literary revival.* But though *The Lake* is an anti-AE book, it is nevertheless dependent, like some of the later pages of *Sister Teresa*, on the perceptions that AE's company and conversation had opened up. Moore's earlier books had shown that he knew his native earth but saw it as unbenevolent, poor as the peasantry. *The Untilled Field* has shown it without vitality. Now, he finds vitality in it: its therapy, its power to change men. (All Europe is making the discovery simultaneously: Gide in France, Forster in England).

A SECOND LOOK AT WAGNER: SIEGMUND AND PARNELL

Moore had arrived in Ireland expecting, in view of his considerable European reputation, to be welcomed as the champion of the Irish cause. Ireland had not risen to welcome him. He had invited attention by his Gaelic *Untilled Field*. Little attention resulted. Angrily he had detonated the religious explosion of his public change of faith. That drew attention but no applause. He had offered himself to Ireland, but had been rejected. He stayed in Ireland till 1910 writing a trilogy to recount the offer and the rejection, and to caricature his literary rivals and their offering. On October 1st, 1908, AE described Moore's "work in progress" to Quinn (the American supporter of the Irish movement): "One half of Dublin is afraid it will be in the book, and the other is afraid it won't." In the outcome only AE and Eglinton "escaped with a halo". *Hail and Farewell* is mendacious, airy, wilfully grotesque. We have to feel for the truth in it, and respond as we do to a poem, above all as we do to a comic poem. Test it by the standards which Yeats proposed in the circular drawn up for would-be contributors to the Abbey:†

[It] should contain some criticism of life, founded on experience or personal observation of the writer, or some

---

Vide, for example, Eglinton, Introduction to *Letters from George Moore to E. Dujardin*: "our convention was that the spiritual attitude of each of us towards the things of the body was detached and contemplative."

†See Lady Gregory, *Our Irish Theatre*, 1914, pp.100-6.

vision of life, of Irish life by preference, important from its beauty or from some excellence of style; and this intellectual quality is not more necessary to tragedy than to comedy.

These requirements are all fulfilled by Moore's comic trilogy. And he intends it as *sacred* comedy. Even though it is an autobiography, he explicitly calls it "a sacred book": "But an autobiography, I said, is an unusual form for a sacred book. But is it? My doubts quenched a moment after in a memory of Paul. . ." With Paul to confirm his intuition, he gives a comedy to Ireland for her scriptures. The prevailing tone of his writing is not vehement, as Paul's tone seemed to him to be, but the beguiling piano tones, the gentle humanity, which had impressed him in Christ's teaching when he sat down and read through the Bible in Dublin on the eve of his "conversion". It is the tone of the Beatitudes, the Beatitudes turned into comedy by Moore's temperament.

The three volumes proceed as if they had no structure but the line of time, as if merely a journal, a sequence of anecdotes and profiles. But Moore was angry with anyone who showed a disposition to treat them as merely that. He had selected his events and organised them with his excellent sense of structure. Following his experiment in *Evelyn Innes*, Moore again works through parallelism, and his frames of reference are Wagner and the Bible. How many readers of *Ave* have wondered why Moore has dragged them with the suffering Martyn through Germany to Bayreuth? The journey seems to lead far from Ireland. In fact, the journey to Bayreuth is a pilgrimage to a holy centre of Messianism. Just as Ireland sought a Messiah, Wagner had sought a Messiah for Germany, and created one who had seized the imagination of the western world: Siegfried—his birth and death celebrated annually at Bayreuth.

Undemonstratively, as though it were only a diary of a summer journey, as though there were no other object but to tease Martyn and to exchange information on polite, agreeable subjects, Moore accumulates his references to Wagner: then at the climax of *Vale* he uses them, disclosing the parallel that has been in his mind:

> . . . I have come into the most impersonal country in the
> world to preach personality—personal love and personal
> religion, personal art, personality for all except for God;
> and I walked across the greensward afraid to leave the garden,
> and to heighten my inspiration I looked towards the old apple-
> tree, remembering that many had striven to draw forth the
> sword that Wotan had struck into the tree about which
> Hunding had built his hut. Parnell, like Sigmund, had drawn
> it forth, but Wotan had allowed Hunding to strike him with
> his spear. And the allegory becoming clearer I asked myself
> if I were Siegfried, son of Sigmund slain by Hunding, and
> if it were my fate to reforge the sword that lay broken in
> halves in Mimi's cave.

And then "the garden filled with tremendous music, out of
which came a phrase glittering like a sword drawn from its
sheath", and he transcribes the Sword motif.

Nothing could be clearer than this announcement of himself
as Parnell's son and the Siegfried and saviour of Ireland. Would
Ireland receive him? Eglinton had called Moore "too much of a
toff". Martyn told him that the Irish were too offended by his
irregular life to take him seriously. Moore replies to Martyn and
the Irish that he has become inoffensive, for—and he places this
story immediately before his vision of the sword—he is over
fifty and a change of life has made him the equal of the priest,
the nun, and the ox. If chastity is a pre-condition of prophecy,
he is now qualified, and being qualified he will preach contraception and the unfettered Protestant cult of personality.

The very character of this disclosure shows that Moore already
knew in the writing of his book that Ireland would not have him
as the Messiah.

To publish his book he had to withdraw, resume his expatriate
life in imperial England. One possible view of *Hail and Farewell*
is that the recognition that he was not the Messiah after all, and
that he would hardly remain candidate for the role in a country

so clogged as Ireland, is part of the comedy; that the book is wholly in his satirical vein; that he himself is satirised and teased with the other dramatis personae. That would be an attractive but an incomplete view. The rejection of the Messiah does not prove the Messiah an imposter. On the contrary, it is a mark of the Messiah that he is rejected. "When the Messiah comes I will not know him", says the Rabbi in Brod's *David Reubeni*. Christ was rejected. Parnell was rejected. The Old Testament prophets were unpopular. Moore's reading of the Bible in Ely Place had disclosed to him an error in his expectations: he had thought that as Ireland's redeemer he would be royally welcomed; the Bible showed him otherwise, and made him content to be isolated in Dublin and finally exiled from it; content that Ireland had given him, and that he had given it, "a sacred book", and that in doing so he had in fact fulfilled the Messianic mission.

SCRIPTURE AS CASTIGATION

To call *Hail and Farewell* a "sacred book" is a high claim, which is justified. A sacred book need not be directly "inspirational". It may be castigational. Ireland had inspirers. It was good then, and is good still, since a literature is effective and continuously relevant long after the hour when it is written, that she also had a castigator in Moore. To Ireland then and to us who read him now it is obvious what Moore did not and could not see. He did not appreciate the strength of the forces mustering under the surface of the nationalism of 1900–10. Repeatedly he gibed at the patriotic school that the Irishman's dreams are always in conflict with reality, a gibe true but trivial, since the Irish insisted—in the manner of T. E. Lawrence (who participated, by emotional displacement, in a nationalist movement not his own)—on compelling reality to take the shape of their dreams. Moore could not follow the dreamers. If he had, he might have been compelled to make peace with his family, with his antecedents, and that was a decisive impossibility: his brother's image is imposed on Ireland: "my mind reverted to the Colonel, and he stood up in my mind, Ireland in essence, the refined melancholy of her mountains and lakes, and her old castles crumbling among the last echoes of a dying language. In his face, so refined and melancholy, I could trace a constant conflict between dreams and reality. . . ." The future and reconciliation being closed to his view, he sees correspondingly more clearly into the past. As in the 'eighties when he wrote *A Drama in Muslin* he is the recorder of the old Ireland, and now with the keenest sensibility, detecting and recording everything with which there should be no reconciliation. *Ruins and Weed* is the thought in his mind at the beginning of *Ave* when he remembers his childhood and speculates on a title for his book. Implicated in the ruins and weed, he could not take adequate part in the life of revolutionary Ireland. But the ruins and weed had a hold on the land and on the Irish mind. It was important that they should be seen, and it is important that they should be seen now where they still ramify in the body social of Ireland under the welcome changes. They can only be dealt with when recognised, and can best be recognised through the work of the writers, and especially Moore who knew them thoroughly because exclusively, and who described them most realistically and most elegiacally. That is the fundamental sense in which *Hail and Farewell* is a prophet's book, that, though with so much subtlety, with dancing shifts of tone outside the range of the Old Testament, it diagnoses an evil.

Moore believes that he not only diagnoses the evils of Ireland but also prescribes the medicine. He preaches personality. It has been said that Ireland, being deprived of all else by England, was left with nothing but personality to cultivate, cultivated it vigorously, and had it before Moore as well as since. Moore himself with his idiosyncracies was a typical product. On that showing Moore's mission to his countrymen was redundant. On the other hand, it is clear from the text that his code of personality is conceived as a blast against Catholicism (which in turn, as indicated above, is conceived as cause and symbol of Irish decrepitude, but is also the target of attack inasmuch as it is equated with his family). On the climax page of *Vale* he lists the faults of Catholic Ireland: "under the spell of the magicians, without will, without intellect, useless and shameful. . . ." So Moore's *personality* is a shorthand sign for the antithesis of Catholic conformity: it means thinking one's own thoughts freely, "being oneself". Even if Irishmen already have "personality", that is, are idiosyncratic and animated, Moore would argue that they don't *know* that they are. "In Ireland men and women die without realising any of the qualities they bring into the world." He is preaching self-consciousness, the free scrutiny of the self, the resultant knowledge of it, the greater capacity to develop in the light of that knowledge, the freedom to take the steps necessary for that further development. It is a weakness of Moore's position that this meaning, if it is his meaning, does not emerge of itself. We are left probing for it. But better than any definition the whole of the trilogy supports this meaning: it is itself a work of personality, progressing by a series of scrutinies and non-conforming reactions.

The subversion of the family is the first step to personality. As ever, the reader finds himself back at Moore's drive to destroy his family when he questions the reason for his positions. But how much he made of it, above all this radiant, gay, penetrating book, the Bible of the old Ireland. In Moore's latest years and after his death Yeats became the castigator of Ireland, more bitterly, more violently, more greatly too—but it was Moore's special genius to spin his hatred with absurdity, fancy, grace; he is the only angry prophet who has ever beguiled. We must remember that Moore was not a public speaker; among a nation of orators he could not make a speech. He is always a host talking to his visitor, Christ talking to the disciples.

Did Moore blaze his own way to his cult of personality? Did he pick it up, like his *Hail and Farewell* remarks against abstractions in literature, from the talk of Yeats, who around 1910 was actively thinking on the subject? Or did he borrow it from Barrès? *Sous l'Œil des Barbares* had first appeared in January 1888. From that date onwards Barrès was writing prolifically and at the period when *Hail and Farewell* was written his public standing in France was high, and his *culte du moi* was common knowledge. Hone tells us practically nothing of Moore's relations with

Barrès, but they certainly existed as we know from the painter and gossip Jacques-Emile Blanche. They await the attentions of a scholar and may be a rewarding study.

It is a curious coincidence that the late development of Barrès and the late development of Moore alike ran to historical romances. In 1914 Moore travelled to the Holy Land to collect material for *The Brook Kerith*. That same year Barrès was in Syria, and found there the material for the Crusader castle story of *Un Jardin sur l'Oronte*. Is there any truth in the preamble to that story, in which Barrès pretends that it was translated to him by a young Irish archaeologist at Hamah in the June of that year 1914? T. E. Lawrence was engaged in archaeology in Syria till the late spring of 1914. There is just the chance that Barrès met Lawrence, who, with his usual chameleon adaptability, would describe himself to a Frenchman as Irish rather than English; that, as he was on his way to see Crusader castles, which Lawrence had studied, they found common ground for a lively talk; and that, though Lawrence, who was no reader of classical Arabic, translated him no manuscript, his presence and talk acted as catalyst on Barrès' imagination.

MESSIANISM RECONSIDERED

The Brook Kerith is a consequence of *Hail and Farewell*. The two books are different in form and treatment, one a sacred comedy in a contemporary setting with overt autobiography to steer it, the other a group of psychological studies in a historical setting with scriptural exegesis as the node of reference. But they belong to each other: they deal with Messianism; they examine the Christian faith, and thus continue Moore's policy of prising at the foundations of his family's existence; they present Ireland— for Pilate's Roman Palestine is reconstructed in terms of Moore's British Ireland. In *The Lake* Moore had already tapped the analogising between the Hebrew fate and the Irish fate current in Ireland at the turn of the century, and now he took the exploitation further. He identifies the Irish and the Jews, two peoples in a similar predicament: their soil occupied by an alien power, their religion invaded by strangers from without and prophecies from within, a desire for independence leading to underground organisations deriving their courage from a sense of an heroic past, the fanaticism of the zealots, the longing for a revelation.

When Moore's Irish acquaintances heard that he was engaged on an enquiry into Christianity and had sailed for the Levant to obtain a knowledge of the locale at first hand, they at once saw a connection with *Hail and Farewell;* only, because they read that as a debunking book, they supposed that its sequel would be in the same spirit. On March 14th, 1914, AE included a word about his journey and proposed novel in a bulletin to John Quinn and commented, jokingly but expressively, "Having desecrated one holy island, he is now going to desecrate the Holy Land in Asia."

Moore's novel was subversive of established opinion, and is informed with his customary note of pleasure in differing from the common understanding and thereby startling the reader. There are, however, other pleasures combined with it to produce its exotic music. There is the pleasure of emulating the rapid, exact style of the mediæval Irish poem, *God's Grandfather,* which Kuno Meyer had read to him in Dublin. There is also the pleasure of the accomplishment of a dream. As a child Moore had been bewitched every time his father described how he wandered Egypt, Palestine, and beyond. His love for his father was entangled with masculine and colourful associations: his horses, especially his race-horses, the fastest in Ireland; the bizarre journeys; the portage of a boat from Joppa to the Dead Sea; the Dead Sea storm. So, possibilised by his need of exact topographical information on the defiles beyond Jericho, which was in turn sought in accordance with those Zola standards that he never quitted even though he quitted naturalism, Moore fulfilled his earliest fantasy and, having been proud of his father, emulated him. In doing that he performed a maturation ritual: he could now write as one who had crossed to the other side of experience: and therefore the pleasure in writing, therefore the sense of elevation and control.

Yet how complex the matter is. *The Brook Kerith* was an

imitation of his father, an act of love and homage, a step across a boundary. But it was still, in continuation of *Hail and Farewell*, an act of Protestantism, an act of revolt against his family. He turns his gaze on the Messiah whom his family worships according to a religion which demands complete faith, complete submission. His probing of the story means a rejection of faith, the claim to probe facts for himself. As we have seen, this Protestantism, this public examination, is an aspect of his anger with his nation, his house, his family, "my brother's untidy mind". Like Blake, Moore had noted the text

> A man's worst enemies are those
> Of his own house and family

and had grasped it; had written by the inspiration of it in *Hail and Farewell*, and planned *The Brook Kerith* in virtue of it. But what follows? *The Brook Kerith* denies, with an artistic sustained pianissimo, the divine birth of Jesus, and denies and exposes in that example the validity of all religious revelation and all the prophetic sayings of the Bible; and the plot is so constructed that one saying is specifically denied, the saying that justifies Moore's assault on his family. Moore shows Joseph's love for his father and his father's emotional concentration on him; shows Joseph struggling between that natural love and Christ's command to drop human relationships; shows Jesus, in the sanity that comes to him after his recovery from the crucifixion, regretting the cruelty of the command.

Almost equally paradoxical is the outcome of Moore's thinking on Messianism. The Moore of *Hail and Farewell* had been both Ireland's Messiah and Ireland's Paul. In *The Apostle* and *The Brook Kerith* the Christ and Paul are separated, become antitheses: Messianism is insanity; Christ through the shock of suffering has become sane and has recognised his error; Paul will never be sane, will live and change the world under the drive of the morbid interior violence that he calls divine revelation. Messianism is violence, which disorganises one religion only to set up another with as great, or greater, constraints and intolerance. The victory of the personality of a Messiah ends in the depersonalisation, the submission of his worshippers. So Moore, while still pursuing the way of the personalist, the Protestant, the man with a message, produces a book which, in plot and in tone, abnegates his position, and says that quiet, solitude, gentleness are best: if there is a divinity in life, it is in tender family relations, in the selfless conduct of the good shepherd. Having been refused by the Irish people, and having claimed the leadership of them by virtue of that very fact, Moore now denies the whole Irish conception of a divine leader. "The Messiah in Palestine", he says, "came to see that Messianism is a delusion; so do I in respect of Ireland." Instead he offered precisely what Susan Mitchell at the same date, in her book about him, was urging him to offer: a humane sense of friendship and affection, the mean between the bauble and the star, for, she notes, "There has always been a certain sterility in Irish ideals; we reach for a star or we scramble lower down for a more terrestrial bauble."

The high point of *The Brook Kerith*, which should be contrasted with the Wagnerian, prophetic climax of *Hail and Farewell*, is the story of Jesus, when he is back at the humble life of the shepherd of the Essenes, carrying home the lamb that has lost its yoe. Borrowing it from the story of Moses and the sheep in the Talmud,* Moore tells this story with an artfulness that should be repugnant, and yet with so much tenderness, and the tone of oriental story-telling as old as man, that it is irresistible. It is strange how Moore, determined to have no children, horrified by the concept of lineage, had the emotion of family love at his disposal equally in the realist *Esther Waters* and in the elaborately musical *Brook Kerith*.

When we read *The Brook Kerith* we are surprised by the unveiled artifice of the manner of writing, even more surprised by our own surrender to it. The "continuous melody", fully achieved in this book after Moore has been working towards it since *The*

*Compare *A Story-Teller's Holiday*, p.209, where Moore remembers how he found this story for *The Brook Kerith*, and then finds the story of Lilith; "A Talmudic tale, I said, a lilt such as a reaper might sing while reaping—a folk-tale told over the fireside, hardly as much."

Lake, has often been praised, but equally compelling is the orchestration of the melody, the sparse, vivid use of strange instruments with exotic voices, a blend of contrasts, of the primitive and the sophisticated, the primitive as reconstructed and loved by a sophisticated mind. In the example of Yeats and Lady Gregory he had seen what effects could be won by the exploitation of folk-art, above all the story-teller's art. This was his first attempt to borrow what he had seen Yeats so successfully manage, and to manage it better. In fact, he does obtain an unprecedented, a strange, appealing dissonance; and successfully because the mode is not the chief focus of the book but the servant of stronger interests. Observe the book's psychological insight: Moore's reticence on such matters as Joseph's homosexual constitution; his accurate study of Pilate, the nationalists, the assassins. Not that it is a perfect book. *Hail and Farewell* is perfect; *The Brook Kerith* is of wider significance and accessible to a far wider public, but it has flaws—especially a clumsiness in the rustic speech of the disciples, which is a hybrid of Kiltartan and novelist's Sussex.

THE TWO COMPLEXIONS OF STORY-TELLING

To show Yeats that George Moore was the better Irishman, in touch with the soil and folk-art, and also the better artist, able to convert folk-art into work of international and permanent interest—that intention, which could just be detected in *The Brook Kerith*, became the leading consideration in *A Story-Teller's Holiday*. The book is a set of stories which Moore pretends that he exchanges with a gifted Irish shanachie in his Irish countryside. With this scheme he casts over the book the light of the *Bucolics*.

In fact, the folk-tales, fables, and "historical romances" that Moore writes in the last fifteen years of his life have a light from the classical Mediterranean suffusing them, even when he is engaged with Celtic forms, idioms, or settings. He implies, with the deftest suggestions, Virgil, Theocritus, Hesiod; the troubadours; and behind the troubadours their Arab predecessors.* "Isn't it

---

*It is evident that his Holy Land expedition had sensitised him to the Arab voice. So quickly he responded to a stimulus.

a basic pleasure of life", he seems to insinuate, "that we listen to songs or stories, listen regardless of the burden of the world? Song and story are the solace of life everywhere." By the use of age-long techniques he brings sunlight to his material. This is his way of giving Ireland the antique sun, which, he had written in *The Untilled Field* and *The Lake*, must open on the land and revive it.

Mid-twentieth-century taste is averse to Moore's deliberate late manner. But the prejudice will dissolve. The next generation of readers will be able to adapt to it just as well (which means not quite effectively, but with a good measure of effectiveness) as to the eighteenth-century style or to Jane Austen's. Then there will be an appetite for writing like the following from *Ulick and Sóracha:*

> The woman is never the same as the girl, she said, breaking into speech suddenly. We make promises that we cannot fulfil, or fulfil indifferently. And until the woman within her dies, every nun dreams of being carried away. She knows that she will be buried in her habit, but she puts a taper in her window and lies down watching it, uncertain whether she would follow the knight if he came, only certain that she is guilty of a sin in putting the light there, though it lure nobody. She falls asleep watching the taper, and finds the charred wick in the morning. So her life goes by. Shall I tell all you have told me, Princess Sóracha, to Sir Ulick de Burgo? I asked. Tell him what you please, she answered; yes, tell him that I burn tapers in my window, knowing well that no knight will climb the pear tree that grows beneath.

It is quick beguiling writing. Yet it is a criss-cross of paradoxes. It is so deliberately a reduction of the traditional story-teller's art, and so evidently "cunning" in its closeness, that it should be merely decorative. But while it *is* decorative (like all the supports Moore collected for his celibate existence: his Aubusson carpet, eighteenth-century chairs, Georgian coffee-spoons), it is also human and vital. It is so formal, and therefore the essence of restraint, that Moore can even relax another kind of restraint previously imposed on himself and allow physical detail into his wanton passages; and that counterpoints the formality with a sense of vitality. Perhaps the most formidable doubleness in Moore's late work lies in the joint presentation of vitality and a condemnation of life, of the warmth of the vitalising sun and the cold of experience. Discernible in Moore's early work, this contradiction makes the essential pattern of the last books. The beguilement, balance, lovely decorative effects are a frame around material as painful as the life of Esther Waters.

This late art of Moore's is a means of enduring as well as describing his material. It is the opposite of the more characteristic art of our time, the art of "the beauty of ugly pictures", where, on the Wagnerian principle that Moore himself loved, beauty is surrounded by a ring of fire, only to be reached by the hero. In Moore's final art a ring of brilliant beauty encircles a freezing nucleus and constrains indignities that might otherwise be totally destructive. At the centre of the sunny blaze are Moore's old, painful themes. He had long dwelled on celibacy and unappeased desires; on castration (for it is clear that he had a personal problem which insisted on masochistic dalliance with the thought of gelding); on the cruelty of man and nature; on loss and grief, which are the greater part of existence. Those French winters that are so sharply described in *Héloïse and Abélard*, the winters of wolves, which invade the cities in their hunger, the winters when it seems no spring will come; then spring, and the keenness of children; life is pulling at the children, and they disappear, gone with the Crusades; then there is the long residue of desolation. That is the year of life as Moore conceives it from his work-table or hospital bed in his old age. He must have thought of his decorative framework, and its sparkle of pleasure, as his triumph. Knowing that the spring is so brief, he could tell, no one better, how to catch it; could catch the pleasure of nature's consolations, the curves of buttocks, the music of the lute or of a meditating mind. But in the end there is the madness of Ulick on his island; there remains only "solitude 'mid rocks and sand where there is nothing pleasing"; and Moore thoroughly believes what he had written, reflecting on Esther's story, before the turn of the century, "that all things that live are to be pitied".

Did he write better in 1894 when he reported this finding, in *Esther Waters*, directly, without decoration, sternly disciplining himself to lend no more pleasure to the story than scrutiny could find in the life of a poor, overworked servant-girl of religious upbringing? It is a matter of taste whether we judge it better to tell truth rigorously, as he told it then, the art flowing in only as a final consequence between the grilles and prongs of the effort, or to tell it artistically, with the compensating pleasures and solaces wreathed around for self-preservation lest the work and life itself break down. It is a matter of choice for us as readers to which of the two modes we give our preference. To Moore as writer there was no choice. A writer does what he can: his technique, his approach is determined by the danger of his vision, the danger that it may destroy him. Sometimes a young man, by a mixture of nerve and ignorance of the magnitude of the danger, can write more nakedly, free of protective devices, than when he is older. Shaw, looking back on *Mrs. Warren's Profession*, once called it his best play: "but it makes my blood run cold; I can hardly bear the most appalling bits of it. Ah, when I wrote that, I *had* some nerve." The Irish Shaw in London wrote that play during 1893 and 1894. The Irish Moore in London, only four years older than Shaw, published *Esther Waters* in 1894. Later he might well have applied Shaw's words to the novel that first won him a large audience. It is the mark of Yeats' stature as compared with Moore that when knowledge increased in his old age, his nerve was not diminished by it; he never called on the beauty of art as a protection, and so won the highest beauty, the poet's new beauty, that was beyond Moore. But Moore's lesser kind of beauty is still considerable, is not to be contemned.

Moore's attitude to his country is the final paradox of his late period. In *The Brook Kerith* he determined against Messianism. But he still preached, even if his message was the abnegation of preaching and any claim to leadership. He has given up an evangelical interest in Ireland, and he looks away to France, the Mediterranean, *medium aevum*, antiquity, but he cannot give up Ireland, and one half of him comes back with every step the other half moves away. After the Easter Rising in 1916 he hurried to Dublin. He describes himself ambling around the ruins of the shelled Post Office as a reflective, sardonic observer. But it was a compulsive visit; and in his account of it in *A Story-Teller's Holiday* the holed masonry merges into his total picture of the "ruins and weed" of Ireland—that "melancholy beauty" which it has been an object of all his subversive mischief to change into active life.

Even in his French historical novels Moore has Ireland in mind. He writes of Brittany and Bretons—a Celtic people. One day in Dublin, during his nationalist and pro-Gaelic phase, he had met a Breton sailor on the quay, had been shown the four-master grainship in which he served, and had been delighted to learn that the crew, all Bretons, talked their own Celtic language: even at the top of the mast in the gales of Cape Horn they shouted in Celtic to each other. Perhaps Moore had begun to associate Brittany and Ireland at a date still earlier than that; perhaps Yeats had suggested the correspondence to him, for there is a reference in *Evelyn Innes* to "a journey to Brittany . . . in search of folk-tales". Literary gestation, especially in a man who is full of ideas competing for preference, is a long process, and it took over twenty years for the *Evelyn Innes* hint to lead to *Héloïse and Abélard*, and for that book in turn to produce its offshoot, *Peronnik the Fool*. The Breton idea came to life at last because he had to write of Ireland and her hopes and destiny even when he had abandoned his part in the Irish movement, and Brittany gave him an oblique way of doing it. He does not write of Celtic Brittany with love. Abélard has lands in Brittany but forgoes them. Yes, comments Héloïse, "so that thy mind might be saved, a mind that would have been dwarfed in Brittany." Moore identifies himself with Abélard—thinker, musician, lover, and victim. When Abélard withdraws, deprived, to Brittany again, it is to a monastery where "the ocean thunders around the rocks and the gulls scream; a country without laws, a savagery". His Brittany and Ireland are barbarian. His voice is hostile; his late sunlight falls on a rusty javelin. A force in him, nevertheless, keeps him prodding at the Irish situation.

There is a close parallel between his feelings regarding Ireland and his perennial worrying on the question of whether a man should continue to live and beget life. Passion says no; reason endorses that no; but an inner, undesired, unaccepted force persists. Moore's persistence in writing about Ireland and Irishness is equivalent to a persistence in offering a lesson and lead to her. When Messianism no longer seemed possible for him, and when he had convinced himself that it was not proper either for him or anyone else, he still—obliquely, mutedly, contradictorily—persisted in the role, or a ghost of it.

Part of the excellence of Moore lies in his freedom from complacency. He often pretends to complacency, but he has none, as these contradictions demonstrate. Right to the end he continued to scandalise. Scandalisation pre-supposes that the status quo is not desirable—and also that it can be altered, that one man, at least, is capable of opening his eyes, seeing clearly, and differing, and that the shock thus given to orthodox opinion will stimulate others and open the way to remedy and change. During the era when scandalisation was a prevalent technique Gide warned that it will not always do what is expected of it, and that gentler methods may be the more efficacious. In his journal for the year 1893 (when Moore was a participant in the Ibsen movement and was colouring *Esther Waters* with a grimness drawn from *Ghosts*, which he had seen in Antoine's production) Gide wrote:

> *Les Revenants* d'Ibsen m'ont fait un grand effet à cette nouvelle lecture; je les ai lus devant ma mère et tante Henry; mais il faut prendre garde de s'amuser trop du scandale. C'est en poussant les choses, non en les heurtant, qu'on les remue. Toujours nous devons tenir compte de l'inertie des ames et des corps. En heurtant bien souvent l'on brise; et c'est tout. Il faut émouvoir.

There were times when Moore, scandaliser by prime impulse, acted, thanks to his artistic flair, on this principle. Elsewhere and more often scandalising is uppermost; certainly it is so in *Hail and Farewell;* but there, and in all the confessional and much other work, to make it efficacious he blends it with comedy. He once pretended to despise humour, and black-listed it as the English vice; but it was valuable to him, and in him to us. Intellectual comedy retrieved, modified, and made comestible and effective his scandalising violence.

Moore's late works, with their doubling of his intricacies, were still unwritten when Susan Mitchell published her book about him in 1916, but, with her bent towards oriental imagery, she compared his first thirty-three years' books with "the banyan tree whose own branches spring up into trees all round it, never detaching themselves from their parent, but in their many lives are one tree." That is just. It is odd, though—or did Susan, consciously or unconsciously, remember the passage?—that in the nostalgic, closing chapters of *Vale*, wandering with the Colonel on his family estate, Moore came on such a tree, imported and planted by his father, and expressed dislike for it: "a tree of vile habit, sending down branches to take root, creating a little jungle." That kind of tree he did not like. Yet neither he nor his brother would fell it. They were, he commented, both tree-worshippers: the Colonel unperceivingly and by habit, he himself with knowledge of the implications, reverenced "the mystery of the vasty height sprung out of a single seed". In this tree, Moore's report of it, and Susan Mitchell's intuition, the enigma of the man is nicely epitomised.

CHAPTER III

ISABELLA AUGUSTA GREGORY

1852-1932

BORN in the same year as Moore, Lady Gregory was the young-
est of seven daughters of Dudley Persse of Roxborough in
Galway. Moore bolted from the landlordism which led him to
write his criticism of the system. The Persses at Roxborough,
the Gregorys at Coole, lived the system and, while benefiting
from it, tried to sustain the best in it while it decayed around them.
Her family was Protestant, but she had a Catholic nurse, Mary
Sheridan, an old story-telling Irishwoman.

She grew in the habit of Christian charity, good works, and
reading. "Quite a student" Sir William Gregory thought her
when he chose her for his second wife in 1880. Gregory's lands at
Coole were a few miles from Roxborough. He was a politician
and administrator, of the same generation, standing, and disposition as Moore's father if perhaps a little smoother and less
individual. "Sir William's travels", commented Moore, "were
not so original as my father's, and the racehorses that he kept
were not so fast, and his politics were not so definite"; but
Moore goes on to compliment his affability, his interest in the Old
Masters, and his knowledge of men and affairs. He had pursued a
conspicuous public career, for five years in the 'seventies had been
a successful Governor of Ceylon. He had friends throughout
Europe and the East, and, taking his new wife to meet them,
he taught her to know the "top of the world", as Yeats afterwards put it—"that top of the world where men and women

are valued for their manhood and charm, not for their opinions".
He was closely interested in the relationship between art and the
State, in the museums and the National Gallery. He transplanted
her from a narrow, intense home, to a larger world where her
energies were suddenly wholly engaged in acquiring from him
and through him larger ideas and social, intellectual, and administrative skills. We know too little about her during this decade of
her expansion. It still awaits a lucky biographer.

Moore was at dinner at Coole during Lady Gregory's married
years and describes her then: "a young woman, very earnest, who
divided her hair in the middle and wore it smooth on either side
of a broad and handsome brow. Her eyes were always full of
questions, and her Protestant high-school air became her greatly
and estranged her from me." The elderly Sir William stood up to
marriage with her for twelve years, then died leaving her with a
son and his estates and even his library (of which he had originally
promised her, on marriage, six volumes of her choice), but not
his best pictures which he gave to the National Gallery shortly
before his death. Now she began to tinker with literature. She
edited and published, in 1894, his memoirs: they unfortunately
stop short at the date of her marriage to him. Then she turned to a
project they had sometimes discussed, but found too unhandy,
during his lifetime, the editing of his grandfather's letters. She
occupied a winter, aided, she says, by patience and the long
evenings, sifting through the box in which they were kept,
selecting the passages she thought most relevant to Ireland's
current history, and linking them with a commentary. Published
in 1898 as *Mr. Gregory's Letter-Box* it offered the first expression,
disjointed but sometimes quick and tangy, of the enthusiasms
hidden under her solemnity. Here she first tried her hand at
reporting peasant stories in the original words.

She met Yeats at Edward Martyn's Tillyra Castle in August
1896. She invited him to come to see her. She also had him bring
AE. Of the two she decided that Yeats was the man Ireland was
waiting for. It is clear that he was the personality that she was
waiting for to direct her stirring energies. Yeats was in bad health

and his finances were meagre; she gave him, for long spells, the peace and good diet of Coole, and when he was not at Coole she sent him wine, biscuits, or bottled fruit, and sometimes, calling, left money on his mantelpiece. She discussed the collecting of folk-lore with him; he saw the ease with which she persuaded the country people to talk, and her industry and accuracy in writing down what she heard. Believing that there would be evidence of the supernatural in her records, he encouraged her to push her collecting forward systematically. He was shown her translations from Gaelic, and encouraged her to more. In 1902 she published her translation of *Cuchulain of Muirthemne*. In his preface to it Yeats said: "When she has added her translations from other cycles she will have given Ireland its Mabinogion, its Morte d'Arthur, its Nibelungenlied". This did not work out as roundedly as he promised, for she was becoming, at the date of printing of this first volume, interested in the Irish theatre, eventually her central passion, but she nevertheless compiled a number of collections: *Poets and Dreamers* in 1903, *Gods and Fighting Men* in 1904, *A Book of Saints and Wonders* in 1906, *The Kiltartan History Book* in 1909, *The Kiltartan Poetry Book* in 1919.

When Yeats saw in 1898 how prolifically she was accumulating folk-lore he proposed that her records should be the basis of a long and authoritative study of the supernatural—since that, he explains in *Dramatis Personae*, is the most violent force in history, but has never been captured in a book, only overheard passing from mouth to mouth. She would be gleaner, he would be editor and interpreter, the book appearing over their joint signatures. It took twenty years to control her findings in two volumes, which were published in 1920, over her signature alone, as *Visions and Beliefs in the West of Ireland*.

Her practical enthusiasm, after a conversation of 1898 which has become a piece of history,* enabled Yeats to make a start with his Irish theatre. When Yeats said the main obstacle was money, she put herself down for £25 as the first guarantor of an annual spring festival of "certain Celtic and Irish plays", and

*See Lady Gregory, *Our Irish Theatre*.

circulated an appeal to her friends. That yielded the 1899 performance at the Antient Concert Rooms of Edward Martyn's *Heather Field* and Yeats' *Countess Cathleen*, and set going the sequence which after five years of perseverance established the Abbey Theatre. Lady Gregory first helped with administration; typed Yeats' drafts and speeches on her old Remington; suggested words to him when he was at a loss; proved especially useful for words with the ring of daily life; then made her own creative experiments. She looked for a gap to fill: there was a shortage of practitioners in comedy; she offered *Twentyfive* in 1902. It was rejected, but played the following year. In 1904 she had her first success with *Spreading the News*, and the next year attempted a historical play *Kincora*, followed quickly by *The White Cockade* and in 1906 by a successful hybrid, comic history, *The Canavans*. She rehandled some of these early works as she got to know her medium better. When she published *Seven Short Plays* in 1909 she dedicated them to Yeats, "because you have taught me my trade", but in fact, as Professor Ellis-Fermor has pointed out, she had rather been taught her trade by the theatre itself and the players, with whom she had busied herself unsparingly. Her playwriting went on steadily and included translations from Molière and Goldoni. Her play, *The Deliverer*, describing Moses as a Parnell, came in 1911. In the middle of the Great War she began to write "Wonder Plays". They date from 1916 to 1921, and their flavour of fantasy and gaiety contrasts sharply with the circumstances out of which they sprang: the Great War and then the fighting in Ireland; the death of her son, Robert, in Italy; the British refusal to release Hugh Lane's pictures to Ireland and her powerful and useless struggle for them. She has commented that *The Dragon*, written only a year after the Easter Rising, must represent "some unseen inevitable kick of the swing towards gay-coloured comedy from the shadow of tragedy", and whatever meaning underlies that applies to the whole group of Wonder Plays.

In the 'twenties she felt her powers failing. She remained a force in Ireland and at the Abbey; she helped to launch Sean

O'Casey's first plays; the published fragments of her journals*
are a fascinating commentary on the new Ireland. She died at
Coole in 1932.

CASTE OR LITERATURE?

Lady Gregory became aware of the voice of the new literature
in 1893. That was a pivotal year for her, and, if her observation
was right, for the whole Irish movement. She had been watching
the newspapers "for some word of poetic promise". She saw
Katharine Tynan's lament for Parnell. She tore it out of the newspaper. It seemed to her the first statement, or the first intense one,
the first worth the keeping, of the passions of the last years. Thirty
years afterwards the fragment of newspaper was still beside her:
"I had unwittingly taken note of almost the moment of a new
impulse in literature." Then Douglas Hyde published his *Love
Songs of Connacht*. It is a hideously designed book, yet to look
through it, with its Celtic text on the left-hand page, its English
on the right, is a joy and the end of any belief that the only
attractive book is the well-produced one. Lady Gregory read the
songs: "I realized that, while I had thought poetry was all but
dead in Ireland the people about me had been keeping up the
lyrical tradition that existed in Ireland before Chaucer lived."
She had so far read nothing of Yeats' work, but *The Celtic Twilight*
was published in 1893, and she obtained that, and, struck by the
folk-lore he had gathered in Sligo, became jealous for her own
county and set to work collecting in Galway.

She had just been left a widow. She turned to literature and
Ireland to replace her marriage. Why to literature? What made
her sensitive to it? She liked to say that it was a French great-
grandmother. Probably a French streak in the blood gave a
younger woman, Virginia Woolf, the special zest of her fancy,
and it may have been the same with Lady Gregory. It was probably
also her old nurse, Mary Sheridan, who had delighted her child-

---

*Select passages were edited by Lennox Robinson: *Lady Gregory's Journals 1916–1930*,
London, 1946. The complete journals would be welcomed by every reader of Irish
literature: they are a major need.

hood with the twists of story-telling and the excitement of rebellion:

> In the home of my childhood there was an old Catholic nurse whose upstairs teaching tempered the strict Orangeism of the drawing-room, and whose eye would flash as she told of the triumphant shouting she had heard in 1798 when it was told at a theatre she had been taken to that the French had landed at Killala. She was only a child herself then, but she remembered how all the audience had stood up and cheered and waved their handkerchieves at the joyful news.

Her early passion for books was inseparable from a patriotic passion. When one of her sisters invited her to choose a book for a birthday present, she asked for *The Spirit of the Nation*. Her sister agreed doubtfully, and wrote on the fly-leaf "Patriotism is the last refuge of a scoundrel". She learned her weekly Bible-lesson to earn sixpence, and went off to Loughrea, the market town five miles distant, and bought Fenian books from the old stationer. "You are my best customer for them", he told her. In 1918 she still had the "little books in gay paper or in green cloth".

Literary nationalism, then, was her secret centre. But we see it more distinctly reading her today than her friends could in 1893, for in her late accounts she inevitably emphasised anything that points to what she regards as most admirable in herself—and by 1918 her work for the literary and dramatic revival seemed the most admirable thing. She was not interested in the stiff and proper self that formed her outward shell. She didn't want to dissimulate, for she was rigorously honest; but was not interested. We can see the outward person, first, in a conscious standing-up-straight in her style; then in casual references, as when she admits that she shared her family's dislike for the ambitious young man who carried off Adelaide, the beauty among her sisters, and became father of Hugh Lane; then from the picture drawn by Moore; then from the antagonism to her among the young women, notably Mary Colum, who idolised Yeats and envied the old lady's ownership of him. Yeats occasionally, under a special temptation, departs from his convention of praising her: for example he tells Olivia Shakespeare:*

> She hates all clergy though she never misses Church, and is a great reader of her bible and, as she believes, very orthodox —furthermore she is a great prude so far as what others say to her is concerned.

This is reported because Yeats wants the fun of discussing a striking exception:

> She suddenly astounded me by saying—apropos of nothing —a couple of weeks ago—and with an air of gratified malice— "That Russell case shed a new light on the immaculate conception"—she evidently felt that a doctrine which belonged in an especial sense to the clergy had been hit—a perplexity with simple laity abated.
>
> If I had said such a thing to her I would have been in disgrace for the afternoon. . . .

Beckoned by literary concupiscence to this anecdote, Yeats discloses both her Victorian, ladylike, Protestant high-school side, and her capacity, intermittent but real, for thinking herself out of it.

In the long run the interest of her life lies in the way she pressed beyond what birth gave her. She might have been satisfied with caste and charity, but was not. Of the possibilities afforded by her traditions, growing-up, marriage, she took those that made for action and change. But we must not see her literary work merely as a stepping-beyond her orthodox self. She managed to carry a strength from her orthodoxy and the complacent power of her class, and assimilate it to the touch of revolutionary poetry in her.

During the twelve years of her married life, and the first seven or eight years of her widowhood and literary experiment, this assimilation was scarcely begun. In her St. George's Place drawing-room in the 'eighties the latest books lay everywhere, but the

*Yeats, Letters, edited by Allan Wade, p. 706.

poets and writers she received were the politer kind. They were men like Sir Alfred Lyall, whose literary reputations Yeats destroyed for her in later years. On the other hand, she was constantly taught in that period to admire strength of personality in political contexts. At the very outset of her marriage her husband was engaged in championing Egypt's national leader, Arabi Pasha. She met both Arabi and his English poet-supporter, Wilfred Scawen Blunt. Just as her husband admired Arabi in Egypt, he had admired (though he had opposed politically) the dashing old O'Connell in Ireland. In January 1889 Gladstone reviewed O'Connell's Correspondence in laudatory language in the *Nineteenth Century*, and Gregory followed that up with an article in the April issue describing the warm impression the Liberator had made on him in private talks (and incidentally exposing his own feeling against religious division in Ireland, a feeling that Lady Gregory took up and developed into a conviction). As regards Parnell, her husband had early in the 'eighties been opposed to Parnell's policies; I don't know that we yet have evidence of his later view of Parnell as a man and leader; and he died only a few months after the great Dublin funeral. But he may have admired Parnell's strength in action no less than O'Connell's before him, and I am certain that Lady Gregory admired it. Parnell had what she was working towards: the strength of caste, the fire of sacrificial performance, and a spark of madness. Her eye was sensitive to those lines of Katharine Tynan in 1893. The image of Parnell grew in her mind when she became a participant in the literary movement. She used it explicitly in two plays (*The Image* and *The Deliverer*) and often as an implicit point of reference. She makes Grania describe the dead Diarmuid:

> he was a good man to put down his enemies and the enemies of Ireland, and it is living he would be this day if it was not for his great comeliness and the way he had, that sent every woman stammering after him and coveting him; and it was love of a woman brought him down in the end and sent him astray in the world.

The passage is resonant with the memories of the 1890–1 disaster, and with the admiration of the inner Lady Gregory for wilful strength.

MYTH IN THE INTERNATIONAL PERSPECTIVE

She tells in her notes to *The Deliverer* the story of the country people who said that Parnell was still living and would come again—the story that Joyce corroborates in the midnight talk at the Dublin coffee-stall. Her knowledge of the drawing-rooms of London and the salons of Venice and Rome had not made her sceptical or contemptuous of peasant myth. On the contrary, the international world to which her husband had given her access, confirmed the importance of popular belief. Her husband's Irish sensibility, deflected from home by his ambitions, had expressed itself in a concern for freedom movements in other countries. He knew the Orient and had seen there how rumour runs, how the belief in a prophet or a Messiah can turn a peasantry or tribesmen into an army. In particular, in his contacts with Arabi Pasha he had glimpsed how a force partaking of Messianism, an ancient expectation of a redeemer among the Nile fellaheen, provided the revolutionary potential of Arab nationalism. Lady Gregory, to whom he had presented Arabi, had glimpsed it too. She often thought of Arabi, and his imprisonment by the British in the troubled post-war days when Irish leaders were in prison. As late as December 1928, she told herself, for pleasure and consolation, in her journal: "On that large photograph upstairs Arabi the Egyptian has written in Arabic that is translated: 'This is my portrait in the days of my imprisonment and my distress and on it I have written in my own hand—I offer it to the gentle and noble Lady Gregory to remind her of what has befallen me'."

So the experiences that had taught her to make judgments in the largest perspective had taught her to value the myths of a people as the basis of political change. In her observation of Ireland, and her thinking in collaboration with the literary movement, she was supported by analogies with other national movements that she had known.

The same knowledge of the world taught her that though these popular forces count so much, they do not count alone: there must also be the upper-level of work and diplomacy. She had seen, and could imitate, the traffic of the *coulisses*. It also taught her, with the help of her innate sanity, that change does not solve much, and that political freedom, though necessary, is a beginning, not an end. A nation is responsible the minute it is free. She often points out, obliquely, that the Ireland of the Union is in the easy position of being able to blame all its misfortunes on the stranger. On one occasion she said of herself that she was no politician, that she had not judged it her business to work for Home Rule, but that she had tried to raise Ireland's sense of responsibility and power of achievement, so that the country should be ready prepared for freedom. There was a mixture of puritanism and informed good sense in this attitude.

APPRENTICE AND CONTRIBUTOR

Moore says that she divined as soon as she saw Yeats that he "would help her out of conventions and prejudices, and give her wings to soar in the free air of ideas and instincts". She offered herself very humbly to Yeats as patron, secretary, and apprentice. She sheltered him and helped him to find his tough inner strength. He showed her how a writer works, gave her the stimulus of his example; gave her some flattery, which he justified to himself by phrasing it in the traditional mode of poet to patron, but also advice and private criticism.

She was, however, not a mere blank on which Yeats set his stamp. Additional to the personal enthusiasms and the knowledge of the world just described, she had at the literary level something of her own, something with which to reciprocate Yeats' teaching. Her interest in Gaelic pre-dated his. As a child she had asked for lessons in Irish, but had asked too timidly, afraid the family would mock. Soon after her marriage she had bought a Gaelic grammar and worked at it with the help of a gardener, but he was slack for *he*, this time, suspected mockery—"for those were the days before Irish became the fashion". A dozen years later her son, due to enter Harrow with a classical scholarship, wanted to learn "and rode over to Tillyra before breakfast one morning to ask our neighbour Edward Martyn to help him to a teacher. He came back without what he had sought, but with the gift of a fine old Irish Bible, which became a help in our early lessons. For we set to work together." She and Robert Gregory read the Irish Bible together and used the elementary grammar prepared by Father Eugene O'Growney, the Professor of Irish at Maynooth College, who with Douglas Hyde and John MacNeil did the work that led to the forming of the Gaelic League in 1893. She knew and admired Hyde. She followed the early work of the Gaelic League, and looking back in 1918 on those meetings of country people to collect Irish songs remembered "an upsetting of the table of values, an astonishing excitement".

The songs and the idea of the wandering blind poet, Raftery, caught hold of her; she went to a mason to have a headstone cut for his grave; and at the mason's cottage found a manuscript book of his poems; and these she read with a working farmer, walking with the pages to his house "on many a moonlit evening". It may be that with all this her mastery of Gaelic remained tenuous. Where a difficult language with an unusual script, learned not early in life, is concerned, a person can, after much reconnoitring of the grammars and the literature, still be unskilled; and so it may have been in this case. Yet the experience brings some sense of the language, a feeling for its flavour, an obscure but strong awareness of the objectives of its literature.

Her translations from Raftery helped to establish this great Gaelic singer as a pattern-figure for Yeats and younger Irishmen. Joyce, who loved to gibe at the idolatry of the Irish literary movement for Gaelic literature, made a decisive exception of the relatively recent Raftery. Yeats learned from some of Hyde's translations of Gaelic country songs and from some of Lady Gregory's translations of Raftery to work for the image that stands sharp and clean in its context. In his contribution to the symposium *Ideals in Ireland* in 1901 he quoted, as an example of the "intensity of emotion" and "strangeness of language" of Irish peasant art, Lady Gregory's translation "into the simple English of the country people of today" of "a lament, that Raftery the wandering fiddler made for a fiddler some sixty years ago":

> The swans on the water are nine times blacker than a black-
> berry, since the man died from us that had pleasantness on
> the top of his fingers;
> His two grey eyes were like the dew of the morning that
> lies on the grass;
> And since he was laid in the grave, the cold is getting the
> upper hand.

Actuality of image is the keynote, even though one or two abstractions are present. Yeats' reading of Hyde and Lady Gregory led to those conversations with Ezra Pound, ten years later, in which the two poets agreed to keep abstractions out of their poetry.

Lady Gregory had her Gaelic interest before Yeats influenced her, and she had her knowledge of peasant speech, alive in her ear from her nurse's story-telling and then from visits and minis-tering to tenants all her life, early at Roxborough and then at Kiltartan. Like everything else constructive in her, the music of the speech was the result of a fusion of pleasure and duty. She judged it one of the duties that go with the rights of a landlord to visit her tenants, and she listened to them as a constant act of service. The music of the talk in the chimney-nooks was a pleasure to her because it brought her nursery memories back and it touched her historical sense and roused images of three centuries of Irish life under the English. Yeats, when he saw her early transcriptions of peasant lore, realised that the idiom had a special power of evocation, and encouraged her to use it in her writing. She used it in her first full-length book, *Cuchulain of Muirthemne*, which she dedicated to her tenantry at Kiltartan. She has tried, she tells them:

> to take the best of the stories, or whatever parts of each will
> fit best to one another, and in that way to give a fair account

of Cuchulain's life and death. I left out a good deal that I thought you would not care about for one reason or another, but I put in nothing of my own that could be helped, only a sentence or so now and again to link the different parts together. I have told the story in plain and simple words, in the same way my old nurse Mary Sheridan used to be telling stories from the Irish long ago, and I a child at Roxborough.

George Moore has savaged her procedure. He has urged that the peasant idiom was either already long familiar or false and artificial. Whether he was right or not, the idiom justified itself by success. Synge told Lady Gregory that when he read *Cuchulain* it gave him the speech he was seeking, and that he made it his daily bread. I shall look again at this remark in the Synge chapter: let us for the moment note it, and the undeniable fact that the "Kiltartan" of *Cuchulain* helped to form an Abbey Theatre style and the world's conception of Anglo-Celtic speech and poetry. What she inaugurated was a convention, a convention on which a genius could build, as Synge proceeded to do.

Moore's charge of bowdlerising is graver. Her own remark, "I left out a good deal that I thought you would not care about . . .", lends credence to it. In fact, while she was an honest folk-lorist, who could legitimately claim for her oral-collecting "I had no theories, no case to prove, I but 'held up a clean mirror to tradition'", and while she feared very little, her caste may have baulked her literary flair where indecency was concerned. Her tenantry may have spared her some things they thought she might not like to hear, while she spared them in her writing. In a comparable way she refined her Kiltartan even though her object was to give it plain and simple. We can see this if we set against *Cuchulain* an occasional example of speech which she has not refined. A coarse-spun passage is this late piece of Irish Messianism, involving General Smuts and Gandhi, from the 1926 edition of the *History Book*:

The man in the skies is settling down things; he is coming from very far out; from South Africa or maybe from India.

There is gold buckles all over his clothes; there is gold rings
in his ears. He'll settle down everything and he'll begin work.
All drink will be stopped. . .

This is crude Kiltartan with abruptness and vigour. Except for
one or two paragraphs like this, however, she purifies what she
uses. In her translations and reports she mellows the crude
vibrancy of the modern speech and makes old harmonies.

A contemporary development compelled her to the purifying
process as she wrote *Cuchulain*. In 1900 the Commission of
Intermediate Education had heard evidence on the Irish language
and its literature. Against Dr. Hyde had appeared a Dr. Atkinson,
a Professor at Dublin's Trinity College, testifying that the early
literature "is almost intolerably low in tone—I do not mean
naughty, but low; and every now and then, when the circum-
stance occasions, it goes down lower than low . . . if I read the
Irish books, I see nothing ideal in them, and my astonishment
is that through the whole range of Irish literature that I have read
(and I have read an enormous range of it), the smallness of the
element of idealism is most noticeable. . . . And as there is very
little idealism there is very little imagination." John Eglinton,
though he lived through the shot and smoke of this battle,
expressed wonder in his *Irish Literary Portraits* of thirty years later,
that Yeats and Lady Gregory regarded Trinity College, "the
naturally friendly entity of Anglo-Irish culture", as the enemy of
their movement. Dr. Atkinson's evidence makes clear that they
had justification. (Trinity had produced Douglas Hyde, but it had
done much damage too. It is horrifying to read Sir William
Gregory's story of the inflammatory anti-Catholic speeches of
Trinity men in his Dublin election of 1842.)*

But I suspect that even without the pressure of Atkinson's
charge of lowness she would have purified *Cuchulain*. It was her
besetting temptation, from which only the stage requirements of
comedy could half-save her. In her creative work there is a
distinction between her tragedies and comedies. The tragedies

*In his article, already quoted, in the *Nineteenth Century*, April 1889.

use the mellowed, traditional harmonies, a consciously literary tone, a continuously noble pace. In her comedies she lets some crudeness come through, imitates speech a little more closely, and the result is more vital. But, for all her capacity to pass beyond her orthodox limits, there is a further area of crudeness and vitality into which she can never enter.

The refinement of Lady Gregory's *Cuchulain*, which is now evident as a weakness, was in 1902 temporarily an asset to the Irish movement in its appeal to overseas interest. With her sense of political strategy, she sent a copy to President Theodore Roosevelt. He was captivated, took it with him on a tour of the western States, sent for more Irish literature. In England Henry Newbolt, discussing it in the *Monthly Review*, cited Yeats and went on: "beautiful as his own work is, he has not yet equalled this fabric of the giants of old, massive and aerial, grotesque and exquisite beyond the power of a later and less generation." English liberals and intellectuals read it and were moved, or their wives read it to them. Mrs. Watts chose it, together with AE's *Earth Breath*, as her favourite evening reading with her husband. "How many beautiful evenings you gave us", she wrote to Lady Gregory. It carried forward the conquest of the English imagination by the Celtic. On the political plane it helped, by so doing, to reinforce the small* but significant and growing body of English opinion in favour of Irish autonomy.

AUTHENTICITY

When Yeats met Lady Gregory he had already for eight years been collecting Irish folk-material, though as often in English libraries as on the Irish roads. He had thought of himself as contributing to a pool of lore on which writers would draw. When he

---

*Gladstone in 1889 computed the English sympathisers with Ireland at "millions and millions". He must have been writing in an intoxicated moment of oriental verbosity. The average Irishman at the same date ran to the opposite extreme of totally discounting English sympathy. John O'Hagan, writing in the *Irish Monthly*, January 1891, spoke of English "scorn and loathing" for Ireland and alleged: "Even when the old dogged John Bullism in its contemptuous attitude towards foreigners, became mollified, and there was full sympathy for the national feelings of Italy, Hungary, Germany, the claims of Irishmen to have a country of their affections still provoked a sneer".

saw Lady Gregory's first notes, and discovered her aptitude for collecting, he pressed her to do more. She would thus provide the material for a "sacred book", a system. She would also provide a pool on which writers could draw, and on which he himself might draw to compose (he told Robert Bridges in 1901), an Irish mythological *Comédie Humaine*. In response she collected, he later estimated, some 200,000 words of material.

She was energetic in her search for folk-lore. She went out to find whatever she heard rumoured. The energy she spent gave something back to her writing. In squeezing information, as she squeezed the secrets of herb-healing from old Bridget Ruane, or in travelling distances to interview a legendary personage, she linked herself with the colours and textures of her land, the habits, absurdities, and tribulations of the cottagers. There was her journey to find the home of the witch, Biddy Early. She drove with her pony to the shooting-lodge in the hills, spent the night there, then next day went "eight strong miles" over the mountain by a wild road. Her pony splashed his way through the red mud of the road, through two unbridged rivers swollen with the summer rains, past purple heather and foxglove, past brown bog. So she came to Biddy Early's village. Biddy had been dead, it turned out, twenty years. Such pursuits as these gave her the overall feel of her work and a multitude of incidental details. At the village inn where she put up her pony that day she saw on the wall portraits of John Dillon and Michael Davitt, and the landlady told her that Parnell had been a third till the priest hinted that he did not think well of her for hanging it. This found its way into the dialogue in *The Image:* "Sure I had his picture on the wall and I took it down after, the priest thinking it did not look well to be hanging where it was." Into the same play came a legendary saying of Biddy Early: "It is a pity neighbours to be going contrary to one another. 'Let ye be at one', Biddy Early said, 'and ye will rule the world'." Lady Gregory is a sort of Irish Queen Victoria and Albert in one, exerting tireless energy and authority. From the persistence and pilgrimages—"one Sunday in Connemara I went a long way to a poor little empty church", she says another time—she brought back sensations, phrase and melody, and knowledge.

Her classical village comedies are such as spring most easily in the narrow, primitive conventions of a religious peasant community, whether in Ireland or Spain or Egypt or Wales: a comedy of the absurdity of human interaction, of the misunderstandings and mis-shapings that occur in an environment where order is so familiar that there is an immense appetite for the shock of disorder, where ignorance is so common that a trivial error or obscurity can precipitate disorder. After two or three years of experiment she had this mode at her finger-tips, and used it for twenty years, never fumbling, never wasting—yet never exalting it. Synge wrote a comedy, and it became a poem. Dylan Thomas concentrated his iconoclastic fancies in a comedy based on village situations comparable with hers, including, for example, the postmistress who opens or interprets all the letters. *Under Milk Wood* is a ferocious divining of life. Her comedy is non-conflagratory. Yet it has a special quality. Yeats said "only one mind could have made it". That praise is too high, but there is a unifying verve in it, a vigour of mind unleashed by pleasure. She relied on her knowledge of rural Ireland for her action, key-phrases, and dialogue. She used memories of festivals regularly celebrated on the country estates, such as the Cregoostha, the annual sheep-shearing that wound up with a dance for the shearers; of a popular wandering piper, who played at the dance given for her tenants when she married and again at her son's coming-of-age; of a melancholy man telling her of his troubles at home and saying: "But I'm thinking if I went to America, it's long ago today I'd be dead. And it's a great expense to a poor man to be buried in America." Then, reciprocally, the business of accommodating these to the stage and developing the play so engaged her conscious mind that her otherwise puritanically-restrained pleasure was liberated and infused the whole work. That is why Yeats could say, in another phrase which is also too strong but just in touch with truth, that her comedies are "a high celebration of indulgence".

Her best historical play, *The Canavans*, is also a comedy, to be performed, as Lennox Robinson has repeatedly said, "extravagantly". Nothing seems erroneous, ill-placed, or unnecessary in this, or in *Spreading the News* or *Hyacinth Halvey*. There is one paradox in her comic method: although she and her colleagues set out to write plays that would banish the old conception of the stage Irishman as a buffoon, her practice admits the element of village buffoonery.

She started to write comedy because the Abbey was short of comedies, and she was craftsman enough to shape what she had to the theatre's needs. *Spreading the News* came to her as an idea with possibly tragic connotations: she "kept seeing" an image of a girl going to market, "gay and fearless", but coming home in the evening with her head hanging and avoided by the crowd because of a story that had arisen from a chance word. It might have made a serious play, but comedy was needed at that time for the Abbey, and Lady Gregory made it her quickest comedy. Quickness and spareness are her assets. Her tragedy has them too. If she had only a limited range of things to say, at least she knew better than to say more. Yeats regarded himself as a sparer, quicker, conciser developer of stage situations, yet whereas he and Moore had made a *Grania* traffic-blocked with characters, she astonished him by making a *Grania* out of three characters and with those three eliciting from the traditional story the Irish father-son problem and her private problem of the appeal of a strong woman.

It is both a limitation and an excellence of her theatre that the allusions depend on her intimacy with the audience. Think of her as a writer thinking of her audience, and you see that she chooses every word with warmth and purpose. In her first draft for a play, *Colman and Guaire*, she conceived herself as providing material for Kiltartan schoolchildren to play to Kiltartan people. Later, even in the most ambitious work, the conception was similar. She hoped that her histories would be played in the schools of Ireland to inform and inspire Irish children. The texts crackle with topical allusion, with instruction and exhortation: the king will "make no settlement that will leave any one of the five Provinces a breeding-ground for the enemies and the ill-wishers of Ireland"; "this tossed and tormented country" has to compose its divisions, to travel "without argument and backbiting and the quarrelling of cranky bigoted men"; the king must do his work with the sword, "striving to cut the name of Ireland in clean letters among the nations", until success makes him free to do it with "nine drops of the water of wisdom". In all this she follows the pattern of point-making established by Yeats' *Cathleen ni Houlihan* (in which she had helped with her advice at the typewriter). Throughout the Abbey work it is assumed that, without any undue stress on the points by the actors—Yeats is insistent over this in his commentary on the right and wrong way of producing *Cathleen ni Houlihan*—actor and audience will be in perfect understanding. This is odd, if we think of the angry misunderstandings between dramatists and audience throughout the Abbey history. But in fact the audiences did in one sense always understand, even when they disliked what they understood. Because of the organic relationship between the drama and the burning problems of external politics and internal social friction the Irish drama was able to succeed. Lady Gregory works entirely on the basis of that consent between author and audience to discuss—even if to quarrel—Ireland and Irish issues: actually, she herself never challenges a quarrel; she never gives less than a whole-hearted treatment of the issues, she never is unorthodox on them, she never goes outside them to use the enriching terms of other interests and other literatures.

THE SAGA STYLE

Andrew Malone called her tragedy, *Grania*, "superior to Ibsen of *The Vikings*, Strindberg of *Gustavus Vasa*, or Hauptmann's *Florian Geyer*".* But praise of a play is less valuable than performance of it, and neither *Grania* nor any of her serious work is played; nor even read very much. Like *Cuchulain* her tragedy

*Andrew Malone, an article on Lady Gregory in the *Yale Review*, April 1925, excellent in its strictures and, with the exception of the sentence quoted, its judicious praise.

should at the least be studied as part of the history of the attempt to write the saga style into English.

I should rather say "into modern English". The saga style is the basis of early English literature, and still audible and powerful in middle English. It was jettisoned by humanism. Milton thought of recovering it, but did not try. Gray tried, but did not quite master it. Wordsworth, whose atavistic Lake temperament might have enabled him to carve it afresh, let the opportunity pass when he dropped his thought of a Scandinavian epic. Arnold and William Morris looked for it and half-grasped it. The Irish took up their work, and more than half-grasped it. They used it in their own way for their own purposes, so that the result was an offshoot from the main stream of English literature; but the sight was an encouragement to twentieth-century English poets, who went on to recover the saga style for English out of the inspiration of the teaching of Anglo-Saxon at Oxford. They inveighed against the requirement to read the old language as part of their Honours syllabus, but they learned from it. Notably, W. H. Auden, the Anglo-Saxon poems stirring the Scandinavian blood in him, re-naturalised the style.

What does the saga style do effectively, and what are its limitations, in English? In a full-length translation like *Cuchulain* versatility and great beauties are displayed in it. It has force, vividness. Often it is sudden and direct. Sometimes teasing, obscure, but compelling, as in the chapter in which Cuchulain, wooing Emer, speaks to her in a cover language, the cover being legendary allusions which the well-reared Emer knows though her maidens do not. But when the saga style is transposed into new writing, it is usually applied for one main purpose: to throw basic passions, basic social situations into high relief. We are invited to consider what is common in them to all of us. Lady Gregory's own practice when she borrows the style for her historical plays shows this. "And what at all is love", she makes Grania say after the death of Diarmuid, "but lies on the lips and drunkenness, and a bad companion on the road?" So naked, so sheer, but above all so general, do problems become when they are seen in this way: they are made less gnawing, the private contortions are smoothed out of them, they are made more tolerable, absorbed into the simple collective experience of all time.

Nowhere is this more forcibly demonstrated than in a sentence written by Lady Gregory after tragedy came to her in reality in 1918. Her son, Robert Gregory, was flying an Allied aircraft in Italy. She had been disturbed about him for some time, waking up in the night feeling that a part of herself was crying far away. In the New Year she began to select the poems that she would print in *The Kiltartan Poetry Book*. It struck her as surprising that among the songs of the people the laments outnumbered the songs of joy: "But before that month was out news was brought to me that made the keening of women for the brave and of those who are left lonely after the young seem to be but the natural outcome and expression of human life." So she summons the saga style to hold her up in her grief, to protect her by giving her a place in the procession of the ages.

In Auden's charade, *Paid on Both Sides*, the saga style works to the same end:

> Often the man, alone shut, shall consider
> The killings in old winters, death of friends.
> Sitting with stranger shall expect no good.

It is easy to see why Auden, writing at the beginning of the 'thirties, a time of sensitivity to collective stresses, of immersion in collective philosophies, should find in his Anglo-Saxon predecessors a means of diminishing the size of the impending war and enduring the menace. One may say that it is even easier to see why an Irish writer, her style formed by the labour of reconstructing the heroic past as a springboard for an heroic future, should become habituated to the use of the characteristic Celtic rhetoric. But actually the matter is not quite so straightforward. We do not find Yeats resorting to that rhetoric. He knows how to incorporate it into his own idiom, but he seldom makes a replica of an old form. For to rely on collective forms *tout simple* is to reverse the process which Moore preached and Yeats and Moore practised: it is to reverse the drive for personality. As between the nobility and heroism of *Kincora* or *Grania* and the nastiness of Joyce's *Exiles*, there could be no question for Yeats that, friendship and Ireland notwithstanding, he must prefer the latter: those contortions of personal suffering must be chosen rather than the collective rituals that tranquillise suffering by congealing it. Must be chosen, that is, if a choice is unavoidable. What Yeats really wanted, as described in his preface to Lady Gregory's *Gods and Fighting Men*, is the use of the collective, yes, but penetrated, shaped, and vivified by the personal. Lady Gregory, for all that she commands respect and gives pleasure, seldom admits personality and idiosyncracy into her writing to transform it. That deficiency led Yeats to write a biographical analysis in *A Vision* which, urgent, excited, and ruthless, contrasts with his eulogy of her in *Dramatis Personae* and two or three poems. He correlated her with Queen Victoria and Galsworthy as an example of the phase where all is sacrificed to a code of personal conduct, sustained by moral strength:

> There is great humility—"she died every day she lived"—and pride as great, pride in the code's acceptance, an impersonal pride, as though one were to sign "servant of servants". There is no philosophic capacity, no intellectual curiosity, but there is no dislike for either philosophy or science; they are part of the world and that world is accepted. There may be great intolerance for all who break or resist the code, and great tolerance for all the evil of the world that is clearly beyond it whether above it or below it. The code must rule, and because that code cannot be an intellectual choice, it is always a tradition bound up with family, or office, or trade, always a part of history. . . .
>
> Men and women of the phase create an art where individuals only exist to express some historical code, or some historical tradition of action and feeling, things written in what Raftery called the Book of the People, or settled by

social or official station, even as set forth in Directory or Peerage. The judge upon the bench is but a judge, the prisoner in the dock is but the eternal offender, whom we may study in legend or in Blue Book. They despise the Bohemian above all men till he turns gypsy, tinker, convict or the like, and so finds historical sanction, attains as it were to some inherited code or recognised relation to such code. They submit all their actions to the most unflinching examination, and yet are without psychology, or self-knowledge, or self-created standard of any kind, for they but ask without ceasing, "Have I done my duty as well as So-and-So?" "Am I as unflinching as my father before me?" and though they can stand utterly alone, indifferent though all the world condemn, it is not that they have found themselves, but they have been found faithful.

It is an indictment of the saga mind which is reflected in Lady Gregory's saga method.

There is, however, one point at which a personal predilection of Lady Gregory's seems to break through the collective, nameless feeling of her dramas. She was strong and she loved strength. Her First Series of *Irish Folk History Plays* she dedicated in 1912 as follows:

> THESE THREE PLAYS CONCERNING
> STRONG PEOPLE OF THE WORLD I
> OFFER TO THEODORE ROOSEVELT
> ONE OF THE WORLD'S STRONG MEN.

Repeatedly in her Abbey work she demonstrated that she could live up to her liking, especially in her successful battle against the Viceroy for the freedom to perform Shaw's *Shewing-Up of Blanco Posnet*. Shaw liked strong women and liked her. All this matches Yeats' analysis. But that analysis supposes that the strength will be applied in the interests of duty. It usually was in her life; but in her art she could conceive of strength in conflict with duty; and then, she loved strength so much, she was ready to prefer it. When she wrote a play on Dervorgilla, the red-haired mediæval beauty whose adultery brought the English into Ireland, she decided, where the legend leaves it open whether the adulteress was willing or unwilling, that she was willing. Lady Gregory could not interest herself in a passive character. For a similar reason she did not care for Deirdre as a dramatic heroine. She chose for her most aspiring play a more positive woman, Grania: "I think I turned to Grania because so many have written about sad, lovely Deirdre, who when overtaken by sorrow made no good battle at the last. Grania had more power of will, and for good or evil twice took the shaping of her life into her own hands." That preference is an Irish, conservative way of joining in the contemporary movement for female emancipation, and probably justifies us in thinking that if, like Shaw, she had skipped her Irish loyalties and become a Londoner, she might in late life have joined the militant suffragettes.* Certainly, her success, limited but real, with Grania was a success for her private passion rather than Ireland's. Grania never became a current symbol as Deirdre did. The Irish needed strength, but the passive, mournful Deirdre held some interior implication which made her a more acceptable national figure than Grania. It was a poet's business to explore the mysterious, popular significance of Deirdre, as Yeats, AE, and Synge did. Lady Gregory was insufficient of a poet for that.

Yet, prompted by her personal drive, she made a remarkable effort to give national significance to the heroine she preferred. Diarmuid calls Grania "as beautiful as the blossoming of the wild furze on the hills". In *Mr. Gregory's Letter-Box* Lady Gregory had sketched an image for religious dissension: "That root of bitterness whose fruit, like the blossom of the furze, is never quite out of season in Ireland". The earlier simile shows how the image in the play implies that Grania's beauty is enmeshed with the bitterness of Irish internecine strife. When Diarmuid is dead Grania speaks that Parnell-evoking epitaph, which I have already

*Some of her London friends, like Lady Layard, signed a petition against female suffrage, printed in the *Nineteenth Century*, June 1889. I do not know whether the absence of her name means that she refused to sign, or that she was simply not consulted or not available.

quoted, and in it nearly catches what an Irish poet sought, and what the nerves of an Irish audience answered, from 1892 onwards, a glimpse of the complexity of the social-moral-political skein. There is a vein of complicating originality in Lady Gregory's treatment of the theme: it was, in her strict upper-class woman's view, female impudence that undermined Parnell and brought him down; but because she loved strength, and especially strong militant determination in a woman, she now glorified that impudent principle as it emerged in the strength of Grania.

The older she got the more she lived her ideal of strength; she began altogether to approximate to the character of her writing. On the occasion in 1919 when the Abbey needed at two days' notice a Cathleen for *Cathleen ni Houlihan*, she said "What is wanted but a hag and a voice?" and adequately played the role for several nights.

She had written in her journal in 1918, the year of her son's death, a list of the things she still wished for. It is a short list:

> I passionately wish for the children's (i.e. her grand-children's) love and happiness. For the return of Hugh's pictures. For the government of Ireland in the hands of Ireland; for the rebuilding to begin.
>
> For the increased worthiness of the Abbey until we hand it over.

The fight for the return of the Hugh Lane Collection was the only fight she lost. When he went down in the *Lusitania* in 1915 his will left his pictures to London. A codicil, which had not yet been witnessed, amended that bequest in favour of Ireland. She pressed vainly through the writing and publication of his biography and a subsequent short book, through hours in the ante-chambers of her influential friends in Dublin and London, for recognition of the validity of the codicil.* But for that lacuna in her life, her last years had their satisfaction. Her plays had been

---

*At the time of writing this sentence, 1957, forty years after Lane's death, the Tate holds the pictures still, some of them out of sight in its cellars. Legally correct, the detention of the pictures is morally unpardonable, the extension, against the will of many Britishers, of Britain's record of offences against Ireland.

translated into several languages, performed with or without permission in several countries. She had seen Yeats recognised internationally with a Nobel Prize, and in Ireland with a seat in the free nation's Senate. She had helped a young writer, Sean O'Casey, to acceptance by the Abbey, so that the story of the terrible beauty was put from the standpoint of the new generation, of the poor and urban, and she had been present in the theatre on March 8th, 1924, when *Juno and the Paycock* had its first performance: "that full house, the packed pit and gallery, the fine play, the call of the Mother for the putting away of hatred, made me say to Yeats, 'This is one of the evenings at the Abbey that makes me glad to have been born'."

Of all compliments paid to her in the conspiracy of compliment, perhaps one from Sean O'Casey in a letter of 1928 was of widest interest: "You can always walk with your head up. And remember you had to fight against your birth and position and comfort, as others had to fight against their birth into hardship and poverty, and it is as difficult to come out of one as it is to come out of the other, so that power may be gained to bring fountains and waters out of the hard rocks."*

A fine Irish compliment, but with truth in it. She had foregone leisure and ease, foregone the alternative of contenting herself with the traditional work of her class. She had been as decisively different as the women in England who began, about the time she turned to folk-lore, theatre, and theatre administration, to turn to Fabian politics, economics, the social services. Yet there is an error in the tribute. After all, it is not so hard to move from comfort into worthwhile work as from poverty. The person who knows comfort is free from the illusion that it is paradise on earth, more readily discerns that the best joy is (as she said) "the joy of work begun, work completed", is more habituated, by the family background of public service and intellectual application, to labour's solace. Yeats was right, in fact, in counting her birth among her advantages. What was difficult, what she had to learn, what shocked her at moments by its dizziness, was the

*For these passages on O'Casey see *Lady Gregory's Journals,* edited by Lennox Robinson.

leap between administrative work and creative work. Administrative work was natural to her. Shaw pointed out that if she had had to be a washerwoman, she would have been an excellent one. She could have said like Tudor Elizabeth, of whose prose she wrote a latter-day echo, "I thank God I am endued with such qualities that if I were turned out of the realm in my petticoat, I were able to live in any place in Christendom." She could not help working assiduously and well. But creative writing is so hard that even a professional, a Dr. Johnson, baulks at it constantly. She saw how she made excuses to put off the instant of getting down to writing. "Anything that is more or less external administration is so easy!" she pleads to Yeats, "Why were we not born to be curators of Museums?". She pressed on with administration, running the Abbey, managing its American tour, providing after-theatre suppers to Yeats and Synge and sometimes binges for all the players, commissioning artists to do portraits when their trade was slack, commissioning a tenant to spin wool for her and others to weave it into a frieze, distributing alms, training the players in the lost art of keening—and busy enough to fill a lifetime with this she could have been forgiven if she had shied at the higher hurdle. But she made the effort. When she had repeatedly made it, it modified her, vitalised potentialities that were outside the norm of her family and her kind. Her life shows how we can discriminate among our data and change ourselves, and strike into the unknown even after forty-five years of apparently regular progress along a common track. Of her creative writing none was so much as sketched or drafted before "the turn", as the Kiltartan villagers apparently call the signal of a woman's aging. She never had the arrogance of youth, which is best for smashing the cordons around the mind, but she had something like its élan between her fiftieth and seventieth year.

CHAPTER IV

WILLIAM BUTLER YEATS
1865-1939

YEATS was born at Sandymount on the Liffey estuary on June 13th, 1865. The house, according to Joseph Hone, was a "genteel", six-roomed, semi-detached semi-villa. His father, J. B. Yeats, was a conscious gentleman, free-thinking and free-talking; had been trained as a barrister, had gifts for the profession and a dislike for it; and practised as an artist—in London from 1868 to 1880, in Ireland again for seven years (living in Howth and painting in a Dublin studio), then in London for another long spell after 1887. Mrs. Yeats and the children moved with him on these migrations, though they also spent long holidays with her family in Sligo on the Atlantic coast of Ireland.

Yeats thought of Sligo as his real home. There he was in touch with the physical world. He went, for instance, to a deep pool in a Sligo river, fishing for eels. A conger trailed over his shoulder as he returned, and he told an old fisherman who met him on the way that he had almost caught a monster. Yes, said the old man, that was the dragon of the bottomless hole. He scoured the fields with a negro girl whose instinct led her to all the plovers' nests. At Sligo he first acquired, and later he developed on the coast at Howth, the outdoor knowledge which made George Moore observe, when they rambled at Tillyra, that he was "something of a naturalist". Through his poetry there runs a system of allusions to the weasel, the fox, the lapwing, the nettle, pointing to vigorous, aggressive, natural life.

E. M. Forster in *Howard's End* explains Mrs. Wilcox's strength:

"she let her ancestors help her". Yeats did that, too; and one way in which he had come to know his ancestors was through the landscape and the folk of Sligo. But his loyalty to Sligo was incompletely sustained—or so he says in the important poem *Under Saturn*. In November 1919, staying there with his wife, he spent a day in silence. The poem explains his gloom to her, so that she shall not blame herself for it:

> You heard that labouring man who had served my people.
> $\qquad\qquad\qquad$ He said
> Upon the open road, near to the Sligo quay—
> No, no, not said, but cried it out—"You have come again,
> And surely after twenty years it was time to come".
> I am thinking of a child's vow sworn in vain
> Never to leave that valley his fathers called their home.

His relationship with Sligo was a microcosm of his relationship with Ireland. All his writing was consciously intended to champion Ireland before the world and to raise Irish dignity. While working at his early poems he had compiled anthologies, published in 1888, through which to reach print and earn a little money, but they had been deliberately Irish: *Poems and Ballads of Young Ireland*, *Fairy and Folk Tales of the Irish Peasantry*, *Stories from Carleton*. When he wrote journalism his themes were mainly Irish. He talked of Ireland and thought of Ireland. The statement that he eventually made to Miss Horniman held good all his life: "I understand my own race and in all my work, lyric or dramatic, I have thought of it. . . I shall write for my own people— whether in love or hate of them matters little—probably I shall not know which it is." When he met an Irishman abroad he sent him, as he sent Synge, to Irish subjects and if possible actually into Ireland. Yet the pattern he lived in was a pattern of oscillation between Ireland and abroad, the pattern to which his father's movements had conditioned him, and to which something in him readily acceded. He was still near enough to his Celtic predecessors to be tempted by the cosmopolitan opportunities of the capital. While dedicated to Ireland, working ceaselessly for her, often returning, he adroitly contrived to live a cosmopolitan life too: exploiting the potentialities of London and drawing nourishment from the city even though disliking it; learning first from Londoners to know Paris and derive something from French literature and theatre; visiting Paris itself; afterwards America; and at the end of his life, breaking away from Ireland in horror of the social failure thrown into relief by the political success, basking in the Mediterranean warmth and history. His most celebrated early poem, *Innisfree*, shows the same sense of disloyalty as *Under Saturn*. Conceived in Fleet Street (the best possible symbol of London's fatal appeal to an Irish writer) it opens with "I will arise and go"—a quotation from the parable of the Prodigal Son!

I shall resume the details of Yeats' life only briefly here, since the following pages, examining his development chronologically, must repeat many points. He was a student of the Metropolitan School of Art, Dublin, from 1883. A short drama, *Mosada*, appeared in the Dublin University Review in 1886 and was then published by his father as a subscription volume. *The Wanderings of Oisin and other Poems* appeared in London in 1889. Volumes of poems continued to appear from him at fairly regular intervals: of distinctive quality, but thin volumes. He was also concerned to excel in prose, thought that his future might lie in the novel and published *John Sherman* and *Dhoya*, wrote articles and essays and issued collections of them, notably *The Celtic Twilight*, the first edition of which in 1893 gave currency to this famous phrase. He studied Blake: produced a lavish edition in collaboration with Edwin Ellis, and a modest work alone, both dated 1893. He pursued his reading in esoterica, and wrote condensed, aureate fantasies out of it; *The Tables of the Law* and *The Adoration of the Magi*, privately printed together in a limited edition in 1897, were picked up by Joyce from a bookseller's cart, and read till he could repeat them from memory; and Yeats had them commercially published in 1904 with an introductory note claiming "I . . . met a young man in Ireland the other day who liked them very much and nothing else that I have written". In 1899 he launched, and then carried forward, as creative writer and practical administrator, the Irish dramatic movement. As the early sketch *Mosada* shows, the dramatic form had appealed to him from the start; at the very outset of the 'nineties, before he had any prospect of a theatre for its performance, he had poured his love for Maud Gonne into *The Countess Cathleen;* then Florence Farr enabled him to write *The Land of Heart's Desire* as a curtain-raiser to Shaw's *Arms and the Man* in her adventurous Avenue Theatre season of 1894. He watched the Avenue Theatre performances, analysed his mistakes, learned from Shaw's adroit audience-baiting though it filled him with exasperation. He conceived an Irish theatre, interested Lady Gregory so effectively that she insisted on immediate action, and obtained the financial support of Moore's cousin, the dramatist Edward Martyn, and of an Englishwoman, Miss A. Horniman.* The new Irish theatre immediately encountered the vociferous opposition that was to dog it for its first thirty years. His *Countess Cathleen* was attacked as heretical, and the Catholic students of University College petitioned (Joyce alone abstaining) against it and demonstrated. From that moment Yeats took on the role of fighter and strategist which he sustained in Irish cultural affairs for a generation. He obtained an opinion in favour of the play from a leading Catholic thinker, Father Barry, and forced the performance through. He won the battle; but discovered that the attacks on his theatre, on moral, political, and nationalist grounds, were constantly renewed. Though he throve on the fighting and grew in stature from it, he never overcame the bitterness of the discovery that he had to fight his own people. It made him doubt the claims he had voiced internationally on Ireland's behalf, and in the end when Ireland was free and no longer needed defence it made him an exile and his people's critic like Joyce (and like Joyce an emotionally involved critic).

Yeats had met in 1889 the beautiful Irish revolutionary Maud Gonne, and until she married John MacBride in 1903 had constantly pressed for marriage with her. She soon separated from her

---

*See page 85 above on Lady Gregory. For a noble tribute to Miss Horniman see Lennox Robinson, *History of the Abbey Theatre,* Sidgwick and Jackson, London, 1951.

husband, but was not free to re-marry until after the Easter Rising of 1916 when he was shot. Yeats then proposed again, and on her refusal, and her stepdaughter's, almost immediately married, at the age of fifty-two, an Englishwoman, with whom an extremely happy and much more productive phase of his life began. George Moore had commented when they first met in the 'nineties that the early poems only sparely represented the profusion of Yeats' conversation. After marriage all Yeats' ideas were completely at his disposal. The award of the Nobel Prize in 1923, the international recognition and the financial comfort it brought, completed his confidence. Everything that he said was now certain of an audience, and he said it all, and towards the end said it violently. In his last letter, dated January 4th, 1939, he remarked: "It seems to me that I have found what I wanted. When I try to put all into a phrase I say, 'Man can embody truth but he cannot know it'. I must embody it in the completion of my life." The poems of his last fifteen years are embodiments of, first, an ecstasy which results from the uncovering of basic human energies, and then, a ruthless contempt for any society or any way of life deficient in those energies. They are also informed with a demand for intellect and a love of it. The reason why man cannot know truth is that he cannot find a formula which accommodates both those crude energies and intellect. But poems can embody both, and Yeats' poems, and the last plays, do.

That is why his late work has seemed splendid to the present generation. The pity is, that during the last twenty-five years the later poems have been praised at the expense of the early poems. This was an unavoidable *revanche* for the inflexibility of his early admirers who, admiring *The Wind among the Reeds* of 1899, which is in fact a perfect volume, would not follow the poet's development afterwards. But it entailed much loss—and a neglect of the importance of the early poems for the generation of poets who grew up on them. One of these, Stephen Spender, gave a B.B.C. broadcast talk in the autumn of 1956 in which, under the title *A Double Debt to Yeats*, he showed, in terms of his own experience, how the early work has value as well as the late: it is different but scarcely less important. His sensible and moving comment may mark the beginning of a new reading of Yeats' verse as a whole.

Yeats was a determined revisionist. He re-worked his poems again and again, as if engaged, said Lady Gregory, in a "competition for eternity". His friends and critics for years doubted the wisdom of his course. In *Hail and Farewell* we hear the AE circle murmuring how his revisions take the freshness out of his early poems. Moore, though himself an indefatigable re-writer, endorsed their protest. "The trouble is", he added, "that Yeats is a clever man, and there is always something to be said for the changes he makes." This is true; but sometimes the changes destroy a pleasant early poem and substitute a later-Yeats poem which is repetitive of some other later-Yeats poem. A case in point is *The Lamentation of the Old Pensioner*. The *Variorum Yeats* which appeared in 1957 was long-needed, and is a useful tool; but it is strictly a scholar's tool. One day there will have to be a new edition of Yeats for the general reader, giving, in the instances where a poem has undergone a sea-change, both versions in readable form. Equally desirable is an edition of the plays, reproducing his prefaces and including information as to performances, sources, and revisions.

THE COMMANDER UNDER THE POET

It may be that Yeats insistently wrote his late, virile self over the early, slighter self because he resented the initial conception of him fostered by his father and admirers like Katharine Tynan. They femininised him. When he was in his twenties there was already a movement afoot for the crowning of "masculinity in literature". But its application at first appeared to be to prose rather than poetry, and the dominant conception of the poet was formed in the image of Shelley. J. B. Yeats seems, for all his notable intellect and for all that he told his son to put Rossetti's "fundamental brainwork" into poetry, to have shared this conception. Look at the way he painted W. B. as a young man. There is one portrait by his father which, placed beside a portrait of Katharine Tynan, leaves the modern spectator uncertain which is which and which has which sex. Like his father's portraits Katharine Tynan's rhapsodical reminiscences make him a paranoiac—because she imagines it praise to show a poet as oblivious of the physical world. She tells in *Twenty-Five Years* how she waited with him for a tram on a rainy Dublin night after they had attended a meeting of the Protestant Home Rule Association:

> . . . I in my smart clothes, my high-heeled French shoes, standing in a pool of water; the wind driving the rain as it does only in a seabound city; Willie holding the umbrella at an acute and absent-minded angle which could shelter nobody, pouring the while into my ears *The Sensitive Plant*.

and a little earlier in the same book:

> He never had the remotest idea of taking care of himself. He would go all day without food unless someone remembered it for him, and in the same way he would go on eating unless someone checked him. That first winter, a hard one, he would come to see me, five miles from Dublin, striding along over snow-bound roads, a gaunt young figure, mouthing poetry, swinging his arms and gesticulating as he went.

Those last words catch the energy of the boy for a minute. But that is a chance glimpse of the truth; she is really after his unworldliness.

There *was* some burdensome dreaminess, but there was more energy, just as there was the early knowledge of earth and the weasels, under the outer simulacrum of "the faun of Sligo". In fact, Yeats imagined his inner self as organiser and commander. We know that his countryman T. E. Lawrence later grew up secreting an inner image of Napoleon. (Yeats had a good deal of sympathy with T. E., by whose side his fantasy's shadow-figure, Michael Robartes, fought. "Young Colonel Lawrence never suspected the nationality of the old Arab fighting at his side." In Lawrence he saw a kindred disposition, and remembered his own images of Napoleon or Garibaldi, behind which gloomed the archetypal figure of Prometheus.) Perhaps his paramount desire at the end of the 'eighties and early in the 'nineties was to realise this inner person, to make him function as an Irish hero. Working in the enemy city, he made it the base of operations against the enemy. The form the operations took was the organisation of Irish societies and public-speaking campaigns in connection with them. To anyone who knows what the meeting of a society in a city means—the few rows of chairs in a drab hall, the dozen faces in a drawing-room—it may sound absurd that the young Yeats could have seen in this the initiation of a large, coherent plan for wresting Ireland from an Empire. Yet he did see his London activities in that light. Two books had conditioned his view: Gavan Duffy's *Young Ireland* and Waite's *Real History of the Rosicrucians*.

Duffy's book describing the Young Ireland movement that broke away from the old Daniel O'Connell was written long after the events, and the opening chapters attempt very finely to indicate O'Connell's genius as well as his failings. The second chapter pictures O'Connell addressing, week after week, a humble and scanty audience: "in his singular career there is nothing more notable than the patience with which this man who had long passed his grand climacteric, applied himself to the task as if he had a lifetime to work it out. . . ." This justified Yeats in his addresses in halls or houses that were only pinpoints in the metropolis or the provinces. Then Duffy describes O'Connell's oratory (and we know from an entry in Elizabeth Yeats's diary for 1888 that the Irish orators, including O'Connell, were read by old J. B. Yeats to the family circle): when he was at his rare best, the "short fierce sentences of concentrated passion . . . fell on our ear like a tocsin". Yeats remembered this in forming his platform style. Then Duffy singles out the virtues which made the tribune's success: "He joined steadfast industry to a capacity with which it is seldom united except in intellects of the first order— the capacity for projecting. He could plan large designs boldly, and work out the details of his plan as if he possessed no other faculty but diligence", and tells how he entered the Irish courts as one of the first Catholic barristers since the fall of Limerick and by a disregard of "the mere trappings of power" gave the Irish people the feeling that they had a spokesman:

> To see the young Catholic lawyer not only hold his own fearlessly with the Bench, but subject officials to a sharp censorship, to see him ready to defend the weak and poor, and always hopeful and confident of final success for a just cause, were important examples to a people struggling back into the atmosphere of liberty; and in old age the consciousness of having done this work was still an inspiration. He was patient, because a long experience of life taught him how difficulties disappear and opinions change, and he was of so vigorous a constitution that no difficulties disheartened him. He was always at his post, and ready for work as for a feast.

Even to a reader who is not an Irishman, and who comes to view a battle that is mainly over, Duffy's attempt to do justice to the old, and to his generation lost, liberator is thrilling. From that can be measured Yeats' feelings. He read while the battle was still uncertain and growing hotter. This chapter gave him a pattern of work. He tried to use its lessons of leadership and campaigning.

When he opened Waite's *Rosicrucians* (1887) the first sentences confirmed how secret societies, though their work seem random and minute as drops of rain, can change the face of the world. "Beneath the broad tide of human history", begins the preface, "there flow the steady undercurrents of the secret societies, which frequently determine in the depths the changes that take place upon the surface." The sentence echoed in his memory over forty years later when Lady Gregory read George Sand's *Consuelo* and its sequel to him; he comments in a letter how "they fill one with reverie—secret societies of the eighteenth century, all turmoil of an imagined wisdom from which came the barricades". In the 'nineties Moore had heard him tell stories of meetings attended with Maud Gonne: "meetings in West Kensington, which in his imagination had become as picturesque as the meetings of Roman and Venetian conspirators in the sixteenth century". In old age he still tingled at their memory, and believed that the meetings had in fact produced the Irish revolution and independence. "My movement", he said in summary of them in a late letter to Ethel Mannin. Note the possessive.

As far as Maud Gonne was concerned the object of the meetings had been political activism. Maud Gonne was one of those girls of courage and sensationalist temperament who enter every extreme movement. She was wedded to espionage, dynamite, and public demonstration. Her unthinking ardour was bound to enthral Yeats: it epitomised dogmatism; it was the animal life of Sligo transposed to a political ground. He was dedicated to Sligo and to Ireland's politics, but not simply dedicated. Literature— though it was also for Ireland—had modified his dedication, and there were things that it would not permit him to do. The relationship in which he stood to Maud Gonne for over a quarter of a century expressed his attitude to Irish nationalism: he loved compulsively, could not separate himself from the devotion and the suffering it entailed, but could not lay hold on what he loved, for he did not really want it: its blaze was destructive of subtleties.

In one poem Yeats imagines that Maud Gonne returns his love though she does not requite it. In another he remembers a moment when

<blockquote>
the wild thought
That she denies
And has forgot,
Set all her blood astir
And glittered in her eyes.
</blockquote>

Perhaps he hallucinated. From her point of view he was unacceptable because he made her sacred, while she needed someone who would secularise her. She found the intercourse of private love less real than the sensations of politics: the brevity of her two-year marriage with John MacBride indicates so. But MacBride could seize her because he was as willing as she was to grip a desired object without reflection: as brave, violent, and thoughtless enough for Yeats to rhyme him as a "clown".

Maud Gonne afterwards claimed that she saved Yeats as a poet by refusing him as a husband, and he made a similar observation in one of his poems. But she so completely embodied unthinking nationalist Ireland for him, he never could have laid hold on her, or if he had she would still have made him suffer. A name that seems to matter more whenever readers of Yeats meet and talk at present is "Diana Vernon". In 1896 Diana Vernon gave him her love, freed him from some of youth's dreamy load, made him ready for the vision at Coole that summer, called out of him the imagery and the metrical nuances of *The Wind among the Reeds*. He also had a debt to Florence Farr, indulgent, knowledgeable about men, who, since he could tell her everything, helped him to feel knowledgeable about women.

POETRY—PARNELL—ARCHER AND CENTAUR

What exasperated Maud Gonne was Yeats' loyalty to literature (and consequently to ethics and intellect) which went deeper than loyalty to immediate political advantage. From the outset his literary discrimination was faultless. Essays and letters covering dates between 1888 and 1905 show that he already found, as a result of his reading, and established as his touchstones, writers and passages which scholarly criticism recognised only some decades later Ulysses' speeches in *Troilus and Cressida;* "Brightness falls from the air"; Henry More; Dame Julian's "old mystical book . . . full of fine distinction, of delicate logic". It was the bent of his mind to assign an Irish relevance to his reading, to consider when he read the Elizabethans how their idiom was still alive in the English spoken in certain districts of Ireland, or when he worked on Blake to discover a possible Irish ancestry for him. Similarly it was his habit to come away from his reading with his understanding of Irish problems or his procedures as an Irish poet illuminated, just as he came away from editing Blake convinced by Blake' example that a poet's business is to pronounce local political truths in the setting of cosmic history. But these were pretexts though dynamic; the constant and central thing for him was his literary sense. It never let him down.

This fact is relevant in assessing Yeats' reaction to Parnell's fall and his death. His significant writing on the subject did not begin till twenty years after Parnell's death. In 1890 and 1891 he was relatively silent. The letters of the time said little, except for an enthusiastic claim that, by standing fast, Parnell "has driven up into dust and vacuum no end of insincerities". His articles reporting British events to the Boston and Providence press said nothing. Yet we know he was excited, or at least that he believed years afterwards that he had been excited; for when he described the furore in Dublin over a gallery for Hugh Lane's pictures he wrote that he had not been so disturbed since the Parnell affair. It appears that he suffered a pressure which he could not at once interpret. When Parnell was buried he had thought it was his duty as an Irish poet to make a statement in poetry. He wrote *Mourn—and then Onward* and had it printed in *United Ireland*.* It was a dreary and unreal poem, using an un-Yeatsian "ye" instead of his more natural "you", and using it because he wanted to infuse an Old Testament character into the statement:

> Mourn—and then onward, there is no returning,
>   He guides ye from the tomb;
> His memory now is a tall pillar, burning
>   Before us in the gloom.

This quasi-Moses image, which was to colour the Parnell legend and to be developed by Lady Gregory in her play *The Deliverer*, was the only vital touch in a flaccid poem. Yeats' critical discrimination warned him that he had tried to find words for the situation too quickly. He never reprinted the poem and attempted no further public formulation of the Parnell incident for a long time, waiting till he understood its significance better. He was not able to understand it until he had suffered from the Irish while working for them, as Parnell had.

It is interesting that Yeats' father in later years expressed him-

*Richard Ellmann has given the text of the poem in *Yeats, The Man and the Masks*.

self against Parnell. In his early days at the Bar he had worked under Isaac Butt, whom Parnell ousted from the leadership of the Irish Parliamentary Party. J. B. never forgave Parnell and wrote him down as an opportunist. If that view ever affected W. B. Yeats, he disregarded it in later years as he formed his ideal of a powerful and scornfully dictatorial leader after the Parnell model.

Almost five years after Parnell's death AE and Yeats exchanged their news of the impending millennium as described in Chapter I. That August he had his Tillyra vision of the galloping centaur and the naked woman shooting and bringing down a star. To the shaping of that image AE's early poem of the Unknown Archer in *Homeward* in 1894, may have contributed. The vision was a crucial experience. He drew on it again and again in his latest work. A statement on history had been made to him by elemental powers, and the statement included a direction on his functions in the development of current history. In Yeats a horse often represents his poetic power. A centaur represents the poet and his poetry in complete fusion. In virtue of the presence of the centaur his vision directs him: "You as poet must bear witness to what you now see!". When as an old man he remakes the vision in the poem *Parnell's Funeral* he uses all the other details from his dream, together with cognates listed in the appendix to *The Trembling of the Veil*, but omits the centaur. For the poem itself is now the centaur.

Just as he could not use the figure of Parnell or the phenomena of his funeral in his poetry for a long time, so he could not at once obey the direction to write the poetry of the Tillyra vision. Yeats' first interpretation of the vision was that it called for action rather than poetry. He responded with a Gonnish activism, and brought her in to help. Richard Ellmann and A. Norman Jeffare have told how Yeats proceeded to inaugurate a cult for the "forerunners". He considered, though did not undertake, the purchase of an island castle in Lough Key to be their headquarters, the "Castle of the Heroes", a place of vigil where the elect would be fortified for their work of linking "the supernal and terrestrial natures". In Maud Gonne's recollection the significance of the castle was to be purely Irish: "only those who had dedicated their lives to Ireland might penetrate". "It was to be built of Irish stone and decorated with the Four Jewels of the Tuatha de Danaan, with perhaps a statue of Ireland, if any artist could be found great enough to make one, which we doubted." But her outlook was wilfully narrow. Reading Yeats and AE it is impossible to doubt that the Ireland-picture and the world-picture merged in their theology: the Messiah would appear in Ireland. All civilisation would crumble around His feet and be remade. The rebirth of Ireland would come in Messianic chaos, whereby the world's great age begins anew.

Yeats, a little over thirty, was young enough still to welcome the prospect of Armageddon. He had the optimism of a young man. Modifying it with a "maybe", a precaution posted throughout his prose, he said at the climax of his 1899 essay, *The Autumn of the Flesh:* "We are, it may be, at a crowning crisis of the world, at the moment when man is about to ascend, with his arms full of the wealth he has been so long gathering: the stairway he has been descending from the first days." We know from his preceding remarks that he wishes wealth to be understood in spiritual, not material terms. But is not a century of optimism, all the impetus of Victorian and materialist England, behind this promise?

INDIGNATION

His heroic and ritualist preparation gave way, while Maud Gonne and others developed their underground military preparations, to drama in the literary sense. In 1899 he and his friends launched the Irish theatre. At once his real struggle began. He had hoped "to write for his own race", and as soon as he wrote he found that he had to fight his race for the privilege of seeing and reporting the world his own way. The earlier works, up to and including *The Wind among the Reeds* of 1899, had rung with private desolation, but—except in *He thinks of those who have spoken evil of his beloved*—not with public indignation. The discovery that nationalist Ireland could be an Ireland opposed to him and to the statement of poetic truth now brought the vitally modifying note of indignation and bitterness into his writing.

In the opening poem of *In the Seven Woods*, dated August 1902, he tells how he finds refuge and quiet in Lady Gregory's woods. Refuge from what? First he names

> The unavailing outcries and the old bitterness
> That empty the heart

This seems to touch on the old private problem: his love for Maud Gonne and her constant refusals of him. But the next problem is

> Tara uprooted, and new commonness
> Upon the throne and crying about the streets

We know from the words "Tara uprooted" that he is pointing to public issues. Very circumspectly, so as not to help England by dividing religious sect against religious sect in Ireland, he is saying that the Church is destroying Ireland's greatness. His point of reference is Chapter XVIII of Douglas Hyde's *Literary History of Ireland*, which shows how early Irish civilisation failed because, like the early Jewish civilisation, it developed religious institutions at the expense of civil institutions. When the priest overrode the magistrate, says Hyde, collapse came—and that was when the palace at Tara was cursed by St. Ruadhan:

> The great palace where, according to general belief, a hundred and thirty-six pagan and six Christian kings had ruled uninterruptedly, the most august spot in all Ireland, where a "truce of God" had always reigned during the great triennial assemblies, was now to be given up and deserted at the curse of a tonsured monk. The great Assembly or Féis of Tara, which accustomed the people to the idea of a centre of government and a ruling power, could no more be convened, and a thousand associations and memories which hallowed the office of the High-king were snapped in a moment. It was a blow from which the monarchy of Ireland never recovered. . . .

It is plain that, thinking how *The Countess Cathleen* was opposed in the name of the Church, Yeats blames the ecclesiastics for the struggle he is having in Ireland. He also blames "new commonness upon the throne". Ellmann takes this as an attack on Edward VII, who had just been crowned. However, Yeats is using the recent coronation as a metaphor, and is attacking with its help the new nationalist leaders in Dublin and their preference for catchwords instead of the spirit of enquiry.

So *In the Seven Woods* utters his first open reproach against Ireland, indicting Churchmen and politicians and mob-thinking. Then, for consolation and support, it makes the first reference in poetry to the vision of 1896:

> I am contented, for I know that Quiet
> Wanders laughing and eating her wild heart
> Among pigeons and bees, while that Great Archer,
> Who but awaits His hour to shoot, still hangs
> A cloudy quiver over Pairc-na-Lee.

It was in the neighbouring estate of Tillyra that he had seen the archer six years earlier. Now that he is resting in that landscape again he is sure that the vision is valid: the Messiah—note the initial of His—will come; there is, at the centre of his bitterness, this point of certainty and repose. But what about Quiet "eating her wild heart"? We shall see the old Yeats recognising the meaning of the eaten heart and using it in the terrible *Parnell's Funeral*. In 1902 it is an image alive in him but uninterpreted, and it is attached to Quiet by displacement.

Yeats never forgot or forgave the attack on *Countess Cathleen*. He believed that from then on the public did not trust him. The attacks on his orthodoxy had spread a poison which made, he noted in 1901, "a very serious difference in my position outside the small cultured class". If that incident had been an isolated one, he might have got over it. After all, at the crisis, he had found friends in the Church as well as opponents: Father Barry had come to his rescue with the pronouncement that "you have given us what is really an Auto, in the manner of Calderon, with the old

Irish folk-lore as a perceptive". But the attack had not been isolated or incidental; it resulted from a chronic condition in Ireland, out of which came repeated assaults against the writers and their works. Nor was it only Catholic orthodoxy that put obstacles in the way of his "movement". The scholarship of Protestant Trinity College, Dublin, was equally hostile. Nor was it only on religious grounds that literary nationalism was attacked. Yeats was appalled, for example, at the evidence tendered by T.C.D. men to the commission considering the Irish language in 1900.

Matching the element in Yeats' make-up which thought strategically and conspiratorially, there was a readiness to scent counter-conspiracy and persecution. John Eglinton has commented sarcastically on it in his *Irish Literary Portraits*. Yeats was very willing to believe that forces were arrayed against him to diminish his reputation (and we know from conversations in *Hail and Farewell* that when the AE group snuggled together they did tear up his character—but so do all literary friends). He was willing to believe that the booksellers were agreed not to handle the books of the movement. A letter★ written to Lady Gregory in 1901 makes this complaint in detail, and includes a significant sentence: "Magee, the [Trinity College] publisher said 'What is he doing here? Why doesn't he go away and leave us in peace?' ". When a man quotes in this way, he is often seizing the opportunity to hear on another man's lips an inner temptation of his own. Does the passage show that Yeats was considering taking leave of Ireland, which received so uncordially what he offered her? Eventually he was driven to that, and this sentence may be a first sign. He undoubtedly considered at once stripping his work of its political purpose; for in the next paragraph he comments "I imagine that as I withdraw from politics my friends among the nationalists will grow less, at first at any rate, and my foes more numerous."

Allan Wade has dated that letter by its postmark May 21st 1901. If the dating is right, it illuminates a question that has con-

★*Letters of W. B. Yeats*, edited by Allan Wade, pp.349–51.

cerned Yeats' biographers: how far his bitterness against his own race and his withdrawal, if it can really be so called, from politics, were due to his distress when Maud Gonne married John Mac-Bride. The marriage was in 1903. This letter and the Seven Woods poem make clear that the bitterness and the mood of withdrawal were smouldering well before that, sparked by the public situation in Dublin. Her marriage may have accentuated, but did not begin, the process.

A great event, curious in the context, occurred between 1901 and 1903. In the first week of April 1902, Yeats' most obviously political and most vividly and simply nationalist play, *Cathleen ni Houlihan*, was produced, with Maud Gonne playing Cathleen, that symbol of Ireland, outwardly a ragged old woman but to those who see true, a queen. Stephen Gwynn has left a fine record of the performance and its effect:

> Miss Maud Gonne, as everyone knows, is a woman of superb stature and beauty; she is said to be an orator, and she certainly has the gifts of voice and gesture. To the courage and sincerity of her acting I can pay no better tribute than to say that her entrance brought instantly to my mind a half-mad old-wife in Donegal whom I have always known. . . . The actors played the piece as it is written; that is, they lessened instead of emphasising the dialect and the brogue; they left the points unemphasised. But they had the house thrilling. I have never known altogether what drama might be before.*

"I went home", says Gwynn in another celebrated reminiscence, "asking myself if such plays should be produced unless one was prepared for people to go out to shoot and be shot." The play rekindled the revolutionary passion of Ireland; the rising of 1798 had failed, but must be attempted again.

Two years earlier Standish O'Grady had uttered "high meaningless words", so impressive to Yeats that they stayed in his mind to the end, commemorated in *Beautiful Lofty Things* and recorded in *Dramatis Personæ*. They were: "We have now a

*In *Irish Literature*, vol. X, edited by Justin McCarthy, Debower-Elliott, Chicago, 1904.

literary movement, it is not very important; it will be followed by a political movement, that will not be very important; then must come a military movement, that will be important indeed." They impressed Yeats and troubled him. With *Cathleen ni Houlihan* he both refuted them and reinforced them. Leaving the political movement to serve wholly in the literary movement, he made a play whereby the literary movement impelled forward the military movement. If the military movement was important, could the literary movement, which impelled it, be less so?

And the play is not only a reaction to Standish O'Grady's challenge. It is also a counter-offensive against the public suspicion of which the booksellers had made him aware in 1901. Though his first notion had been to put politics aside, and he acted on it, he simultaneously—and this is illogical but common human practice—set himself to recapture the lost political ground by writing an indisputably patriotic play. For years afterwards Yeats inscribed "author of *Cathleen ni Houlihan*" on his banner, and it sometimes opened a way through difficulties.

Again, it reunited him, for the last time as things turned out, in a joint task with Maud Gonne. It was a victory. But he continued to move apart from the Irish: the Seven Woods poem, dated only four months later, shows that. From then on he worked no less for their cause, but in ways different from, often opposed to, often contemptuous of, theirs.

Between 1903 and 1914 he was continually in action in Ireland. He belaboured his people for ignorance, narrowness, pettiness. He fought to establish a place amongst them for imaginative work which would, he believed, correct their faults. George Moore said, a year or two before Yeats was prepared to admit it openly, that Ireland was inimical to art, inventing in illustration the story of the statue smashed by the model's angry brothers, and blazing out "This is no place to live. It is no country for an educated man. It won't be fit for a man to live in for another hundred years." By 1905 Yeats reached a comparable position. He made an issue out of Synge's plays, and, as is well-known and will be repeated in the next chapters, he fought that issue successfully.

But when row had followed row—the *Playboy* row followed by the turmoil over Hugh Lane's art gallery, and so on—he doubted what the end would be. Neither the wild Maud Gonne nor the tight-minded men in the nationalist underground, neither the traditional Church nor the new political constellation, would countenance the amorality of art. He had to recognise that the nation liberated might be even less receptive of his values than the nation oppressed and struggling.

Discouragement crept upon him, at its worst during the squabble over the gallery for Hugh Lane's pictures. There is a double motive in his poetic commentary on this episode. Hugh Lane was Lady Gregory's nephew, and Yeats had to fulfil the office of poet on behalf of patron, an antique office which he loved, and find verses for the occasion. But the tone of the poems, the dejection and snarl in them, leave no doubt of the personal concern as well. He saw the gallery dispute as epitomising the insolence of Ireland towards art and thus towards all he stood for.*

The volume *Responsibilities*, published in 1914, collected the verses written out of the intermittent anger and despair of ten years of public action in Dublin. It is quantitatively a scant poetic outcome; the real poetic consequences were reserved for middle age and old age, when, retrospecting, he used in poetry both his country's quarrels and his quarrels with his country; if he could not write out of immediate stimulus, he had the power to scoop out the past long afterwards. But though thin, the book has a new masculinity. He had dreamed of stiffening the backbone of Ireland. He found Ireland dead set against his innovations, all "dirt and slop and general shiftlessness", as the hostile Kipling said in Dublin in 1911†; and in reaction *his* backbone was stiffened. Thereupon, to fight the contemporary Irish defects he employed an Irish tradition both pugnacious and intellectual. The diction and accent of eighteenth-century satire had shown for a moment in that poem written in the Seven Woods. In *Responsibilities* they

---

*See Lady Gregory, *Hugh Lane's Life and Achievement*. This book is the essential if incomplete background to the Yeats' gallery poems.

†See C. E. Carrington, *Life of Rudyard Kipling*, Doubleday, 1955, p.326.

resonate. For example, in *To a Shade*, an address to Parnell. It begins as though it might become a sonnet; then shoots Augustan satire through its parenthesis—

> If you have revisited the town, thin Shade,
> Whether to look upon your monument
> (I wonder if the builder has been paid) . . .

Then, where the sestet might have come, it swings into a long accelerating movement, an accumulation of angry reproach— poetry meaningfully, extendedly angry and vituperative for the first time in English since Pope—as it describes Dublin's treatment of Hugh Lane, who

> has been driven from the place,
> And insult heaped upon him for his pains,
> And for his openhandedness, disgrace;
> Your enemy, an old foul mouth, had set
> The pack upon him

"Your enemy" means, of course, Parnell's enemy, which is the mob-mouth of collective Ireland.

Shaw, another Protestant Irishman, was cudgelling and vituperating in prose with Augustan turns to it, and Yeats probably had learned something from it, so his praise of a Shaw letter to *The Times* in 1907 suggests,* but knew he could hit harder with poetry. He proved it with the tail-poem to *Responsibilities*. And this *is* a sonnet. Yeats is a master of the sonnet, in the sense that he has compelled it to new functions. It is a telescoping of that compact, statuesque form with the lope, the punching, the dung-throwing of classical satire and with the tocsin effects of Irish oratory. It snubs the worthless society of Dublin, whose behaviour it defines with a phrase from Ben Jonson, "the fling of the dull ass's hoof" (from time to time Yeats will now appropriate from some earlier poet images of this colloquial force, especially if rooted in the basic life of farm or covert or kitchen, and will include an acknowledgment to the source as part of his verse, thus saying in effect, "I think as the few best, whose heir I am,

*See *Letters of W. B. Yeats*, p.500.

have always thought"). Then follows the well-known phrase of his own: undreamt accidents have made him

> Notorious, till all my priceless things
> Are but a post the passing dogs defile.

Placed at the end of the volume, this sonnet is a dramatic gesture: it is Yeats as the traditional Irish orator from Grattan to O'Connell, confronting, however, not the aliens but his own people.

A little earlier another form of Augustan vituperative has appeared in his work: the epigram. In *The Green Helmet* of 1910 came the first, the not quite successful *On Hearing that the Students of our New University have joined the Agitation against Immoral Literature*. The right combination of distance and destructiveness is obtained in the 1914 volume when he attacks *Those that Hated 'The Playboy of the Western World'*, the pictorial vehicle of which was suggested by a drawing of Charles Ricketts:

> Once, when midnight smote the air,
> Eunuchs ran through Hell and met
> On every crowded street to stare
> Upon great Juan riding by:
> Even like these to rail and sweat
> Staring upon his sinewy thigh.

Labelling his opponents eunuchs, which implies surety of his own virility, he shows how he has outgrown those portraits by his father and later artists which represent him as feminine. In the famous Sargent portrait of 1908, he is half-way through the change: he looks absurdly young, though his actual age was forty-three; but the inept femininity of his father's 1900 portrait is changing into pride. By 1914 the domestic turmoils of Ireland have hardened his mind, made it a sinewy cock, which jerks in writing and speeches.

Hone has pointed out that in the Dublin schools in the 'eighties "Pope was the only poet since Shakespeare", and in that city and in the other urban patches and the scattered manors of Ireland the eighteenth century lingered presidially. The tradition was extant for Yeats to spring to when the need arose. Out of need he became a satirist, not for pleasure nor out of any theory of its value or tradition's value. Like Swift he writes the satire of public emergency experienced as personal emergency. It is all the better because it is not solely satire.

In identifying the voice of his anger we can go further. At least two centuries earlier than Swift satire was a favourite mode of poetry in Ireland. Lady Gregory had briefly hinted at this un-forsaken Gaelic tradition in *Poets and Dreamers*, a collection of papers published in 1903. She had named O'Higinn, whose tongue was cut out by the men of Sligo when they had suffered from it, and O'Daly "who criticized the poverty of the Irish chiefs in the sixteenth century until the servant of one of them stuck a knife in his throat". Yeats was close to her when she compiled these notes. He was always quick to seize on a hint and graft a technique on to his work.

While the English eighteenth century gave the patterns of the satire which Yeats, Shaw, and sometimes their Irish contem-poraries, wrote, an earlier Irish voice spoke in them, too, sharpen-ing the bite, rudening the vilification. It might be examined one day whether the drive which prompted the Augustans themselves to satire came entirely from their emulation of the Romans. May not the filth, the immediate social and personal relevance, the dynamic, have swirled to Augustan London from Dublin with the literary toing-and-froing between the cities? The English eighteenth century, imposed on Ireland, flourished there. How much the more natural that seems if we regard its character as in part of Irish ancestry, if we detect something of Ireland enfleshed in it.

TATTERDEMALION

The date under that Augustan poem, *To a Shade*, is September 29th, 1913. It has taken Yeats nearly twenty-one years to awaken the dormant image of Parnell. He has at last discovered functions for Parnell: to point, as a betrayed hero, to the disgrace of the betrayers; to imply the "Shakespearean contempt" for the crowd which he will later attempt to shape into a political attitude; to suggest a masculinity in which self-respect speaks out like arrogance because otherwise it would not be understood.

Simultaneously there enters a new image: it is a lusty tatter-demalion dancing beggarman. He was present as fiddler or crone in the rather bloodless early Yeats ballads. Now he has taken on lust and knowledge. He rummages in his rags, cracks fleas, frenziedly sings, mixes lice and blood, stumbles on his crutch. He is allied to Synge's tinkers, those lust-brimming tinkers of Ireland who rallied annually to exchange their wives. His final incarnation in Yeats' late period is Mannion, the Roaring Tinker, whose name shows his relationship to the old Irish divinity Mananaan. He is kin, too, with the gypsies and shares their lore. He may be one of the Thirty-Six Tsaddiqim wandering the earth, according to Jewish legend, in who-knows-what guise. "Did an Avatar ever sit on a throne? Have they not always gone about the world as vagrants?" asked AE later. Yeats and AE both use the knowledge gained in the study of esoteric doctrine: that saint or god appears as beggarman and that the delighted lust of the beggar secretes purity. AE was never as energetic as Yeats in his use of it, yet he has his beguiling moment in a poem for Krishna:

> I saw him pass from love to love;
>   and yet the pure allowed his claim
> To be the purest of the pure,
>   thrice holy, stainless, without blame.
> I saw the open tavern door
>   flash on the dusk a ruddy glare
> And saw the King of Kings outcast
>   reel brawling through the starlit air.
> And yet He is the Prince of Peace
>   of whom the ancient wisdom tells. . . .

It is significant that this theme comes alive in Yeats with the stirring of the Parnell memories and their Messianic associations promising the birth of a hero. Messianism involves the hour of the beggar and the orgy.

Did Yeats consciously intend this connotation of his theme when he published his first tinker-beggarman poems in *Responsibilities?* He certainly intended it in his later apocalyptic writing. Here he may have had the intuition before he could wholly interpret it. Let us notice as a fact that in the same volume there is an overtly Messianic poem, *The Magi:*

> Now as at all times I can see in the mind's eye
> In their stiff, painted clothes, the pale unsatisfied ones
> Appear and disappear in the blue depths of the sky
> With all their ancient faces like rain-beaten stones,
> And all their helms of silver hovering side by side,
> And all their eyes still fixed, hoping to find once more,
> Being by Calvary's turbulence unsatisfied,
> The uncontrollable mystery on the bestial floor.

It is a sharp, haunting vision, a holding-together of the static and mobile. But how the mood has changed since the 'nineties when he made the confident promise to the Secret Rose "Surely thine hour has come". This poem tells of a dour prolongation of the search for the Messiah. Yeats had realised that the hopes originally formed for Ireland, and pursued in simple conviction till the Irish harried him, were inadequate, yet he trusted that something lay behind them and was straining to descry the shape.

Meanwhile he had been trying to write—in prose and as a piece of systematics—the Sacred Book that must either be borne in the hands of the Irish Messiah or be furnished Him by evangelist or lieutenant, to illuminate His road and be His message to the world. We have heard Eglinton and Moore and their cronies discussing this Book in Ely Place,★ and we have seen Moore writing his version of it. On December 22nd, 1898, Yeats had invited Lady Gregory to collaborate with him in *his* version. It was to consist of a major report on the spirit-world, evidence supplied by the peasants of Ireland and correlated with the findings of folklorists elsewhere and with esoteric traditions. He conceived Lady Gregory's part as relatively servile. He warned

★See page 17 above.

her, "One hand should do the actual shaping and writing—apart from peasant talk—and I would wish to do this. In some cases my opinions may be too directly mystical for you to accept." She was to be the apprentice; yet he knew that any peasant material he could collect alone would be meagre compared with the results of her tactful industry. She agreed to his conditions and worked hard collecting. In the spring of 1911 in Paris they jointly made an effort at "putting into final shape the big book of Fairy Belief". A year later he was preparing an introduction for it, but a change had occurred: it was now "Lady Gregory's big book of Fairy Belief". He had transferred it to her in honesty since he recognised that all the compilation was hers: it should be published as hers, and he would contribute explications fore and aft. But also he had transferred it to her less ingenuously, recognising that for all its interest it was not the Sacred Book of Ireland. He would have to write that alone in his own way when he saw its character more clearly than he then could. Pale and unsatisfied, he strained to descry the mystery on the bestial floor. If it was clouded, that was because he did not yet take literally enough the word "bestial". A more complete accoutrement of filth was wanted.

LOST MOON—AND NEW IMAGE

He had moments of fear that his writing would be permanently lame as a result of the loss of contact with the Irish public. That is the sense of his *Lines Written in Dejection*. He laments that "The holy centaurs of the hills are vanished"—that is, the poetry is gone or is unsatisfying. This is because "Heroic mother moon" herself has gone and, at the age of fifty, he is left with "the timid sun". We know what significance he attaches to moon and sun from a passage in his preface to Lady Gregory's *Gods and Fighting Men*. The moon, he said there, represents the songs of the folk, the collective; the sun "the individual soul turning itself into a pure fire and imposing its own pattern, its own music":

To lunar influence belong all thoughts and emotions that were created by the community, by the common people, by nobody knows who, and to the sun all that came from the highly disciplined or individual kingly mind. I myself imagine a marriage of the sun and moon in the arts I take most pleasure in; and now bride and bridegroom but exchange as it were, full cups of gold and silver and now they are one in a mystical embrace.

He has rejected collective Ireland on finding the commons bound to Church or politics, neither of which, he says, "can of itself create minds with enough receptivity to become wise, or just and generous enough to make a nation". But the result of his rejection is that he cannot celebrate the mystic marriage: one of the partners has been driven out.

In the Collected Poems Yeats places, two pages after this lament, a dramatic lyric widely recognised as one of the great consolation-poems, *The Fisherman*. Whipping his Irish audience which has disillusioned him, he offers himself an image of support a man in touch with nature, physically skilled, stable, meditative

> The freckled man who goes
> To a grey place on a hill
> In grey Connemara clothes
> At dawn to cast his flies

Two ghosts are elicited and fused: the boy Yeats who fished the deep pool that morning in Sligo, who swore never to leave his father's home; and the meditative man who would have developed from that stay-at-home life, a life that would have been without colours but without oscillation. The grey hills, the grey clothes predicate the hope with which the poem *is about to* end—that he may be free enough, and yet though free (with mystic marriage rejected) still powerful enough, to make a cold neutral poem Yet the actual ending is

> Before I am old
> I shall have made him one
> Poem maybe as cold
> And passionate as the dawn.

By interposing "passionate" at the last moment Yeats alters the significance of his image. He discovers—the act of making the poem enables him to discover—a different future than he had foreseen when he mourned the moon. He had been imagining the neutral man. But what is a neutral man—one fortunately free from the assaults of passion, or a man who experiences passions but holds them in total control? Which did Hamlet mean when he loved Horatio?—

> Give me that man
> That is not passion's slave, and I will wear him
> At my heart's core, aye, at my heart of hearts,
> As I do thee.

As *The Fisherman* moves forward in the key of grey, it appears to be aspiring towards the former meaning. But when Yeats met in life people who might be called neutral or stable in that sense, he did not care for them. AE was stable in that way; for all their early intimacy Yeats did not really like him. So the last line of the poem makes its astonishing modulation. It is suddenly obvious that the valuable thing is not to be free of passion, but to hold it under. Yeats had remembered Parnell: no one was so passionate, no one had so complete a control of his passions when confronting the public. At least, so Yeats believed. The stories that he sketches with furious strokes in *A Vision* stirred as he completed *The Fisherman:*

He made upon his contemporaries an impression of impassivity, and yet a follower has recorded that, after a speech that seemed brutal and callous, his hands were full of blood because he had torn them with his nails.★ One of his followers was shocked during the impassioned discussion in Committee Room No. 15 that led to his abandonment, by this most reticent man's lack of reticence in allusion to the operations of sex, an indifference as of a mathematician dealing with

★Compare Joyce's description of Gabriel Conroy in *The Dead:* "his arms were trembling with desire to seize her and only the stress of his nails against the palms of his hands held the wild impulse of his body in check."

some arithmetical quantity, and yet Mrs. Parnell tells how upon a night of storm on Brighton pier, and at the height of his power, he held her out over the waters and she lay still, stretched upon his two hands, knowing that if she moved, he would drown himself and her.

Yeats began moulding his consolation, his image of support, on the model of the self dedicated to stay in Sligo, but he finished it in the image of Parnell. And he elaborated the image into a theory in subsequent years. Whoever is truly strong, intellectual, tragic, he inferred, holds down passion, and it is a most intense passion that he holds down. When Yeats rehearsed actors in his plays, he instructed them to speak as if they were mastering *hysterica passio:* "the passion of the verse comes from the fact that the speakers are holding down violence or madness. . . . All depends on the completeness of the holding down, on the stirring of the beast underneath."

The temptation to a neutral life was strong in 1914 and 1915 He wondered whether to go away from Ireland permanently He spent a great deal more time in England again. The Noh play to which Ezra Pound introduced him was probably the more seductive because he was weary of Irish preoccupations,* and because he was weary of crowds and it could be played to a few elect in a salon. The stylisation and ritual of Noh, its dances and impassive masks, offered themselves as an embodiment of neutrality; but what had happened with *The Fisherman* happened here they became, instead, an expression of the holding down of passion. Yeats so tautens the action and poetry as to suggest the concentration and muscular tension involved in controlling force which is only just less strong than the controller. And, foreign form, they were converted into a medium for Irish material.

The poet who in rancour and dejection had thought of quitting Ireland began to negotiate early in 1917 for the purchase of an old Irish property, the square tower at Ballylee. The transaction was

*Note Eglinton's sneer, when he points out that Yeats' first statement on *Certa Noble Plays of Japan* bears the date of the year of the Easter Rising, 1916.

settled for thirty-five pounds by June of that year. He had visited the tower "two or three times" (which I take to mean twice, possibly once) in 1899, to enquire into a saying of Biddy Early*, the nineteenth-century wise woman of Clare: "There is a cure for all evil between the two mill-wheels of Ballylee." Questioning the old miller, he had learned that the cure lay "in the strong cellar" of Ballylee, which was a great hole where the river sank underground. So the man whose home was Ballylee would be in contact with power: the cure for all evils would be by his door, and there too the caverns measureless to man, the depths of the rivers of Egypt. He recalled the hole where he had fished for eels—for the dragons—when he was a boy in Sligo. He settled himself in 1917 at a holy centre of Ireland and of the universe.

This reversal of his distinct drift away from Ireland must have been due to the Easter Rising. He had been absent during the Rising, he was indignant that he had not been consulted by the conspirators, he was ambivalent in his attitude to it, but on one point he was at once clear: that its political consequences would be crucial. Charles Ricketts noted in his journal on April 28th that Yeats assured him that the revolt was serious, and that he reassured Yeats that all would pass, both the Rising and the Casement trial, and that an amnesty after the War would bring back general tranquillity and the status quo. Ricketts later annotated the entry "I was an idiot"; Yeats had been the better judge.

Eglinton gibes that Yeats somewhat hurriedly invoked his muse, regarding himself as national laureate, and produced *Easter 1916*. His letters show that within a few days of the news of the Rising he framed the motif "a terrible beauty is born" and related images moved in his mind. But the date of the final manuscript is September 25th; reflection and anxiety evidently went into the making; while the oxymoron of the refrain, "a terrible beauty", reconciles the two opposing impulses which the poem considers, everything else in the poem fails to reconcile them. It perpetuates the sense of sanctity which, following the execution of the leaders,

---

Compare page 98, in the Lady Gregory chapter. And for the legend of Ballylee compare AE's poem *The Well of All Healing* in *The Divine Vision*, 1904.

wreathed Ireland that summer and hallowed the military movement; yet it condemns military sacrifice as always coupled with
hatred; and sacrifice and hatred, it says, narrow the vista, obliterate
essential landmarks. Yeats speaks at some length of the Irish
landscape as if trying to recover wider vistas, in the perspective of
which to remind the Irish of the original ideals of nationalism. He
comes on the image of sacrifice as a stone in the stream. Here his
two conflicting attitudes should have met and established a relationship. But there is confusion instead of contact. A sequence
like the following seems to be adumbrated: (1) sacrifice is a stone;
(2) in the whole landscape of Ireland, which stands for nature
or truth or perfection, or at least for the fount of Irish action, the
stone has its proper place, but only as a detail, a very small fraction
of the whole; (3) in the individual's heart, however, a stone is a
stoppage of the lifestream. This has to be felt for by the reader,
so uncertain is the poet of it, and even when found it is not con-
vincing. But though the obscurity troubles the poem it does not
destroy it. That two unresolved, perhaps irresolvable, reactions to
the Rising wrestle through the stanzas, neither able to oust or to
mate with the other, is a reason why it has compelled readers for
forty years.

But Yeats knew that he had left an incomplete argument. He
worked at the problem for a year and dealt with it again in a
Noh play, *The Dreaming of the Bones*, imposing it on the old Irish
theme of Dervorgilla, whose adulterous love for Diarmuid
brought the first Norman invaders into Ireland and so precipitated the 700-years' subjugation. On her lay Ireland's suffering and
the blood of the martyrs, Wolfe Tone, Emmet, and the leaders of
1916. A young man who has escaped after the Post Office fighting
is crossing the mountains. In the hour before dawn he meets
Dervorgilla and Diarmuid—two ghosts separated, never to kiss
each other till someone of their race forgives them. He has the
opportunity to forgive them and dissolve the 700-years' curse.
And

> I had almost yielded and forgiven it all—
> Terrible the temptation and the place!

but he resists, confirms the sentence

> never, never
> Shall Diarmuid and Dervorgilla be forgiven.

There is a dizzying invitation to forgive. There is the decision not to forgive. When Yeats wrote to Lady Gregory about the play he confessed "I am afraid [it is] only too powerful politically". We might be doubtful whether he thought it dangerous because it invited or because it refused forgiveness, but for a letter written to Clement Shorter, in May 1918, predicting that there will be more bloodshed in Ireland. Yeats has heard an old cabinet-maker say: "There will be more wild work. The young men are made jealous of their leaders for being shot." He tells Shorter, what he will admit in later poems, that he is pained and perplexed that earlier plays and verse of his—his "movement"—have led to the Rising, the killing, the martyrdoms, and to all that will now ensue. He will refrain from any statements that could lead further in that direction: "Times are too dangerous for me to encourage men to risks I am not prepared to share or approve." This is unmistakable. As the appealing poetry given to the lovers' ghosts suggests, the bias of his mind when he wrote *The Dreaming of the Bones* had turned towards forgiveness. When he wrote to Lady Gregory he evidently thought that this would be clear to his audience and unpopular. In fact, however, the play leaves it in doubt what choice should be made, only ending with a prediction of events:

> I have heard from far below
> The strong March birds a-crow.
> Stretch neck and clap the wing,
> Red cocks, and crow!

—the imminent violence, first of the insurrectionary struggle against Britain, then of the civil war.

John MacBride, who had taken part in the Rising, had been shot. Maud Gonne was free to re-marry, and Yeats made a proposal. Never was he less likely to be accepted. She was in Normandy, but afire to be back in Ireland in her natural place among the martyrs. He was developing an ambivalence incredible to her. He also made proposals to her stepdaughter Iseult, and when these were refused married Georgie Hyde-Lees on October 21st, 1917. It was a complete statement of ambivalence: he broke with the Gonnes, symbols of Ireland, and married an Englishwoman, but renovated the keep at Ballylee for her home.

Residence there was partial. The river at the base made Ballylee suitable only in summer. He and his family were much in England for two or three years. But he confirmed his renewal of residence in Ireland by also taking a house in Dublin early in 1922.

A SACRED BOOK BUT NOT FOR IRELAND

The rebellion and the civil war were the beginning of Irish freedom. They produced what the Irish writers had been promising. But always at this point in the history we have to face the fact that the writers read their people's success as failure, and that their disillusion began when they realised that violence (which as young men they had welcomed as a necessary Armageddon) was the means to success.

Looking at the circumstances from outside we can demur that they were too exacting. Ireland became a free nation by means no less and no more objectionable than other nations, and when she began to live her independence she was no less and no more fault-mottled than other nations. But the writers had believed and had promised the world, that she would be superior to other nations, a light to the Gentiles, a model of dignity. They could not bear her normalcy and condemned it as her failure and theirs.

Yeats' poems on the insurrection and civil war are troubled and angry over the breakdown of values:

> O but we dreamed to mend
> Whatever mischief seemed
> To afflict mankind, but now
> That winds of winter blow
> Learn that we were crack-pated when we dreamed

and again, epigrammatically:

> We, who seven years ago
> Talked of honour and truth
> Shriek with pleasure if we show
> The weasel's twist, the weasel's tooth

His Civil War poems question all his previous beliefs in the light of the facts. They are poems of fluctuation as he tries to determine what was durable in his faith, what illusory, and what revisions he must make. The next generation of Irish writers pointed to them as evidence of a fatal shortcoming. Sean O'Faolain reviewed them in the *Criterion*, April 1930, and charged that "in the inevitable poet's fight . . . between personality and genius" Yeats had dodged a decision. "All his life he has fluctuated between what his will might do and what his destiny would do." This may be a valid charge against a man, but not against a poet, whose discoveries may depend on his fluctuations, which are a function of hyper-sensibility. Yeats was in a phase of transition, and came out of it changed and even distorted in views and powerful as a poet.

He worked in Ireland during the fighting and assassinations, but grew estranged from her. But while public conditions were difficult, marriage had made his private life satisfying and concentrated his capacities and put them at his free disposal. For all his adult years to the age of fifty-two his sexual life had been restricted. Now that enjoyment was regularly available he revelled in it, regretted the wasted nights of half a lifetime. With that his other interests, notably his psychic explorations (which we might have glibly labelled substitutes for marriage, but for this evidence to the contrary) jumped to an unprecedented activity. His wife produced automatic writing, through which a cohort of spirits communicated, supplying information, such as he had always sought, about the processes of human history.

He had already begun to doubt whether the book of faery beliefs to which he had summoned Lady Gregory would be the Sacred Book. Now he realised that the spirits speaking through his wife—or we may prefer to say the projections of his fantasy released through his wife—were furnishing the material of the real Sacred Book, which would plot the rise and fall of cultures and would analyse the two latest cycles of history: the cyle that began with the Annunciation to Leda and ended with the Roman Empire, and the cycle that began with the Annunciation to Mary and is ending now. The convictions of 1896, it will be noticed, underlie this presentation: the supposition is, still, that a new Messiah is due, bringing a new age out of disorder. But though the recent world war and current struggle in Ireland could have encouraged him, as it sometimes encouraged AE, still to maintain that the Messiah would come to the world through Ireland, he did not do so. His Sacred Book, *A Vision*, eventually published in 1925 after much excited writing and much reading for supporting evidence, is written as a book for the world (or at any rate for the western world) with no suggestion that Ireland has a special part to play in the new annunciation. This was the immediate result of his disillusion with the violent events in Ireland and the coarsening, as he regarded it, of Irish feeling.

Publicist-minded, he began, while *A Vision* was in the making, to prepare the world for it. He inserted hints in his interim writing that a Sacred Book was to be expected. In *The Trembling of the Veil*, issued 1922, he released the 1896 dream of the Archer. The very title of that autobiography was an index of his intentions. He described how he had found it in one of his old diaries, then asked: "Is it true that our air is disturbed, as Mallarmé said, by 'the trembling of the veil of the Temple', or 'that our whole age is seeking to bring forth a sacred book?'" But although he signposted its coming, *A Vision* was largely ignored when it came. According to a letter to Olivia Shakespeare, only AE gave it a serious review. "*A Vision* reminds me", Yeats told her between disappointment and worldly humour, "of stones I used to drop as a child into a certain very deep well. The splash is very far off and very faint." Despite its re-publication in further and revised editions, the reputation of the book has stayed on a par with that reception. *A Vision* goes unread or is not taken seriously. From the earliest years Yeats had had a love of pseudo-mathematical diagrams: that had been an incentive to his adoption of astrology and secret-society rituals; that also was why he had imagined his shadow-figure, Michael Robartes, living among the Judwalis (an Arab tribe whose name means Diagrammatists). It probably contributed to his formal skill as a poet. But it could not make him a mathematician. Yet *A Vision* has more than its rudimentary division of the 2,000-year cycle into twenty-eight lunar phases. It has human protraiture. Its biographical studies are excited, robust. They are written in a prose free from the excessive richness, the over-mellifluous falsity of his earlier prose style. The thoughts race forward in tight-packed sentences. And though it omits Ireland from a formative part in history, the best biographies are Irish, and they are part of the mad and entertaining archives of the Irish Literary Revival.

If composing *A Vision* diverted some of his poetic energy, the research for it provided him with material for poems and the position he developed in it provided him with an outlook in terms of which to write. Most of the poems determined by his thoughts for *A Vision* come later, but two that are most famous were written at the same time. *The Second Coming* (1919) looks back to *The Magi* and picks up the word "bestial" and enlarges it into the rough beast slouching towards Bethlehem to be born. The Magi have their answer. Yeats was aware, as we shall see later, of the beauty of the conventional Christian image of the Messiah as infant, of the song of Simeon; but he is preoccupied at this date with the Messianic turbulence, dirt, and odour of blood. In *Leda and the Swan* he dramatises the Annunciation to Leda—"bestiality" in another sense—and the divine engendering of Helen, out of which came the Trojan War and the chain of deaths and civilisation. He had been thinking and writing of Helen of Troy for thirty years already: had once identified her with Mary Hynes,* the loose beauty of Ballylee, loved by the blind poet Raftery, and simultaneously and by a double comparison with Maud Gonne, whom he blindly loved (he being the modern Raftery and perhaps

---

*A. Norman Jeffares, starting from a clue in *The Celtic Twilight*, has written admirably about her in *W. B. Yeats, Man and Poet*.

the modern Homer). In the light of the earlier poems we might sense the vestige of a thought that Maud Gonne, as the modern Helen, marked a new cycle of history; and if this is so, Ireland might still be said to have a part in preluding the new cycle. An allusion to Mary Hynes in *The Tower* reinforces this possibility. However, it is vestigial; Yeats does nothing to insist on it.

In 1919 Yeats had obtained the first performance of *The Player Queen*, a confused work. It had been written and re-written for ten years, altered from tragedy to comedy, tailored to fit Mrs. Patrick Campbell. Some typical Messianic material survived the confusion: hints of bestiality, a unicorn coupling with a Queen; a beggarman, perhaps genuine, perhaps an imposter, who rolls on his back in a fit of uncontrollable itching and brays the bray of Christ's donkey when one king is to be replaced by another. On the stage Yeats now made it his problem to reconsider the Messianic theme and to present it more incisively, as the under-standing of *A Vision* made possible. In 1925 he wrote *Resurrection*. Christ comes out of the tomb, walks through a street where "Asiatic Greeks", the poorest of the poor, are mating at random and lacerating themselves, amid music and dance, to bring their antique god back to life. He comes to the Apostles to show them his beating heart. Let those who doubt that the Messiah is corporeal, and corporeally resurrected, put their hand on that heart: they will find it beating, through that *shock* they will *know*. This is the play that carries the two Songs, that have become independently famous, expounding the cyclical extinction of discipline and tolerance in the turbulence of rebirth. They are *A Vision* in brief.

THE REASON FOR THE LEGEND

The Irish writers had an exaggerated sense of failure when they saw the look of free Ireland. But there is use in a sense of failure: it gives rise to self-criticism. And one of the uses of national freedom is that self-criticism becomes significant, whereas it has no place in the thinking of a subject people, who naturally blame the occupier for their defects. As soon as Irishmen controlled Ireland, Yeats assumed castigatory functions, proper to a writer although not included in his theory of "there is no great art with-out praise". The new leadership displayed little to praise: ignorance and mediocrity. An Irish Minister requested his acquaintance. "We met", he commented fourteen years later, "but my con-versation shocked and embarrassed him. No, neither Gogarty nor I, with our habit of outrageous conversation, could get near these men." The censorial inclinations of his people angered him. Drawing attention to two cases in his regular article for a Dublin paper, he found the editor afraid to print, and thereupon passed his text to T. S. Eliot, who published it in the *Criterion* for April 1926. It told how the old carol of Mary and the cherry-tree had been burned as heretical, and how Lennox Robinson, having written his story of the peasant girl who believes herself pregnant of God, had been threatened with ejection from his post at the Carnegie Library.* What did these reactions to religious art mean? asked Yeats. They showed that the attackers and censors did not believe, as they imagined they believed, in the Incarnation or the Second Coming. If they put their hand on the heart of Christ resurrected, they could not endure the shock of its throb. Bigotry—and Yeats was careful, almost always, to say that he applied this word equally to the Catholics and Protestants of Ireland—bigotry, littleness, lack of imaginative faith, constrained his country. Intellect was persecuted.

In the Irish Senate he hoped to do something to better the position. His frustrations there, where he could not out-argue or out-manœuvre commercially expert fellow-Senators, are recount-ed in the address to Ezra Pound that begins—it rings ironically today—"Never become a Senator".

He re-read his Civil War poems and was appalled at their bitterness. His intellect was too active to bear narrow Ireland. On the Mediterranean coast he might be able to sing of "joyous life". So when his term as Senator ended in 1928 he sailed to Byzantium. The Rapallo period began. Perhaps he was at fault: to sustain his role as national critic most effectively, a man should stay at home in the ruck. But the dynamic of that lifelong

*The Lennox Robinson episode is also described in Lady Gregory's journal.

oscillation in his affair with his people carried him away from Ireland.

The Mediterranean climate and the artistic history of Italy worked on the curious medley of things he had done and read in the past and produced *Oil and Blood* and *Veronica's Napkin*, poems fretted out of gold. *Byzantium* is a too ambitious projection of the same delight in manipulating the richest treasures an ornate civilisation can offer. George Moore's enthusiasm for mediæval craftsmanship was kindled in Ireland: critical of nearly everything else in Ireland, Moore could sympathetically contemplate her mediæval glory, the smiths, the illuminators, the armourers, of the age of Marban. Yeats went abroad to discover his passion for the mediæval smith. He imagined behind the fulsome Byzantine art a society where artists are welcome, integral, so that they become "almost impersonal, almost perhaps without the consciousness of individual design, absorbed in their subject-matter and that the vision of a whole people". Their relationship to society is in fact the polar opposite of that in the new Ireland, where the artist is essentially personal and against the public and rejected by the public. The Byzantine poems are anti-Irish as well as non-Irish, their fulsome brilliance a dream of the collective art that might have been permitted Yeats in a different, mediæval order of society.

I do not know whether it was in virtue of the poems of this class that AE hailed *The Winding Stair*. "In the new poetry", he said when he reviewed it, "plain things shine as by some inner light, as if they were lustrous by themselves." In the same volume there are also overtly Irish poems. For instance, *Remorse for Intemperate Speech*, dated 1931, avows that though he has broken out of Ireland and chosen a "fit audience" instead of the mob, he has not been able to alter what he was born with:

> Great hatred, little room,
> Maimed us at the start.
> I carry from my mother's womb
> A fanatic heart.

The lines are elucidated by an entry in Charles Ricketts' diary fifteen years earlier. Yeats had harangued him that every Irishman is born with a grudge, with an incurable disease implanted by oppression; and Ricketts had recorded his boredom at the repetition of the theme and guessed that Yeats was bored too. Yeats *was* bored, grew more so, hated Ireland's hatred, but could not stop thinking Ireland.

He thought that his movement had failed in success; he had a heavy sense of responsibility because, through his *Cuchulain* and his *Cathleen ni Houlihan*, it had sent out men to be shot; but he had not completely turned away from it. He held that the activist had selected from the tendencies of the movement only a part, insurrection and sacrifice, and had neglected all the cultural implications—fineness of thought, intellect, openmindedness. A hope presented itself to him that a future generation might renew the movement and carry it through totally. He set out to support that possibility, and his method was to establish a legend, engraved in lyric, of his movement and its ideals. He judged that the Irish would accept the legend if he wrote it as a personal tradition. As early as 1909, stimulated by a passage in Synge's preface to *Poems and Translations*, he had been considering the importance of personality in literature. He worked at the issue in correspondence with his father. J. B. insisted on "intimacy" as the sign of fine literature, and W. B. concurred, understanding it as the personal: the uniqueness of individual experience as opposed to "generalization". The doctrine of the Rhymers' Club, he felt, had been "that lyric poetry should be personal"; and when he exposed the story of some of the Rhymers in *The Trembling of the Veil* he defended his candour by pointing to their own high valuation of personality. In 1913 when Katharine Tynan published the first volume of her reminiscences he wrote to her: "I have often felt that the influence of our movement on the generation immediately following us will very largely depend upon the way in which the personal history is written. It has always been so in Ireland." This last sentence is the foundation of his tradition-building. He would have relied on it, and on the Synge dictum which inspired it, if asked to defend the biographical bias of many late lyrics, the use of events in his life and his friends', the investing of their sayings with the aura of apocrypha. He was resolved to perpetuate their personalities. He found help in the naming practice of the old Gaelic poets. That in turn was the tail of the ancient epic, saga, Biblical pageantry of names, based on the genealogical, clan mystique of primitive society. Poetry has always been trying to preserve this practice and make it newly significant. Yeats succeeded. His first list of names occurs in *Easter 1916*; he adopted the technique under the stress of national crisis and obtained a joint old and new quality through it, linking the nationalist dead with their ancestors. Now he developed the technique to establish his tradition.

At the centre of the legend he put the trinity: Lady Gregory, Synge, Yeats. There are fascinating fringe-personalities, too: members of the Rhymers' Club; associates in psychic experiment; the organisers of the Rising. Behind there is the powerful and formative figure of Parnell. But the trinity counts most. Allusions to it begin to appear in, for example, the "Open Letter to Lady Gregory" communicated to the *Irish Statesman* late in 1919. Then in 1923 Yeats had an international forum at his disposal, and decisively phrased his myth. He told the Swedish Royal Academy in his Nobel Prize address:

> When your King gave me medal and diploma, two forms should have stood, one at either side of me, an old woman sinking into the infirmity of age and a younger man's ghost. I think when Lady Gregory's name and John Synge's name are spoken by future generations, my name, if remembered, will come up in the talk, and that if my name is spoken first their names will come in their turn. . . .

It is international legend-making, work which proceeds till his death, its elaborate "heart-smitten" culmination *The Municipal Gallery Revisited*.

It is worth repeating: the purpose is not only vanity, not only the love of being remembered as long as poetry in English is read, but that the movement, though swamped in his own time by the short-term concerns of the politicians, continue to ferment and obtain its results with some later generation, young men and women who will read it and be fired to persist in the work, as Yeats had been fired by Duffy's *Young Ireland* to continue the work of Davis. That is why he often said in the 'twenties and 'thirties that he was writing for the ardent young, the future equivalents of the ardent young Parnellites of his past.

There is only one other poet in English who in anything like the same way has presented himself and his friends through his poems as a legend. That is Pope. The drama that he, Swift, Arbuthnot, Gay, lived, burned in him equally passionately; he equally felt it to be of public significance; felt that it must be commemorated, perpetually to throw out a light in the general darkness. His attempts failed. The tradition dimmed and lapsed. Dr. Johnson recognised its existence but ridiculed it. After Johnson many scanned Pope without noticing the personal claims he recorded. Whether the Yeats tradition will lapse quickly, one cannot tell. There are advantages with Yeats that make for durability: he began his effort earlier, continued it longer; he incorporated the tradition into lyrics, a form that easily seizes the memory; he built a considerable prose literature around the lyrics; he worked in the particular field of Irish affairs at the crucial moment when the country broke out of 700-years' subjection into freedom, and he is likely to be read as the poet of liberation, and therefore his allusions may be kept alive.

When he began to write the legend into lyrics, Yeats was reading a great deal of eighteenth-century work, mainly writers associated with Ireland. He had gone to Swift, Goldsmith, Berkeley, Burke, to extend the tradition of his movement backward and give it ancestors and sharpen its definition. What qualities did he postulate in these deliberately-sought eighteenth-century ancestors and write into his movement? They were wild singers or talkers; they were haughty; haters of the "levelling

L

rancorous, rational" Whig, i.e. democratic, mind;* they knew
the poor, the beggars, and mimicked their voices, thus catching
the basic wisdom of the human race; they represented the purity
of intellectual fire. Out of his meditation on them came his prose
play, *The Words upon the Window pane*, a play tight-drawn in
construction (a "rapid movement to crisis" was his claim for his
drama) and urgent in language. Detained in an old Dublin house
the ghost of Swift re-enacts scenes of his tragic life. He tried to
change Vanessa from her natural self, "without intellect, without
moral ambition", into the embodiment of classical intellect: "I
rebuilt Rome in your mind". The experiment failed, she insisted
that she was a natural, passionate woman. Then the play asks:

> Swift was the chief representative of the intellect of his epoch,
> that arrogant intellect free at last from superstition. He fore-
> saw its collapse. He foresaw Democracy, he must have
> dreaded the future. Did he refuse to beget children because of
> that dread? Was Swift mad? Or was it the intellect itself that
> was mad?

Just as in *The Dreaming of the Bones*, turning thought into art,
Yeats outlined an alternative to his own opinion, so here. Personally he regarded intellect as the answer to Ireland's weaknesses,
arguing that it was the principle of greatness in her finest men
in her finest century. But the play, while embodying the power
of Swift, embodies his tragedy too, and opens up the possibility
that intellect may not be a pure fire, but tyrannical and mad.

As a thinker and controversialist Yeats affirmed, however,
more and more positively from now to the end of his life, that the
intellect is heaven's supreme gift, and that the nation that would
be sound must accept the hegemony of the few who are endowed
with it; that democracy is a wasteful illusion and that only an

*The associations of "Whig" are illuminated by p. 90 of vol. I of R. Barry O'Brien'
Life of Parnell (second edition, London, 1899):
    "No Irish nationalist, be it said, can apply a more opprobrious epithet to another
than to call him a Whig. To call him a Tory would be almost praise in comparison
In Ireland the Tory is regarded as an open enemy: the Whig as a treacherous friend
It is the Whigs, not the Tories, who have habitually sapped the integrity of the Irish
representation. So at least the Irish think, and in 1876 there was a growing suspicio
in the country that the Irish party was gliding into Whiggery."

intellectual oligarchy can govern fitly. That was the result of his difficulties in Ireland. Seeing no cultural health in the new Ireland, he lamented an opportunity thrown away. In free Ireland intellect could have been granted a lease of power. Instead power fell to the servants of the throng.

At the end of his life in 1938 he imagined the opportunity renewed. If ever again revolution makes Ireland "molten wax", he polemicised, let the able men take control: "These men, whether six or six thousand, are the core of Ireland". Let them take control and work from their intellect, giving natural kindness, but otherwise never a thought to the people, rather despising the people "with that old Shakespearean contempt"—and the people will love them the better for it.* Politically as well as procedurally the final Yeats resembled Pope in the late *Epilogues*. He adopted a social theory that looks back to Pope and Swift only a few years after T. S. Eliot, thinking from different premises coloured by different national and personal circumstances, had printed, in the early numbers of the *Criterion*, essays rehabilitating Bolingbroke, Chesterfield, and other notable Tories, and deploring Whiggery and democracy. In several places in Europe comparable views were appearing.

His reaction to disappointment over Ireland took its final aristocratic and despotic form partly through an inherent conservatism which his father had long noted in him; partly through love of the refinement of Coole, to which Lady Gregory had introduced him, and a consequent belief that culture is only fully developed by favourable circumstances in a favoured few; partly because Parnell had set the pattern of a leadership reserved and unconfiding, haughty, fierce and tyrannical, expecting obedience as its due. When Yeats had met in Ireland the ignorant mob-opposition which rejected Parnell, he had fought it by assuming the Chief's dominating and contemptuous demeanour. The rela-

---

*Rex Warner gives a line rather like this to his dictator in *Men of Stone*. His novel, for all its brevity and slightness, is a very beautiful exposition of the problem of dictatorship, one aspect of the problem being that there is an element of positive virtue embedded in the otherwise undesirable dictatorial position. In fact, the book illuminates the history of Europe from 1920 to 1950, and, as part of that, the history of Yeats, Pound, and others.

tionship between the ruler and the ruled became in his final view the relationship that had existed between Parnell and the Irish rank and file. Standish O'Grady, the ideological father of the literary movement, had thought and harangued during the 'eighties and 'nineties in terms of a responsible aristocracy, and that had impressed the writers; but Parnell dramatised the conception of a paternal, heroic despotism, and this stands vividly superimposed on O'Grady's thesis in the late work of Yeats.

THE CONDITIONS WITHOUT THE MESSIAH?

Though Yeats now was preaching Swift, he exhibited one striking difference. Swift was appalled by excrement and the pudenda. Yeats was delighted, read, thought, and wrote about them insatiably. Since 1925 he had identified them with joyous life. His letters to Olivia Shakespeare in the middle 'twenties, quick and splendid throughout, are especially so at every opportunity to describe oddities of sex. He drags in a *cause célèbre* of the divorce courts. He drags in a drawing, seen at Coole, "of two charming young persons in the full stream of their Sapphoistic enthusiasm", and tells how "it got into my dreams at night and made a great racket there". He discusses Gaudier-Brzeska's "greater pleasure in the act when the woman's body is muscular and dry". He recovers youth in this correspondence, re-lives it with an unreined gusto and virility that his "dreamy load" once made impossible. This correspondence contains drafts of *A Woman Young and Old;* sexuality naked, the simple fleshly foundation of human conduct, makes some of his most satisfying poems, written from 1926 onwards.

In *The Tower*, railing at old age, he says

> Never had I more
> Excited, passionate, fantastical
> Imagination, nor an ear and eye
> That more expected the impossible

and goes on to tell the bizarre, Hardyesque story of Mrs. Frencl and the farmer's ears in the covered dish. In the bizarre and sexual, particularly if founded on biography spoken or written, he finds the "vitality" which was the cry of literature when he first practised it in the 'nineties. His late fantasies are ecstatic and vital. But they have spiritual overtones, the more resonant in proportion as they are more physical and rude. When Yeats described the Coole Sapphists to Olivia Shakespeare and hinted at his dreams of them, he immediately added "yet I feel spiritual things are very near me". The earlier realisation that the saint is a beggarman, the beggarman a lecher, and therefore the saint also a lecher, rang in him, and, mixed with irony and a secular enjoyment, yielded such tough passages as this (in *A Vision*, concerning the Renaissance Popes):

> Three Roman courtesans who have one after another got their favourite lovers chosen Pope have, it pleases one's mockery to think, confessed their sins, with full belief in the supernatural efficacy of the act, to ears that have heard their cries of love, or received the Body of God from hands that have played with their own bodies.

Joyce's *Ulysses* had quickened him. There is the often-repeated story that the young Joyce told Yeats: "We have met too late. You are too old to be influenced by me." A strength of Yeats was that he was always able to learn and absorb a technique, and he read *Ulysses* and learned the art of obscenity. For he saw the purpose of the obscenity. In his *Criterion* article of April 1926 he thought of Joyce "lying 'upon his right and left side' like Ezekiel and eating 'dung' that he may raise these men to a perception to (sic) the infinite". There had also been older forces directing Yeats this way: his reading of Donne when Herbert Grierson's edition came into his hands in 1912, his reading of Blake twenty years before that, his friendship with Edwin J. Ellis whose talk was wholly religion and sex, his preoccupation with secret societies and the occult and mystical. The interpenetration of his religious and literary interests had brought him by steady stages to the lecher-saint theme, which in turn brought his poetry to juxtapositions which give a shock of reality like the Saviour's beating heart:

> For love has pitched his mansion in
> The place of excrement.

We know from the plays that Yeats remembers in these poetic discoveries that promiscuity as well as disorder is a condition of the coming of the Messiah. *A Full Moon in March* (1935) is a Messianic play; the title at once indicates that, referring to the tradition described in *Resurrection:* "Three days after the full moon, a full moon in March, they sing the death of the god and pray for his resurrection." A swineherd prophesies to a virgin queen that she "shall bring forth her farrow in the dung", and when she angrily beheads him she is fecundated by a drop of blood from his severed head, and the fulfilment of the prophecy begins. Yeats is re-phrasing the old tradition that the Messiah must pass through filth and evil, go down among the dragons in the rivers of Egypt. It has been an effort of our age to recover an under-standing of this fact after eighteenth-century rationality and nineteenth-century morality had lost sight of it. A very different writer, E. M. Forster, has contributed to its recovery no less than Yeats, with his recognition of the importance, in the Hindu ceremony that rehearses Krishna's birth, of "the spot of filth without which the flesh cannot cohere". Forster's writing on the subject is beautiful in its combination of excitement and coolness. Yeats' writing is rampant; he is trying to push to the furthest recess of a passionate belief which has involved him and his country for fifty years.

All the conditions of Messianism are enacted in his late work, but it is hard to decide whether he any longer believes in the Messiah. His statements are contradictory. On the level of practical politics he comments like a sceptic and repudiator of much mistaken Messianism around him. On June 10th, 1927, for example, a man he respected and counted a friend, Kevin O'Higgins, Vice-President and Minister of Justice, was murdered on his way to

Mass. Yeats brooded on O'Higgins' frequent remark "Nobody can expect to live who has done what I have done", piecing it together with comparable sayings by Irish leaders, and decided that the cult of sacrifice, planted in 1916, had possessed the politicians, so that, as soon as they were in power, they almost invited their own assassination. He expounds this to Olivia Shakespeare, advises her "Read O'Flaherty's novel *The Martyr*", which, he adds, is "very mad in the end". The end of *The Martyr* is that an Irish leader, who has chosen to sacrifice himself rather than to persist in civil warfare, dies the death of Christ on the cross, believing that his martyrdom will re-Christianise Europe. Yeats' dismissal of the climax as mad is surely a refusal to acknowledge the Messiah he has promulgated. It is as if he argues to himself: "Describe the cult: that's a historical fact. By describing it you may curb it. But it's madness to write that the martyr actually makes Christ's sacrifice." He too hesitates before the shock of the Messiah's heart.

In *Parnell's Funeral*, published in 1935, he recalls how the star fell over the lowered coffin; repeats the dream of the archer of Pairc-na-Lee; makes clear that Parnell is the sacrifice, him the archer shoots, his heart devoured by the public will beat in his successor the Messiah. Then he denounces both the public crime in dragging down Parnell, and his own fable of the rebirth that should have followed the downfall:

> Come, fix upon me that accusing eye.
> I thirst for accusation. All that was sung,
> All that was said in Ireland is a lie
> Bred out of the contagion of the throng. . . .

But having denied the truth of his life-long fable, the poem makes one more turn-about: there *would* have been a rebirth, in the sense that there would have been harmony, intellect, and discipline in Ireland, if Parnell's heart had been eaten; but the fable was not lived to that conclusion, the leaders did not take it up and eat it:

Had de Valera eaten Parnell's heart
No loose-lipped demagogue had won the day,
No civil rancour torn the land apart.

Had Cosgrave eaten Parnell's heart, the land's
Imagination had been satisfied,
Or lacking that, government in such hands,
O'Higgins its sole statesman had not died.

Had even O'Duffy—but I name no more—
Their school a crowd, his master solitude. . . .

No poet has more completely condemned his country and his generation and the results of a political drive in which he has participated.

The interpretation of Yeats' final position rests especially on the three last plays: *The Herne's Egg, Purgatory, The Death of Cuchulain. The Herne's Egg* is a tragic farce, planned with *The Player Queen* in memory. At the climax the donkey of *The Player Queen* is astray on a mountain. On the mountaintop the King of Connacht dies. A virgin, pledged like Leda to an eagle, can catch the king's soul for human rebirth if a man will lie with her instantly. She calls a Fool to her, but he is terrified, and while he falters the donkey brays

—there, down there among the rocks
He couples with another donkey.
That donkey has conceived. I thought that I
Could give a human form to Congal
But now he must be born a donkey.

The parturition of a nation, a literary movement and revolution and civil war—and the new Messiah will be a donkey:

All that trouble and nothing to show for it,
Nothing but just another donkey.

Purgatory is the story of an old man, rapscallion, tinker, who once killed his father, and now kills his sixteen-year-old son with the same jackknife

> because had he grown up
> He would have struck a woman's fancy,
> Begot, and passed pollution on.

The night is the anniversary of his mother's wedding when his father begat him in drunkenness. Just as Swift's spirit in *The Words upon the Windowpane* re-enacted the crises of his life, so the tinker re-lives continually the trauma of that begetting and detests all begetting. It is the nihilism of the Swift play. That Schopenhauer Manichaeanism of George Moore, of T. E. Lawrence, which has dogged the Irish writers though it seems out-of-place in them, swells in the late Yeats. *Purgatory* has nothing to set against it. The violent fantasy ends in

> O God,
> Release my mother's soul from its dream!
> Mankind can do no more. Appease
> The misery of the living and the remorse of the dead.

a prayer for extinction.

The Death of Cuchulain was finished only just before he died. His creative mind had lived with Cuchulain, making a new Irish literature out of him, for nearly half a century. Cuchulain re-interpreted had inspired the fighters in the Post Office. Yeats' last undertaking is to kill Cuchulain. And this signifies the definite end of a 2,000-year cycle of history. For the "historical" Cuchulain died in the second year after the birth of Christ. So when Yeats shows him dead again, at the hour of his own death, it means "Now I make way for another cycle of history".

Borrowing a gambit from Pirandello, Yeats warns the audience that this "is the last of a series of plays which has for theme his [Cuchulain's] life and death" and that "they must know the old epics and Mr. Yeats' play about them". The play quickly passes in the terse, enigmatic poetry of an old master, till Cuchulain is knifed for twelve pennies by the Blind Man out of *On Baile's Strand*. And now an extended finale probes Ireland in Yeats' time and Yeats' place in Ireland. When Emer has danced rage, adoration, triumph before Cuchulain's severed head

... she stands motionless. There is silence, and in the silence a few faint bird notes.

The stage darkens slowly. Then comes loud music, but now it is quite different. It is the music of some Irish Fair of our day. The stage brightens. Emer and the head are gone. ... There is no one there but the three musicians. They are in ragged street-singers' clothes; two of them begin to pipe and drum. They cease. The Street-Singer begins to sing.

It is the song "the harlot sang to the beggarman", beginning as a Catullus-like comment on the Irish who buy her; and as they are called "Usna's boys" we know that she is a metamorphosis of Deidre. The measure changes, and after a pipe and drum music she concludes with four questions and an ambiguous epitaph:

> Are those things that men adore and loathe
> Their sole reality?
> What stood in the Post Office
> With Pearse and Connolly?
> What comes out of the mountain
> Where men first shed their blood?
> Who thought Cuchulain till it seemed
> He stood where they had stood?
>
> No body like his body
> Has modern woman borne,
> But an old man looking on life
> Imagines it in scorn.
> A statue's there to mark the place,
> By Oliver Sheppard done.
> So ends the tale that the harlot
> Sang to the beggar-man.

Everything depends on the answer to the first question. I have talked with devoted admirers of Yeats who are sure that it must be "No", because if it were "Yes" it would make him a mere materialist and he hated materialism. But as I read it the answer is, like Molly Bloom's, "Yes". Yeats is saying at the end that everything in a man's life is illusion except the thing he adores and loathes, which in his case was Ireland; that out of that passion he had created Cuchulain, awakened his ancestors, changed Ireland; that it was all, viewed against eternity, as little as the tale of the harlot to the beggarman; but it was also as much as that— was a harsh, resonant vibration of life.

Cuchulain appears in one of the last poems, *Crazy Jane on the Mountain*, and the effect is similar. Crazy Jane sees Cuchulain in a carriage drawn over the pass with his wife Emer, who is described with the Homeric epithet "great-bladdered". Now when Yeats was much younger he had written an explanatory note to that chapter of Lady Gregory's *Cuchulain of Muirthemne* which tells of the wooing of Emer. His interest had centred on the riddles with which Cuchulain wooed, and he had elaborated on them: "that esoteric speech brings the odour of wild woods to our nostrils". . . . "Till Greece and Rome created a new culture . . . one was less interested in man, who did not seem important, than in divine revelations, in changes among the heavens and the gods, which can hardly be expressed at all, and only by myth, by symbol, by enigma." That was a Yeats amorous of the esoteric. At that stage of life, he liked riddles, i.e. a cover-language, because they seem to catch a power we sense but do not know enough about to name—or worse, if we try to name it without the cover-language, it seems common and simple, which we suppose to mean without power. At the age of seventy-two when he again meditated on the wooing of Emer, his focus had changed:

> In a fragment from some early version of "The Courting of Emer" Emer is chosen for the strength and volume of her bladder. This strength and volume were certainly considered signs of vigour. A woman of divine origin was murdered by jealous rivals because she made the deepest hole in the snow with her urine.

Here he uses words to express, not to conceal; drops disguises; is avowedly amorous of physique and other odours than wood; delights in physical nature and human appetite. Out of these

considerations, documented in *On the Boiler*, he made his new
poem:

> Last night as I lay on the mountain
> (Said Crazy Jane)
> There in a two-horsed carriage
> That on two wheels ran
> Great-bladdered Emer sat,
> Her violent man
> Cuchulain at her side;
> Thereupon
> Propped upon my two knees
> I kissed a stone;
> I lay stretched out in the dirt
> And I cried tears down.

Cuchulain and Emer are now simply vigour incarnate, and the
sight of them makes him shake from head to foot, begets the
ecstasy, the dissolution, so compelling in Yeats because emotion
has to burst the dykes of the dignity, intellect, and coldness that
have been reared to contain it. Given that the *hysterica passio* is
held down as long as possible, there is nothing more wonderful
than its ultimate jetting and over-surging. Yeats may have had
this in mind when he spoke of tragic ecstasy. "I have aimed at
tragic ecstasy and here and there in my own work and in the work
of my friends, I have seen it greatly played." But, though there
is a spare excitement, so much is stripped away at the end that
sometimes the result looks like destruction, bomb-blast.★

But there are late pieces of writing where gaunt energy is not
the only consideration, where there is a proportionate luxuriance:

★It is sometimes asked whether the hard-hitting of his last years was activated by the
Steinach operation which, with his keen empiricism, he underwent as soon as he read
about it in 1934. A physician friend writes in answer to my enquiry; "The operation
consists of the tying on both sides of the duct which leads from the testes to the base of
the penis and along which the seminal fluid flows. The idea of the operation was that the
blockage of the duct would result in the secretions from the testes going back into the
blood-stream and this somehow would rejuvenate the body. So far as I know, and I have
spoken to a number of geriatricians about this, the operation was never proved to be
the least bit of use and has been completely given up. This, of course, is at variance with
what seems to have happened to Yeats, but one of the physicians that I spoke to explained
Yeats' reaction as a psychological response, not a real physical one."

The Municipal Gallery Revisited, News for the Delphic Oracle, Hound Voice. And there is at least one place where the Messiah is recognised with ecstasy. It was Yeats' habit to read to his children poetry and stories that he had known since he was a child. In October 1933 he read William Morris' *Sigurd the Volsung* to his daughter Anne—"and last night when I came to the description of the birth of Sigurd and that wonderful first nursing of the child, I could hardly read for my tears. Then when Anne had gone to bed I tried to read it to George and it was just the same." Recovered from the past—and how marvellously it deserves to be recovered, and Yeats' understanding of Morris will eventually result in that poet's rehabilitation—it stayed in his mind through the metamorphoses of his last seven years. For a moment as he wrote *On the Boiler* he stopped ranting and quoted it in a paragraph shot with the ecstasy of that night in 1933. It seized him because it describes a miraculous child. It is a song of Simeon. And for the old Yeats, who had gone through a lifetime of hopes and disappointment, its special appeal was that this Messiah was born not of God but of man, and of the best of men; was "the best sprung from the best".

On the Boiler goes on, drastically, to link the poem with the teaching of the Eugenics Society, urging that to prevent the dilution of talent in Europe only the ablest and healthiest be permitted to procreate. If this is to be taken seriously, he who once urged the claims of the spiritual over the material, has finally materialised his Messianic doctrine and favours a Messiah selected by man's control over himself. He wrote: "Eugenical and psychical research are the revolutionary movements with that element of novelty and sensation which sooner or later stir men to action. It may be, or it must be, that the best bred from the best shall claim against their ancient omens." The nineteenth-century optimism that possessed AE motivates these sentences; they ride on the hope, mixing beauty and absurdity, that men will actually see the babe born to rule. The accent is on the word "rule". Yeats is pursuing to a logical conclusion the political belief expounded since *The Words upon the Windowpane*, offering instead of democracy, which swamps intellect, the rule of the ablest few, and those few perhaps whittled down to one only.

If we had only the letters and *On the Boiler* to judge by, we would certainly think that at the end of his life Yeats clung strenuously to his earliest Messianic faith but had resolved it from a heavenly miracle cracking the order of life into an unpopular but realisable political and social doctrine, and that he believed in perfectibility. But much of his creative work of the same epoch is, as we have seen, the opposite in temper and implication: it scorns life with a bray; it slips constantly towards nihilism; is just saved from that by irresistible ecstasies at the sight of a figure lewd, primitive, giant-size, or, less frequently but richly, at memories from the Victorian or Edwardian past, or beautiful Renaissance bodies seen from a Joycean rere angle, or a saga child.

CHAPTER V

AE—GEORGE WILLIAM RUSSELL

1867-1935

In the last thirty years of his life AE was a great figure. He was not the most famous living Irishman, but he was the most famous Irishman who permanently lived in Ireland. Shaw and Joyce were abroad, Yeats was at home only for a period. It was clear that AE was not a poet of Yeats' order nor so idiosyncratic a personality, but he was better-loved as a man and perhaps better-respected as a thinker and humane arbiter. He was consulted on private and public problems, and wrote in the Press on all the issues of the day like a man who knew himself to be the national conscience. It is lucky for a nation if it has an AE to admonish it; but such work sometimes dies with the man, and the next generation cannot easily understand what made him so important to his contemporaries. By giving the greater part of his energy to arbitration and polemic he neglected his poetry and painting; he wrote poetry and painted for refreshment in scanty intervals from public life, whereas Yeats—or Eliot—made public pronouncements secondary to, and developed from, their work at their art. So his poems and paintings grew only a little; at the end of his life they still seemed much what they had been at the outset; and by the 'twenties they already had a faded air, and were loved for his sake rather than their own. Now they are largely ignored. In the course of these notes I shall refer to the interest of his poems and some of their qualities, but must admit that his mood is so different from the prevailing mood of our time that only three or four of his poems come to my mind as I go about life—and a test of a poem is whether it does this—and that if words of his come unsolicited to my help, they are more often from his polemical prose.

AE was an Ulsterman, born at Lurgan in Armagh, April 10th, 1867. His father was book-keeper in a Quaker firm of cambric manufacturers, his mother had been employed in a general store. They moved to Dublin when he was eleven, and there, after he left Rathmines School in 1884, he attended, like Yeats, art classes at the Metropolitan School. He always spoke of painting as his natural activity, which he would have made his profession but "... as my people were poor I gave up art and turned to literature in the odd hours a busy life left me for reverie."* There is a story that his first job was a clerkship in a Guinness brewery, and that he quickly threw it up, his sensibility outraged. Between 1890 and 1897 he was in the warehouse of Pim Brothers, drapers, working twelve hours a day and then going home to the Dublin Lodge of the Theosophical Society (where he was living and serving as Librarian and a leading brother) and keeping its library open till 11 p.m. Out of these burdened hours came the poems, mostly short lyrics, which were published in his first volumes, *Homeward: Songs by the Way*, 1894, and *The Earth Breath*, 1897.

In the winter 1897–8 Horace Plunkett was looking for a man to organise the co-operative movement in the Irish villages. He sounded Yeats, who adroitly dodged the suggestion that he himself should do the work, and nominated AE. AE accepted, though with grave doubts, which Yeats dissolved for him. He settled down to the work; married Violet North on its security; toured the villages, learned the face of Ireland, organised co-operatives with skill for seven years until his health gave in. Then Plunkett made him editor of his co-operative paper, the *Irish Homestead*. Assisted by Susan Mitchell, he poured thousands of words into editorials and notes of the day, and made the dowdy-looking farm-journal a public force. In 1923 it merged with the *Irish Statesman* under

*See *Letters from AE*, edited by Alan Denson. Throughout this chapter, as elsewhere, I am indebted to the generosity of Alan Denson, whose ten years' search for AE's correspondence and notebooks and the oral tradition, at a time when he is out of fashion, deserves the gratitude of all readers of Irish literature.

his editorship. The *Statesman*, like the *Homestead*, had financial problems, and when it successfully defended a libel action (a complaint against its reviewer's estimate of a book of Gaelic songs) the legal expenses proved too much, and it closed in 1930.

Charles Weekes, who believed implicitly in AE and published the first edition of *Homeward*, had tried at an early date to persuade his friend to join him in London, there to have a bigger pulpit and wider audience and to prevail and benefit like Shaw and Yeats. AE understood the arguments, but resisted the invitation to cosmopolis. Even more than Synge he was "that rooted man". But at the end of his life he left Ireland. First necessity compelled: he accepted an invitation to visit the United States in order to meet the costs of his wife's last illness. Later, when there was no longer a wife to look after and no *Irish Statesman* to edit, he stayed much of his time abroad, feeling out of sympathy with the new Ireland, and he died in England.

THE MOTIVE AND MEANS OF SELF-EDUCATION

By middle age AE talked and wrote, as a result of many experiences as arbiter and consultant, with the *ex cathedra* assurance of a Dr. Johnson. The comparison can be extended. A modern reader may recoil from AE's pontifical manner, and construe his affability as complacency, his indignation with shortcomings as self-righteousness. But under the persona there was a suffering man. Eglinton quotes[*] his admission "I have a continual headache and am always wondering how I can go on". He had been in childhood and youth a sensitively distracted and radically protesting spirit. Through an extraordinary inner struggle he worked out standards with which to guide his conduct, and they were good enough to hold him together in a long, militant life, but to the end there were internal tensions and echo-enactments of his original quarrel with his environment.

A paper in Yeats' *Celtic Twilight* describes AE in struggle at a date near to 1890. It tells how AE "latterly had neither written

---

[*]In *A Memoir of AE*, Macmillan, London, 1937. It contains some beautiful Eglintonian writing, and Macmillans produced it attractively, as they produced nearly all their Anglo-Irish titles.

M

nor painted, for his whole heart was set upon making his mind strong, vigorous, and calm, and the emotional life of the artist was bad for him, he feared. . . . He was a clerk in a large shop. His pleasure, however, was to wander about the hills, talking to half-mad and visionary peasants, or to persuade queer and conscience-stricken persons to deliver up the keeping of their troubles into his care". He said to Yeats, so the account goes on: "I prepare myself for a cycle of activities in some other life. I will make rigid my roots and branches. It is not now my turn to burst into leaves and flowers".

That is an AE so frightened of the world that he would rather not grow than suffer its stimulus. Are we to trust the picture? Yeats is not always trustworthy when he speaks of AE, nor AE—completely—when he speaks of Yeats. The young AE had felt the attraction of Yeats; had valued him so much that he was jealous (his jealous rebukes involving sexual imagery) of his corrupting London acquaintances like Symons; had deliberately effected a mental separation from Yeats in order not to be modified by him. Though they had started out together to revive Irish literature and strengthen Irish thinking, it gradually became clear that neither approved what was essential in the other nor what the other approved. "What one likes the other hates", said Synge.* Passages in AE disclose that the young man suffered from a fear; but it was not fear of growth, as Yeats construes it in that essay; it was fear that his growth might be touched and altered by another person. He was terrified by the Abelard story. He was afraid of deformation by Yeats. He was afraid of the influence of a wife, and, though he married, kept a routine which, says Eglinton, seldom included private hours at home. He became the hater of everything that appears to change the inner man, including alcohol and physical love and great poverty and great wealth and magisterial authority and ecclesiastical authority. He was drawn to anything that promised the development of the inner man without intermediacy. His type is anxious for his inner self as if

*See *Journal and Letters of Stephen MacKenna*, edited by E. R. Dodds, Morrow, New York, p.36.

it were frail, and develops it very strongly in reaction to the fear.

The circumstances in which he grew up had compelled him to self-belief. The atmosphere of Christian observance in his home, with frequent resort to both church and chapel, instilled him with a horror of the narrowness of the Christian media of worship (on the other side, it instilled him with a passion for right conduct, but he was conscious only of the horror and protest). In Lurgan, and perhaps in Dublin during the first years, he could believe only in himself and the earth and sky on which he projected himself. One would say that the consequence was a wild over-valuation of himself, but for the positive results which he won—and this can be the merit of a situation like his—by the effort to be as good and great as he thought himself.

Observers like Katharine Tynan, noting how his poems and paintings came to him in waking dreams and detecting the special voice of prophetic illumination, promptly compared him with Blake. He read Blake in 1887 and recognised his own image in the confine-kicking, self-educating Protestant, the man who insists on seeing for himself. The effect of Blake on Yeats was to show how the underground esoterics, whom he had already begun to study, pointed to the Messianic explosion and the New Jerusalem. The effect of Blake on AE was to set him reading Boehme and some of the other esoterics and correlating them with his eastern reading, and to impress him with the thesis of Lucifer's rebellion, a thesis which was the Protestant development of an ancient tradition.

His pseudonym belongs to the tradition. It was originally Aeon, but a compositor could not read it, and left it AE, which Russell accepted and always used. Why Aeon? According to Eglinton, Russell had made a drawing of the apparition in the Divine Mind of the idea of Heavenly Man. He lay awake considering what title he should give it. "Something whispered to him 'Call it the Birth of Aeon' ". A fortnight later his eye caught the word "Aeon" in a book in the National Library, and that led him to Neander's *History of the Christian Religion* with its passage on the Gnostics and the doctrine of the Aeons. In a letter to Carrie Rea★ he analyses the word into the elements of the primal language (which, as a self-educator, reconstructing human knowledge from the foundations, he had discovered by introspection):

A	—sound for God
AE	—is first divergence from A
Au sound	—continuity for a time
N	—change

Thus Aeon represents revolt from God, the passage of the separated soul through its successive incarnations in man homeward to God, and God's consequent amplification. Or, as he translated it to Carrie: "So Aeon would mean that the spirit would continue for a time and finally be absorbed into God again. This would apply to the incarnated Aeon, Christ." That last sentence defers to Carrie's religious susceptibilities, but there is no doubt that AE's pseudonym claimed for him the Christhood which is also Luciferhood. He and Yeats were both influenced by the Rosicrucian view that every man is God and his life's work is to find his inner Christhood.† Neither he nor Yeats borrowed this doctrine in humility, but in sanction of their innate pride and ambition, which Blake encouraged.

AE implies, in various retrospective statements, that his first, and for some time his only reading, was in "eastern literature". The literature of the East is a seduction to any boy set on self-education. The West, conscious of limitations, has an immense, vague respect for what it imagines to be a fully-developed secret knowledge in the possession of eastern adepts, whose literature is a cypher for it rather than a literature. Superstructure of disease and poverty, the eastern scriptures have their answer to the permanent human questions, but not the complete and unguessed one the westerner expects. What they have to suggest has been

---

★See *Letters from AE*, edited by Alan Denson.

†See George Moore's pages on this subject in *Evelyn Innes,* e.g. p.245 in the original Fisher Unwin edition; "he told her how the Rosicrucians greeted each other with 'Man is God, and son of God, and there is no God but man' ".

helpful in the early part of this century to the Harvard school, to Paul Elmer More, Babbitt, Eliot, who have made a disciplined approach. To the Irish, the deficiencies, diseases, and virtues of whose society had an oriental character, it might have been especially meaningful; and one Irish writer, MacKenna, and the great scholar who wrote a Memoir for him, Dodds, did make the disciplined approach to Plotinus. But, MacKenna apart, the writers of the Revival generation exploited rather than understood the eastern material that had captivated their fancy. In the 'eighties and 'nineties they wanted it to yield, and made it yield, not instruction but justification for what they were and dynamic inspiration towards what they hoped to become. Moreover, it gave them ritual, *kalpa*, filling the gap left when they rejected Christian ritual.

Yeats, the performer, the man who lives for an effect, knew that he was merely exploiting the smatterattera that he cleverly picked up. He played the part of a believer in order to dazzle, and gained flamboyancy. AE's case was more serious. He had a sane side, which grew in strength from 1896, and it advised him to look sceptically through the flamboyant and deflate delusion in himself or anyone else. Nevertheless, he managed to deceive himself that what had been fortifying to him at a crucial period of adolescence had been a universally valid experience.

He admits in a late letter that he was already "pagan" and "eastern" before he read eastern books: "I had a natural mysticism of my own before I knew these Indian seers". In another letter (I am quoting from the Alan Denson collection of letters, which may be consulted for fuller evidence on these points) he puts a striking claim: "When I was very young I began to read eastern literature and for about ten years read little else." If this is literally true, he must have begun to read his orientals at the age of twelve, for by twenty-two, at any rate, and probably before, he had read Arnold (Matthew as well as the Orient-loving Sir Edwin), Tennyson, Wordsworth, Blake, Goethe, Carlyle, and others. He had the Dublin libraries at his disposal, and his claim may be true, though it is unusual for a schoolboy actually to read the sages, not merely to be delighted by the thought of reading them. I am half-doubtful whether he really passed beyond the encyclopaedias and perhaps an hour or two of browsing. But if he did, then I cannot forbear the comment that for the western mind to come to eastern scripture tender, before it has had the discipline that belongs to its nearer traditions, is dangerous; and that the faults of AE's poetry and prose, above all of the early prose, may be due to it, since often the English versions of eastern work are soft and steamy, involving the transposition of a technique which carries exaltation or profundity in the original to one which is associated in our language with a vain escape from experience: the one pours out a balm upon the world, the other vexes it. But I must acknowledge, too, that it is all the more to the credit of AE that from such a dangerous beginning he found his way in time to the stronger style of his controversial prose, which is in touch with the Anglo-Irish eighteenth-century tradition.

There was an important western addition to the materials with which AE educated himself: he looked with curiosity and hope into three American writers, Emerson, Thoreau, Whitman. In the late 'eighties he delighted in the fraternalism of Whitman. Whitman, he told Carrie Rea, is "The greatest friend I have. . . . I am sure when you read him that you will find in him 'the friend you were wanting' as he himself says". He spoke with less camaraderie of Emerson—one does not hob-nob with guardians of the faith—but with great devotion. He saw Emerson as a western leader whose natural strength had been doubled by contact with eastern thought. He hoped to grow in his image to be leader and shaper of Ireland.

SHAPER OF IRELAND?

He hoped to grow in Emerson's image and trained himself on the eastern texts of the Theosophical Society's Library, but only gradually realised half-way through the 'nineties that it was for the purpose of shaping Ireland. "I could not have named the Lord Lieutenant when I was twenty-five"—i.e. in 1892. Of the preceding year Eglinton comments: "The event of 1891 was not,

for Russell, the death of Parnell, but that of Madame Blavatsky."
That oblivion of public affairs apparently persisted up to the
appearance of his first volume of poems in 1894. Though I have
sometimes wondered whether one or two poems in it deal with
the death and funeral of Parnell, I accept Eglinton's comment,
taken with AE's own avowal of neglect of external Ireland, as
decisive. And Yeats, at the first reading of *Homeward*, evidently
felt that part of its value to the Irish literary movement lay in its
freedom from obvious patriotic fervour as well as from literary
pretentiousness: "It is about the best piece of poetical work done
by an Irishman this good while back. It is the kind of book which
inevitably lives down big histories and long novels and the like.
It is full of sweetness and subtlety and may well prove to have
three or four immortal pages".*

A year later Yeats moderated the verdict. "A very notable book,
but not specially Irish in subject", he now said. By that time AE
had opened an eye to public affairs, and was probably ready to
agree that Irish writers should, while avoiding what he called
the "boy-scout" poetry of Young Ireland, be Irish in subject or
sensibility. Responding to the new feelings gradually gathering
since the Parnell catastrophe, he had begun to look at the Gaelic
epics. The current Parnell mythology and the antique Celtic
mythology connected with his nine years' reading in the underground esoterics, especially in Madame Blavatsky. In *The Secret
Doctrine* he had met the prophecy, Madame Blavatsky's crude
version of a Messianic tradition, that Great Britain and France
would fall into their "Iron Age" and would be desperately
involved in an international conflagration. Irish popular thinking
had for some time been making use of this tradition (which had
come down by other routes, though I do not know which they
were). Out of it had grown the Fenian political theory that when
Britain was preoccupied with an international struggle Ireland
would succeed in breaking away from her. Blavatsky confirmed
Irish political myth, Irish political myth confirmed Blavatsky,
Blake gave energy and light to both. The imagery of Armageddon

Letters of W. B. Yeats, edited by Allan Wade, p.231.

suffused AE's fantasies.* In a letter which Professor Dodds dated 1913 AE described "a series of visions" of "about twenty years ago":

> I saw a figure descending from heaven and standing on the earth, and at that moment a mother held a child in her lap. Then I saw the old Queen Victoria toppling from her throne, and other things—then a gigantic figure stalked across Ireland beating a drum and there were flights and alarms and smoke and burnings; then after a silence the mountains flung up their rays as Brigid saw in her vision. . . .†

Richard Ellmann has placed Yeats' enthusiasm for Armageddon between the years 1893 and 1896.‡ Perhaps Yeats touched off the fusion of the nationalist and theosophical interests in AE's mind; perhaps the development had already begun as a result of AE's own enquiries, and when they exchanged their thoughts the two men advanced each other's zeal, as they certainly did in the summer of the Avatar, 1896. Yeats' thinking had been the more adventurous, quick, and rich up to that year. Then AE stole a march on him. He saw the Avatar first. His letter of June 2nd claimed "a vision" of the Avatar "some months ago", and was followed by a memorandum, marked "Private" and "Don't spread this about":

> The Celtic adept whom I am inclined to regard as the genius of the renaissance in its literary and intellectual aspects, lives in a little white-washed cottage. I feel convinced it is in Donegal or Sligo. There is a great log a tree with the bark still on it a few feet before the door. It is on a gentle slope. He is middleaged has a grey golden beard and hair (more golden

---

*See Eglinton's *Memoir*, op. cit., p.134: and compare Moore's *Salve*, p.92, on "the nationalism begotten of a belief that a European conflagration might give birth to a hero who would conquer England, and, incidentally, give Ireland her freedom".

†*Journal and Letters of StephenMacKenna,* edited by E. R. Dodds, p.141. What were the "other things"? I suspect that the phrase may conceal sexual imagery, which AE decorously suppressed. The giant figure is evidently the Jewish Golem or an analogue.

‡Richard Ellmann, *Yeats: the Man and the Masks*, Macmillan, New York, 1948, p.97. I am here resuming and adding to the brief sketch of the events of 1896 in my introductory chapter, and am relying partly on Dr. Ellmann's book, partly on Mr. Denson's researches.

than grey) face very delicate and absorbed. Eyes have a curious golden fire in them, broad forehead. . .

Yeats received the news with ardour and jealousy. As the self-appointed leader of the Irish movement, it was time he had a vision, too, and he hastened to Ireland, where it was vouchsafed: —a vision less simple, made of obscure but powerful images that slowly radiated meaning and poetry through a thirty years' process. Out of the communication and rivalry of the two poets that summer the Irish literary movement made its most important lunge forward.

AE had, he claimed in the letter of June 2nd, seen the Avatar earlier that year. It may have been some little time before April 15th. On that date the *Irish Theosophist* carried his poem, *The Message of John*. It is an awkward mixture of felicities and clumsiness, as AE evidently recognised later, for though he gave it a place in *The Earth Breath*, it was discarded, all but a fragment, from the Collected Poems. Historically, however, it is invaluable as a demonstration of the new evangelism of the Irish literary movement in this crucially formative year. It marks the beginning of the Irish writers' conception of themselves each as John the Baptist (they were, in their more modest hours, prepared to accept this alternative to the role of Messiah). In lines reminiscent of Blake's individualist re-interpretations of the New Testament, AE offers to clarify John's vision of the God in man:

> I flow before the feet of Light;
> I am the purifying stream.
> But One of whom ye have no dream,
> Whose footsteps move among you still,
> Though dark, divine, invisible,
> Impelled by Him, before His ways
> I journey, though I dare not raise
> Even from the ground these eyes so dim
> Or look upon the feet of Him.

In particular, it tells how the hero-Messiah is to be known: by

the glory round his head
Like a bird with wings outspread
Gold and silver plumes at rest;
Such a shadowy shining crest
Round the hero's head reveals him
To the soul that would adore him. . .

The details were remembered and used, in the country cottage setting, when AE wrote his last prose-work, *The Avatars*, long afterwards.

In the June 2nd letter AE transcribes what he calls his "first definitely Irish poem". It is "The children awoke in their dreaming", published the next month, on July 15th, in the *Irish Theosophist*. A psychologist would read in this record of a fantasy or dream the promise of a massive release of energy; and AE understood it that way, with the important difference that he thought it was the energy of the nation, not his own, so completely were the conceptions of the new Ireland and his unfolding self identified.

For all the hillside was haunted
    By the faery folk come again;
And down in the heart-light enchanted
    Were opal-coloured men.

They moved like kings unattended
    Without a squire or dame,
But they wore tiaras splendid
    With feathers of starlight flame. . . .

The lights were coming and going
    In many a shining strand,
For the opal fire-kings were blowing
    The darkness out of the land. . . .

The metrics are borrowed partly from Swinburne, partly from Arnold and Morris; the mediaeval trappings are borrowed from Morris and the faery trappings from Yeats; but the borrowings are modified by AE's personal nuances.

Fourteen stanzas in this manner report the vision. Then

follow three stanzas in which AE changes from his early self, the
fantasist, and moves towards his later self, the adviser. Having
listened to the opal fire-kings debating how they will weather
"The ship of the world to its rest", he tries to convey the waking
from the dream, the opportunity and difficulty of translating it
into reality. To do it he uses that "sane" side of himself which is
to be so important when he later becomes Ireland's public debater
and counsellor. The modulation may be interpreted as foresight
that when his fire-kings come alive in him they will make him a
good counsellor rather than a perfect poet. The three concluding
verses sum up the problem of AE as poet. For AE there was no
counselling without moralising, and these are moralising stanzas.
May a poet be so plainly a moralist? Provided that he has a
rhythm and an image which transcend the moral. And there *is* a
queerly Victorian, Kingsley-like, song and domestic light in the
last stanzas. They are a little nesh as well as beautiful. But they have
a poetic quality, however moderate and imperfect, half-knit with
their sanity.

The allusions to the new leader or the new birth persist in his
work to the end. But the tone of 1896 gradually changes. In an
early essay, such as *On an Irish Hill*, it is still wet with its
theosophical and saga origins clinging round it like the gelatine of
the Messianic birth. He tells of a tradition that once there was a
complete sympathy between man and the elements and at every
great deed of hero or king the three swelling waves of Fohla
responded. He addresses the waves: "O mysterious kinsmen,
would that today some deed great enough could call forth the
thunder of your response once again! But perhaps he is now
rocked in his cradle who will hereafter rock you into joyous
foam." For the next twenty-five years he prophesied the growth
of that marvellous infant, "our man of destiny", a big man emerging in Ireland to do big things. But there was a gradual, partial
secularisation of the image. About 1914 he was whipping his
countrymen for lack of thought and curiosity, and his prophecy
became a warning that the expected leader would not arrive till
the national intelligence quickened: "We will get our man of

destiny in Ireland when we begin on our own part to recognise him when he comes". Unfortunately, he adds, the present generation can't distinguish "between genius and flapdoodle".*

Nothing could illustrate better than that last phrase the difference between the Russell of the early esoteric reading and the later public Russell. The fighting vigour is what he has made of the energy the opal fire-kings promised him. The first traces of it can be detected in the correspondence of the second half of 1896, the period of assimilation of the dream of the Avatar and the first Irish poem. He now knows that Emerson's significance to him is that he is the model national shaper, whom he must emulate in his own work for Ireland. In October 1896, asking Yeats to collaborate in a movement to mould the ideals of Ireland and protect her against the temptations of mercantilism, he wrote: "We can do for the young men in the literary and Gaelic societies what Emerson did for the New Englanders. Only of course in our own fashion and with reference to the Celtic spirit." And again in December: "What Emerson did for America by his declaration of intellectual independence we can do here with even more effect." In these sentences public ambition has become alive and conscious, and the note of vigour which characterises the public AE is heard for the first time. The dream of the Avatar has transformed him. Early in 1897 he tells Yeats that he has discovered his controversial power: "a faculty of vehement invective which I would like in the name of brotherhood to use". How use? To batter the forces that are restraining the development of Ireland. Still unexercised in politics, and therefore unaware that no writer, least of all a Protestant, could attack the Church without aiding Britain in her classic policy of ruling Ireland by dividing her religions, he selected the priests as his first target: "I . . . am going to assail the priests in pamphlets, not on theological grounds but on the point of liberty. We are simply a race of slaves here. . . . I believe you may expect my violent death in the future as I get more irritable, brooding over this point. I will say things in print to make people's hair stand."

*Editorial in the *Irish Homestead*, September 11th, 1915, pp.596–7.

The dire controversies that he threatened were delayed—only delayed, yet the result of the closer knowledge and the sense of diplomacy gained during the delay was that they were never as dire as he first intended—by the appointment which he received from Plunkett at the end of 1897. The co-operative movement to which he hired his abilities was pledged to the economic betterment of the country, its members sinking their partisan interests. Thus Plunkett who was a Unionist and AE who was a nationalist worked together for the common economic good and abstained each from using the co-operative platform for political statements. In fact, out of the experience of working in the economic field the co-operative organisers found that they shared a sentiment: a hatred of professional politicians, whom they saw again and again setting expediency and party or personal gain before the public advantage, or short-term public advantages before long-term.

AE had promised in 1897 to make people's hair stand on end; but he did not have a great deal of material at his disposal. While he toured the countryside during his first years as co-operative organiser he lacked time to set hair standing; but he gathered material which he had never had before, the facts of the deficiencies and mismanagement of Ireland. He also learned of qualities which he had not sufficiently appreciated before. He still felt, when he came back to writing in the editorial chair of the *Irish Homestead* in 1905, that the Church was a retarding influence in Ireland, but he had in the meantime met parish priests of all kinds, and some of them had excited his admiration, given him their friendship and won his. He had met distress greater than he had imagined, but he had also met generosity and kindness greater than he could have guessed. Amid all the squalor there was, comparable with but more interesting than that "dignity" which the literary movement had imagined for the peasant, a tone superior to the tone of the nation's public and political life. The upshot of seven years' laborious struggle was that AE finally came to write the energetic invective he had conceived out of the dream-kings, to write it with more wisdom and more purposefully than the one-sided development of the Dublin Lodge years would alone have permitted.

At the moment of accepting Plunkett's invitation to join the Irish Agricultural Organisation Society AE had struggled bitterly against his fate. Afraid of the extinction of his sensibility in toil, appalled by the first contact with rural poverty, he wrote his horror to Yeats. Yeats implored him to persevere: "remember always that now you are face to face with Ireland, its tragedy and its poverty, and if we would express Ireland we must know her to the heart and in all her moods. You will be a far more powerful mystic and poet and teacher because of this knowledge."* As a writer of public prose, as a public force, AE gained what Yeats promised him, and I will shortly show him at work as an effective controversialist. But did he become a more powerful poet?

Alike in the two volumes published before his work for Plunkett started, and in the later volumes, AE's poems lie within a very restricted range. A limitation can also be a definition, if it is notably personal, and AE's best poems are perhaps recognisable as his own by the circumscription and the one or two personal touches within it. His vocabulary mainly depends on the romantic postulation of the vision of the heavenly courts. His imagery is of the same order, deriving partly from nineteenth-century English poetry, partly from English translations of oriental literature; it is only occasionally sharpened by the sights and sounds of the everyday world. AE once spoke of his highest delight as the "intoxication" of the Sufi, and some of his poems evidently hope to catch that divine intoxication; but only one or two kindle with it. There is nothing in the tradition of English literature to help a poet to write with the Sufi note, for the English imagination has found other routes into ecstasy; and AE was not the great technical innovator who opens a new route for future poets. He had three or four forms at his disposal: compact quatrains, such as Blake sometimes used so magnificently; compact six-line stanzas; a

---

*Letters of W. B. Yeats, edited by Allan Wade, p.294. The whole of the letter, colourful and suggestive, is worth consulting.

five-line stanza, occasionally and experimentally; couplets. Now and then he writes couplets eight trochaic feet to the line, the lines long and raking enough to dazzle, the poems short enough for the dazzle to enchant, not to overpower.

At their best the poems have a double effect: they are contained by their compact patterns, and yet we see their vision as if the compact cage were momentarily broken. When that happens AE gives the feeling that the mystical poets traditionally give, that they have riven a cleft into the frame of the universe and we look into celestial spaces:

> . . . suddenly the veil was lifted.
> By a touch of fire awakened, in a moment caught
> and led
> Upward to the wondrous vision: through the star
> mists overhead
> Flare and flaunt the monstrous highlands: on the
> sapphire coast of night
> Fall the ghostly froth and fringes of the ocean of the
> light:

But these moments, in which the poems transcend the conventions of their period and kind, and catch the timelessness which they invoke as a solvent for the wrongs of time, are few.

Yeats hoped for him that, taught by the reality which he met in the villages, he would learn to write of the wrongs of time. That happened in the prose, but seldom in the poetry. There are one or two poems which deal with an actual incident, a local or a national problem, a living person, and where AE's imagery and metrics are not a flight from the world but explore an attachment to it. In *The Divine Vision*, which appeared in 1904 when he had been engaged on his co-operative work for some time, the poem *A New Being* has, though slender, that quality, and *An Irish Face* has it with a touch of power: in a young face he sees the sorrows, Deirdre, Cuchulain weeping the friend he slew, "and all the lovers on whom fate had warred", and

> . . . The old protest, the old pity, whose power
> Are gathering to the hour
> When their knit silence shall be mightier far
> Than leagued empires are.
> And dreaming of the sorrow on this face
> We grow of lordlier race. . . .

Eglinton thought his best poem one which, by exception, expressed his indignant reactions to a public situation not in prose but in verse, and in the result combined the eighteenth-century debating strength of his prose, and its appeal to the sense of propriety, with the subtlety of the best lyrics. This was the poem *On Behalf of Some Irishmen not Followers of Tradition*. It reproves the suicidal impulses of the insurgents and offers a version of his hope of the Avatar:

> We would no Irish sign efface,
> But yet our lips would gladlier hail
> The firstborn of the Coming Race
> Than the last splendour of the Gael.

The poem has imperfections, but a memorable vigour. We could have welcomed more like it.

He was also capable of a humorous poetry of public commentary. We see traces of it in his correspondence; if a short volume could be collected, it might please many readers; but he never thought it valuable enough to publish. Perhaps his problem as a poet was that, right to the end, he only valued the esoteric in poetry. Though as a man he had wrestled with reality effectively, he did not entirely approve of what he had done, and had a nostalgic preference for the theosophist-poet of 1894. The best of his late published poems are the natural partners of the best of his early poems, as if his life had undergone no change. Possibly his most superb verses are those on the last page of *The Candle of Vision*:

> No sign is made while empires pass.
> The flowers and stars are still His care,
> The constellations hid in grass,
> The golden miracles in air.

> Life in an instant will be rent
> When death is glittering, blind and wild,
> The Heavenly Brooding is intent
> To that last instant on Its child.

The verses have a hammered quality, which expresses the workmanship of God which they celebrate. They are written towards the end of the Great War, and the prose that precedes them shows that AE has been reflecting on the significance of that Armageddon and the terrorism and sacrifices in Ireland. "Powers that seem dreadful", he says, "things that seemed abhorrent . . . will reveal themselves as brothers and allies." But for all their excellence the stanzas do not show that AE has lived and developed for twenty-five years since he wrote the poems in *Homeward*. If they had appeared in *Homeward*, they would have seemed the best of the book, just as they seem the best of all AE, but they would not have been conspicuously maturer than the work around them nor out of place, whereas the poetic prose-sketches of early AE look almost a century apart from his mature prose. In his poetry, then, he did not find Yeats' prophecy fulfilled, or did not allow it to be. Just a poem here and there assimilates the new understanding and energy that turn his prose from feminine to masculine.

POLEMIC: HONESTY—HERESIES—ALCOHOL

AE's best prose is pragmatic. As co-operativist and editor he came up against tangles, inefficiency, dishonesty, specious arguments to cover dishonesty. A typical issue over which he battled was the quality of seeds. The Irish Agricultural Organisation Society discovered that sixty per cent of the seeds put into the ground in Ireland were worthless, and set out to get the distributors of the bad seeds blacklisted by the Government's Department of Agriculture. AE pummelled the Department in editorial after editorial. Its leading executive happened to share his name, Russell. AE made a debating point of that, flaying the inefficiency of his namesake and labelling him "the Playboy of the official world". The civil servants hesitated to act, it appeared, because "if they proceeded to blacklist impartially half the dealers in agricultural seeds in Ireland would be blacklisted". AE was determined that this should be done. He got his way in 1915; it had taken him some years.

Out of struggles of this kind he drew the not altogether surprising conclusion that Irish public life was corrupt. When he had a talk with a well-known novelist, possibly H. G. Wells, in 1912, he was impressed by a comparison between America and the British Isles: "Public life in America, he [the novelist] said, is corrupt, but in these islands public life is so corrupt, so much is corruption a part of the national atmosphere, that public men do not know they are corrupt."* AE set out to clean the stables. Irishmen must be roused from their lethargy. He demanded more honesty in Ireland, and, in furtherance of that, more intellect in Ireland. "More intellect in Ireland" was his cry for ten years. In 1924 after Ireland's independence was secure, AE was still demanding public honesty, public sanity, and the vivification of public intelligence. "We want the quality of mind we find in Bishop Berkeley, in Bernard Shaw and in many others who had that aristocracy of mind which probes truth for itself".† Shaw, who had once seemed too brisk and therefore too shallow to the Irish poets, now seemed, so much had they adjusted their thoughts to the national predicament, a model of intellect in action.

In fact AE as editor and polemicist had been something of a Shaw: less agile, adroit, and knowledgeable; clumsy; but powerful in his very clumsiness as a belayer of corruption and folly. There will always be some readers for whom he is at his greatest in his twenty middle years of editorial polemicising. He compels attention as every brave confronter of the public compels it, by talking straight and angrily, by denouncing with an Old Testament certainty that heaven appointed him to correct kings and magistrates. Satire's oblique ways of dealing with error are more entertaining and efficacious, but it is striking to watch a man doing it AE's direct way. What a simple, priggish mind a man

*The *Irish Homestead*, September 14th, 1912.
†In the *Irish Statesman*. See Lady Gregory's approving note in her *Journals*, edited by Lennox Robinson, p.84.

must have to be so sure that he is right! But if he has it, he can wield his words like clubs, and that affords a fine spectacle.

His favourite form was the Open Letter. A display of public fraud or pettiness would excite him and he would sit down to the job. He fired one in July 1912 at John Dillon, Irish Parliamentarian, popular from the outset as the son of a rebel, a notable Parnellite for a while, then one of the anti-Parnellites, and in 1912 respected by the House of Commons as one of its elders. On July 5th Mr. Lewis Haslam, Liberal Member for Monmouth, had asked why the Department of Agriculture and its Vice-President, T. W. Russell, were discouraging a grant of funds from the Development Commissioners to the Irish Agricultural Organisation Society—a society which, he went on to say, was fostering the growth of a business intelligence in rural Ireland and therefore was preparing the way for Home Rule. Dillon had risen in reply to this, and attacked the society as a hotbed of Unionist propaganda: it had interfered with private traders; tried to set the farmers against the towns in Ireland and thus created a new sectarianism destructive of the unity of the country; and undermined the faith of the countryside in the Nationalist representatives by denouncing "politicians as self-seekers and enemies of the people, and politics as the curse of Ireland". ("Hear, hear", interposed one of the jingoist M.P.s). Haslam jumped up to say that three-quarters of the members of I.A.O.S. were Nationalists. "That has no bearing whatever on the question", retorted Dillon. He proceeded to a bitter attack on Sir Horace Plunkett as a man who had failed in every business transaction but was a born statesman—"a Unionist statesman". Then:

> A fortnight ago in every newspaper in London, and in all the magazines, there appeared suddenly, like an outbreak of German measles, a series of articles praising Sir Horace Plunkett and exploiting his propaganda. I recognised that they were all written or inspired from his office in Dublin. . ."

and he quoted passages, attacks on politicians and their "aching vanity", from recent articles in the *Spectator* and *World's Work*.

"Are these articles written", asked Haslem, "by persons directly concerned with the Irish Agricultural Organisation Society?" Dillon replied:

> The articles are anonymous, but I recognize the style. They are written to order, all of them, and this particular one [i.e. the article in *World's Work*] if I am not greatly mistaken is written by one of the chief prophets and organisers of the movement.

Viscount Helmsley repeated Haslam's question: "How does the Hon. Member know this came from the organisation society?". Dillon repeated "I know it by the spirit and the style".★

Although this must have been one of the rare occasions when the House of Commons has relied on literary criticism for its judgments, and an Irishman was the moving spirit, AE was angry when he read the report. His reply was an Open Letter to John Dillon published in the *Irish Homestead* on July 13th. His real object was no doubt to defend the Society for which he worked and Plunkett, the chief for whom he worked; but he was able to write as a man personally impugned because Dillon had evidently referred to him when he spoke of "one of the chief prophets and organisers of the movement". AE pledged his word of honour that he was not the author of the article in *World's Work*. On the strength of that he went on with a righteous trouncing of Ireland's elder statesman. "You were once called 'Honest John' ", AE tells him, "but you have lost the right to the title. Sir, try to think honestly"—

> When you descend to the methods of your speech in Parliament, when you deliberately deceive and mislead, the suspicion, long kept under, that you have in you merely the soul of the little country trader defending his class under the guise of high politics rises in one's mind. The writer who addresses you does not like to think so. He would rather believe you have distorted your soul in a mistaken effort to serve your cause.

★See Hansard 1912, vol. XL, pp.1534–63.

AE has found the only answer to Dillon's attack on his movement: that the politicians are really leagued with the private traders whose former profitable control of the village economy has been undermined by the co-operative movement and its low-interest credit-banks. It could be flung back at AE that he too is writing for his job, as a hired pen; but, helped by the form of the Open Letter and by his utterly genuine assurance that he is God's spokesman, he is armoured against that sort of charge.

Let us look at another Open Letter, of the same year. It is addressed to Kipling, about whose attitude to Ireland something must be said in preamble. Kipling, with Irish in him from his mother's side, wrote some poems on Irish political themes: poems which are vehemently Unionist, anti-nationalist, and the obverse of everything that Yeats and AE believed. In the 'nineties Kipling had appalled them as the servant of barbarously materialist England; it seemed incredible to them that poetry could serve such interests. When we look at Kipling's writing two generations later we can see that poetry could serve them and be superb. Poetry was not only on the side of freedom. It was also on the conservative side, and no less fine for that. Poetry was matched against poetry in the Irish struggle—though Kipling is perhaps the only great practitioner on the reactionary side at that date when most humane minds were seized by the appeal of liberty for small nations.

When, early in 1890, a Government Special Commission, reporting on an enquiry that had occupied it for eighteen months, cleared Parnell of charges of complicity in the Phoenix Park murders and terrorism, and he was being congratulated all over England, welcomed to the clubs and fêted, one clear and bitter voice was heard against him, Kipling's in the poem *Cleared*. It is headed "In memory of the Parnell Commission". Every one of the seventy-six lines is a lash:*

*Rescued from the waste-paper basket after reluctant rejection by *The Times* and definite rejection by Frank Harris's *Fortnightly;* first printed by Henley in the *Scots Observer,* March 8th, 1890. See *Rudyard Kipling's Verse 1885-1926,* Doubleday's edition, Garden City and New York (1927), pp.259-63. C. E. Carrington takes this as an anti-Gladstone poem, but I cannot read it that way; see *Life of Rudyard Kipling,* p.119.

Cleared in the face of all mankind beneath the winking skies,
Like phoenixes from Phoenix Park (and what lay there)
    they rise!
Go shout it to the emerald seas—give word to Erin now,
Her honourable gentlemen are cleared—and this is how:—

They only paid the Moonlighter his cattle-hocking price,
They only helped the murderer with counsel's best advice,
But—sure it keeps their honour white—the learned Court
    believes
They never gave a piece of plate to murderers and thieves.

They never told the ramping crowd to card a woman's hide,
They never marked a man for death—what fault of theirs
    he died?—
They only said "intimidate", and talked and went away—
By God, the boys that did the work were braver men than
    they!

As propaganda and argument, as rhetoric with its clever mimicry of Irish turns of phrase, as indignation and as poetry, it is brilliant. Yeats and Pound eighteen years later were calling for the avoidance of abstraction and vivid images; in this anti-Parnell and anti-Fenian poem, Kipling already teaches them how to write, with his realistic colloquial touches—"cattle-hocking", "card a woman's hide". Perhaps Yeats, adroit enough to learn from his enemy, learned from him as well as from translations out of Gaelic.

    AE was still in his tormented youth when that poem was written, had not lifted his head to politics, and in any case had no technique for reply, nor the standing. At intervals Kipling, easily incensed over the Irish situation, returned to the charge. On April 9th, 1912 he threw his influence in the scale against Home Rule with a poem *Ulster*, published in the *Morning Post*. There he claimed to speak for the Ulstermen, promising to oppose Home Rule by force and die rather than to submit to the oppression he imagined for them under Dublin's rule:

> We know the wars prepared
> On every peaceful home,
> We know the hells declared
> For such as serve not Rome—
> The terror, threats, and dread
> In market, hearth and field—
> We know, when all is said,
> We perish if we yield.★

AE was big enough now to face the old master, and of the whole poem this stanza, with its classic attempt to force the wedge between Protestant and Catholic Ireland, must have determined him to hit back. He hit harder than he could hit Dillon, in proportion as Kipling was the long-standing enemy of his cause, as he was internationally celebrated, and as he was a poet and therefore by vocation committed (in AE's understanding) to decency. His Open Letter has its ups-and-downs, its slips into mush, but it is a powerful rebuke:

> You have blood of our race in you, and you may, perhaps, have some knowledge of Irish sentiment. You have offended against one of our noblest literary traditions in the way you have published your thoughts. . . . After all this high speech about the Lord and the hour of national darkness it shocks me to find this following your verses: "Copyrighted in the United States of America by Rudyard Kipling". You are not in want. You are the most successful man of letters of your time, and yet you are not above making profit out of the perils of your country. . . . In Ireland every poet we honour has dedicated his genius to his country without gain, and has given without stint. . . .
> I would not reason with you, but that I know there is something truly great and noble in you, and there have been hours when the immortal in you secured your immortality in literature, when you ceased to see life with that hard cinematograph eye of yours, and saw with the eyes of the spirit,

★See *Rudyard Kipling's Verse 1885-1926*, op. cit., pp.266-7.

and power and tenderness and insight were mixed in magical tales.

. . . I am a person whose whole being goes into a blaze at the thought of oppression of faith, and yet I think my Catholic countrymen more tolerant than those who hold the faith I was born in. I am a heretic judged by their standards, a heretic who has written and made public his heresies, and I have never suffered in friendship or found my heresies an obstacle in life.*

The last paragraph is splendidly clear. AE could not always write with that force, but he struck it sufficiently often to command attention throughout his middle life.

Both Dillon and Kipling had offended by mixing commercial advantage with their "high speech". In 1915 a leading Irish commercial interest, supported by Irish Members of Parliament, exploited nationalist sentiment to its advantage. Although the story is a lengthy one I will tell it here as a further example of AE's method in polemic. It shows how drastically he could write when his puritanism was shocked.

In the spring of 1915, when England had been at war eight months, the Government became alarmed at the lag in production of munitions and ships. Inspectors reported that absenteeism among the workers was responsible, and it was believed that high wages were making heavy drinking possible, and this causing absences and poor work. A powerful group of shipbuilder magnates urged that alcohol should be prohibited, or in some way controlled. A Liberal Government was in office, and the Chancellor of the Exchequer was Lloyd George, whose Welsh supporters would welcome legislation to reduce drinking and who had been interested in anti-alcohol legislation from early in his career. Action was planned. On April 1st, the 241st day of war, the newspapers published a letter from the King to the Chancellor, offering to set an example to the nation by giving up alcoholic liquors himself and ordering the Royal Household to give them

*See the reprint of this letter in *Imaginations and Reveries*.

up. *The Times* headlined the report WAR AGAINST DRINK, and supported the news with a third leader urging the public to follow the King's example and so obviate the need for legislation. Next day the Minister of War, the public idol Lord Kitchener, announced that he had forbidden alcohol in his household. A group of businessmen and employers, including Runciman, Cadbury, Shrubsole of the Pearl Insurance, Lever, took a full page in *The Times*, appealing to "every man and woman who has a spark of patriotism" to write to Lloyd George and prove that public opinion would be with him if he suspended drink, which was "a greater danger than all the German submarines". On April 3rd the editor of *The Times* gave his first leader to the problem and recommended total prohibition of spirits and a reduction in the strength of beer. April 4th was Easter Sunday, and the Primate in his sermon at Canterbury commended the King's example to the country; and the King's Pledge was, according to the Press, brought into effect on April 7th. On April 8th Canterbury, York, Cardinal Bourne, and the President of the Free Church Council issued a united appeal for abstinence.

But now, after a week of mounting zeal, a counter-challenge was sounded. Hugh Cecil urbanely wrote to *The Times* that, though all self-denial was admirable, liberty was better, and he did not intend to abstain. Manchester City Council rejected the official appeals, and wine was served at its luncheon. *The Times'* correspondent in Belfast described "resentment among the distillery and licensed trade in Ireland". A delegation from the spirits trade, J. Jameson of Dublin representing the Irish interests, waited on Lloyd George.

The advertising group of Liberal employers took alarm as they saw the strength of the opposition gathering (and presumably, from their angles of vantage, they saw more than the Press items report). They bought space again in *The Times* of April 10th, bannered

> Shall the MIGHT
> of the Liquor Millions
> trample RIGHT under foot?

They claimed that a plebiscite in Inverness had counted 8,647 in favour of wartime prohibition, 628 against. And:

> Nothing short of TOTAL SUSPENSION of intoxicants during the war can assure us of a quick and complete victory.

The effect of the notice must have been offset by the concurrent *Times* first leader, which differed markedly from that of a week earlier and showed the inroads of counter-agitation: the root of the munitions shortage was neither drink nor the working-man but lack of foresight and organisation. A report from Glasgow warned that the Scottish banks would be badly affected by the prohibition of spirits, since they had several million pounds in the whisky industries.

The controversy had produced one prompt result. There had been a run on supplies. Many suburban dealers had cleared every bottle of whisky from their cellars. For the next three weeks while the issue swayed in the balance the demand on the stores was enormous. During disastrous fighting at Ypres, wrote a man at the front, it was shocking to the troops to learn that the prime news in Britain was "Rush to buy spirits".

The Times had by now definitely decided against Lloyd George. On April 17th it was urging BACK TO A SENSE OF PROPORTION and loading its influence against such "costly and complex" schemes as Government expropriation of licensed houses. Driven from total prohibition the Government was now considering alternative measures of this kind. Lloyd George evidently gave an immense amount of time to the problem, but was driven back and back till there was only a little left him beyond the conventional procedure of taxation. On April 30th he announced his proposals: (*a*) the duty on spirits to be doubled, (*b*) a tax on beers graded according to specific gravity, (*c*) the duty on wines to be quadrupled, (*d*) the maximum legally-permitted dilution of spirits to be raised from 25 to 35 under proof, (*e*) the Government to take powers to close—against fair compensation—or control the public houses in munition-producing areas. In recommendation of these he addressed the House of Commons for two hours. Mr.

Bonar Law for the Opposition said that he would not express an opinion till he had studied the proposals and the supporting statistics. But the Irish members—here I had better quote *The Times:*

> The Irish members, without waiting for fuller details, condemned the proposals for increased taxation. Mr. Redmond said that no case had been made out against Ireland, and the proposals of the Government would destroy root and branch a great Irish industry. Mr. William O'Brien lamented the striking of an unjust and possibly fatal blow at this industry; and Mr. T. M. Healy also offered vigorous criticism.

and led by O'Brien and Healy the small ginger-group of Independent Nationalists from Cork immediately forced a division—the first since the outbreak of the War. Although the other Irish members did not vote with them, their action was interpreted as a sure sign that the Chancellor's proposals would not secure acceptance without extensive modification.

At the week-end, mass protest meetings were held in the Irish cities. Next Tuesday the Irish Parliamentary Party called its sixty members together and resolved to oppose the taxation as "grossly unjust and oppressive to Ireland".

The Opposition leaders had meanwhile met the principals of the licensing trade, had been convinced that the taxation would be tantamount to its annihilation, and, through Austen Chamberlain, told the House so when it met to discuss the Budget. Lloyd George announced that he would defer to the widespread feeling against the taxes. He spent May 5th meeting deputations from the trade. On May 6th he offered the House a compromise, discarding his tax on wines, but holding out for a surtax on heavier beers (which would include Bass and Guinness) and perhaps a surtax on immature spirits. His offer was crushed by the Irish members, who gave no quarter. Their tactics were to obstruct his Bill for the State control of liquor in munitions and transport areas until he assured them that the tax proposals for beer and spirits would be rescinded. "It was an old-time Parliamentary crisis", reported

The Times. "The Government had to bend before the Irish storm". On May 7th the Chancellor agreed that the new whisky duties be cancelled, and the new duties on beer and wine withdrawn.*

AE had been watching the jockeying from his Dublin office. On April 17th when the issue was still indeterminate, he had noticed in his *Irish Homestead* editorial that "some crawling journalists, in the interests of the drink trade, are trying to make out a case for differential treatment of Ireland, if total prohibition should be adopted by the Government". The Irish, he pointed out, wasted about £14 million yearly in drink. Prohibition for one year would release "a blaze of energy" in Ireland. "To exclude Ireland from the most moral act ever contemplated by an English Cabinet would be a greater wrong to Ireland than its treatment during the great Famine." (But the shrewd commentator in him added: "the talk of total prohibition supposes an energy of virtue which is not to be found in our Government.")

Now in May when the Irish intervention in Parliament ensured the bafflement of nonconformist teetotalism, he was horrified. He could scarcely credit that every party and interest in Ireland had combined on the common platform of protecting the country's drink trade. He had always detested alcohol. We have noticed the story that as a young man he had quitted a brewery clerkship in disgust. Later, travelling through the villages for the co-operative movement around 1900, he had seen everywhere the signs of a general addiction to alcohol. What, for example, was the centre of every country-fair? A drinking-booth. Whenever a fair was

---

*The details of this very minor episode in Lloyd George's life are not reported by his biographer, Thomas Jones, who contents himself with two paragraphs summarising what was salvaged of his original grand scheme. He claims: "When Lloyd George became Minister of Munitions (i.e. on the formation of a new Government three weeks after the failure of his proposals) a Central Liquor Control Board with far-reaching powers was set up: drinking hours and facilities were reduced drastically; to economize grain, beer and spirits were diluted; taxation was increased. In Carlisle 'the trade' was acquired by the State, and this arrangement continues today. So successful were these regulations that excessive drinking ceased to be a glaring social scandal. Although the Lloyd George Cabinet accepted a recommendation of the Control Board that 'the trade' should be purchased— and Milner with Waldorf Astor and others had a bill drafted—it was not introduced. In 1917, yielding to pressure from two Tory brewers and politicians, Younger and Gretton, Lloyd George dropped the bill . . .". See Thomas Jones, *Lloyd George*, O.U.P., London, 1951, p.68.

I call it a "very minor episode". But it is significant of a politician's inability to implement, when he reaches power, the ideals he cherished most at the outset of his career.

organised special licenses were asked and granted—for "the countryman . . . is regarded as a creature whose highest joy is to get drunk". From 1906 he had been attacking in his paper the soddening of the villages, the filth of the tavern, and the unproductive expenditure of Ireland's meagre pocket-money on drink.

So his ingrained hatred of alcohol was inflamed by the events of April and May 1915. But whether we think he was sane or pussyfoot, there is no question that he had two real grounds of complaint against the course his countrymen adopted. First, they had acted as the servants of a commercial interest, and to do it they had gone to extreme, advertising-agency lengths of blarney. William O'Brien had been reported as saying in his speech of April 20th:

> Any doctor, he believed, would say that no more fortifying medicine than good Irish stout could be prescribed for delicate persons or hardworking men. Yet it was to be penalised in order to satisfy a knot of self-righteous prohibitionists. As to whisky that was properly matured, there was no better hygienic tonic. (Laughter).

Worse, they had used the argument of *national* interest to protect *particular industrial* interests. By these two undignified steps they had gainsaid the case which Ireland had for decades been presenting to the world, claiming her freedom in virtue of the purity of her thinking as contrasted with the vulgarity of England.

Here is AE in full cry in his *Irish Homestead* editorial of May 8th:

> During the last fortnight we have had the most degrading exhibition of the worst elements in the Irish national character we ever remember. One felt ashamed to belong to a people whose prominent representatives got up in Parliament to declare that there could be no Irish nationality without copious drinking, that political freedom depended on the prosperity of the publicans and distillers. There was something horrible in the spectacle of these old men dilating in Parliament like commercial travellers paid for the job on the special virtues of the varieties of alcohol produced in Ireland,

and declaring if there was any limitation in the drink traffic that there would be an end of the Irish nation. We had ultimatums of the Irish publicans warning the representatives of the nation who it was supported them and kept them in power. We had meetings all over the country, with wretched creatures like the Mayor of Limerick telling the young men of Ireland that if they wanted to fight and die, the cause of alcohol in Ireland was the noblest of any. He said: "At the present day there were a great many young men training to be soldiers, and he advised them to assist the licensed trade in its hour of distress and to fight for their liberation and rights. I think that would be a far nobler action than to join any other army". What kind of a town is it makes such a creature its representative citizen? Island of saints and heroes, of fighters for lost causes in every clime, the last cause your children are asked to die for is the right to be as drunken as publicans can make them.

He goes on to point out that normally the Irish Agricultural Organisation Society cannot interest the Press in food production. The *Freeman's Journal* in particular had previously attacked the co-operative movement as encouraging overproduction of food! Now when alcohol was at stake the *Freeman's Journal* had called on people of all creeds in Ireland to unite—"How can that religion which denied its Paradise to the wine-bibber and the drunkard be called upon to defend the manufacturers of whiskey (sic) we don't know, but the *Freeman* assumes that it is the duty of Christians to unite in this cause". In a climax phrase he protests against "this masquerading of Bung as Kathleen ni-Houlihan".

A week later, on May 15th, he writes that the Germans have been trying for some months "with indifferent success to overcome the British Empire, but alcohol has done it in a couple of months. Alcohol is the oversoul of Ireland and dictates her policies." Still persevering at the problem on May 22nd he produces figures to rebut the licensing trade's claim to be the backbone of Irish industry. As against the 2,423 persons in distilling and 6,451 in brewing and malting, he contends that Ireland has 31,213 in fishing ("But whoever among our brazen-lunged politicians described fishing as among our main industries?"), 75,192 in textiles, 41,836 in clothing and millinery, 40,000 in shipbuilding, 14,300 in the building trade, 11,696 in railway construction, 9,445 bakers. With his notable practical side uppermost he offers these facts—and having offered them remarks that they will be disregarded by a nation which parrots every nonsensical cry the new aristocracy, the publicans, put out.

He never forgot the disgrace of this crisis. Echoes are heard through his later work—and in Joyce.* Six months later he was again hammering at a rather similar case. Dublin elected, in October 1915, a publican for its new M.P. AE roared into a tirade. Two weeks later the new member made his first speech in the House of Commons and, according to AE, said that "if his little pub. had only paid he would never have sought election". "Degradation", wrote AE in his editorial on October 23rd, "is a state individuals or nations impose on themselves by their own acts. We were degraded as a nation when our representatives in Parliament declared a few months ago that Irish nationality depended on the trade in alcohol. We were degraded and insulted by our last representative who intimated he would prefer running a public-house to representing his country".

In many issues of the *Irish Homestead*, AE was simply the convinced, quietly-arguing, pegging-away-at-the-same-thing official of Plunkett's co-operative movement. But at intervals, his sense of justice or decency racked, he used his paper as the platform for the aboriginal AE. Then he did not spare language. He was afraid of neither libel action nor assault. Lacking the completely educated mastery of the language that marked his eighteenth-century predecessors, he nevertheless caught their qualities of assurance and invective. In his polemic he gave the Irish their first acquaintance with conscience. Joyce at the same period was slowly working out his more massive draft for a

*See pp.270–71 below. And note how Joyce's early story *Ivy-Day in the Committee-Room* anticipates on the local scale the next national scandal that occupied AE—the election of a publican.

national conscience. By contrast with what he made he thought AE's attempts rudimentary, and so they were; all the same, his greater achievement contains a good deal of AE. And AE's value was that his polemic was immediate: he wrote at once in response to the event; thus Ireland could watch the reactions of this rudimentary conscience throughout fifteen pre-*Ulysses* years and obtain some guidance from it. His polemic was not the Sacred Book for which Ireland was waiting, but it provides a body of case-law.

THE GODS ARE TURNED AWAY?

The emphasis of AE's prose is on intellect as the discriminator of right conduct. The Irish, over-occupied with religion and politics, were liable to prejudice—intellect was the best corrective. Their nationalist mythology bent them towards destructive manias—intellect was the best antidote. AE was splendid in his appeal for a sane public life. But can a man be the prophet of Armageddon and the Messiah, the "poet of a new insurrection" (which Yeats, writing in the centennial anniversary year of the 1798 insurrection, had, in those words, promised AE would be), and the master of moderating intellect at the same time?

Yeats and AE were both up against this disrupting problem during the quick evolution of Irish politics after 1910. They continued to think of their original Messianic vision and to desire its fulfilment, and to deplore its fulfilment when they saw the reality. AE told MacKenna that early dream of Queen Victoria toppling, which I have already quoted on page 174, precisely because he saw the fulfilment approaching in Ireland of 1913:

The land is shaking with the tramp of volunteers. Labour is drilling. The Hibernians are drilling, so are the Sinn Feiners. The Ulster men are also at it still. Ireland seems to have forgotten it had any brains, but places all its confidence in its muscles. I am all for other methods; but all my friends are so enthusiastic that I can only look on and hope that the Lord means something good for this unfortunate country out of it. . . . It is a new Ireland shaping itself rapidly before our eyes, like a country re-forming itself in an earthquake where old hills are rent in twain and fissures open in the long established plains—and there will be more fissures and cracks to no end before we get the new human formation. . . .

The para-militarists were doing what he and Yeats had recommended around 1900, making ready to live the heroism of Cuchulain. "The drilling put me in mind of these twenty-year-old visions. But I am horribly sad at heart over Ireland just now."

When the Great War came a year later he saw it as Armageddon, and expected the fighting, as Eglinton has reported, to clog up as "stalemate and general revolution", out of which would come a settlement for the world, including freedom for Ireland. His comments on these vital political changes are the oddest amalgam of demonological credulity and shrewd foresight. Soon after the outset of war, on October 10th, 1914, he told Weekes that Ireland would have "one more heart-searching trial, baring our lives to the very spirit, and that within the next few years". Within two years the Rising had occurred. When the life-and-death battle for freedom began with that, he did his best to minimise violence and obtain freedom through arbitration; found neither the British Government nor the terrorists nor any other party concerned willing to give an inch of ground. At that discovery—the discovery that, in fact, Armageddon must take its course—he stood back, making one last earnest appeal to the British, one last angry rebuke to the Cuchulainists. To the Cuchulainist MacLysaght he said on February 1st, 1918, "Ireland is going to descend into Hell and I won't help it in that direction. It may rise again and I believe it will but by other minds than those engaged in its troubles today." To the British Prime Minister, Lloyd George, he wrote on February 5th:

. . . we have for the first time in Ireland a disinterested nationalism not deriving its power from grievances connected with land or even oppressive Government but solely from the growing self-consciousness of nationality, and this has with the younger generation all the force of a religion, with the carelessness about death, suffering or material loss which we find among the devotees of a religion. Any Government established which does not allow this national impulse free play, will be wrecked by it. . . .

Privately he felt that his commitment was to Ireland free by violence rather than Ireland not free, but the reckless intransigence, barren of intellect, on all sides, permanently embittered him. In the columns of his newspaper he quoted (and Lady Gregory in her journal appreciatively echoed) the oracle "The gods are never so turned away from man as when he ascends to them by disorderly methods." The Alan Denson *Letters*, from which I have drawn the Weekes, MacLysaght, and Lloyd George quotations, are revealing on the evolution of AE's feelings throughout this period. I believe that the failure of his arbitration first implanted the disillusion, confirmed when he eventually measured the new Ireland against the Ireland he had imagined, which resulted in his voluntary exile at the end.

We have already seen Yeats working out his reactions to Easter 1916 in a famous poem. AE's three poetic statements on the Rising have never gained wide currency, though the old J. B. Yeats praised one of them, *Michael*, as his most "delightful" work. Yeats was abroad when the news of Easter reached him, AE was in Ireland, though not in Dublin, for he had been invited —perhaps to keep him out of danger and out of intervention (for his host was in touch with the activists)—to spend the week-end in County Clare. But he returned to his home, half a mile from the fighting, during that critical week. During the last stages of the Post Office siege AE's rooftop office in Merrion Square was according to Katharine Tynan, all too near to the scenes of the rounding-up of the young Irishmen. Writing Susan Mitchell's obituary in the London *Times* (March 10th, 1926), Katharine Tynan said: "She suffered tragically in the Irish Rebellion of 1916 when the rebels were being hunted over the roofs of the Merrion Square houses."

To Quinn four months after the Rising, AE commented like a detached observer:*

> ... The psychology of the Rising interested me. People got a kind of dilated consciousness from the sound of guns, bombs, shells, and the burning of the city, and in this dilated consciousness the most extraordinary rumours took root and people did the most amazing things and believed the wildest tales which were pure fiction but were no wilder than the reality. I know, for example, of a sane businessman, head of a big mill outside Dublin, who was so overcome by the Rising that he came in glaring wildly and said "I am getting a revolver. The first man I meet who does not do exactly what I tell him, I will shoot him dead on the spot" .... Lord, what creatures we are! We must rewrite psychology when the war is over. ....

There was an embryonic psychologist in AE, whose discernment was activated by the crisis, and the account is interesting. But acute observation is often a cover-reaction to protect a man when he is uncertain how to respond to a situation with his whole self. To look below the detached notes, and to see the whole which AE working as poet pieced together from the torn emotions, we have to go to *Salutation*, to a poem which Alan Denson pointed out to me in the American periodical *Foreign Affairs* (January 1929), and to *Michael*.

Salutation was published, like Yeats' *Easter*, by Clement Shorter in twenty-five copies for private circulation. It does not appear in the Collected Poems, but is in Eglinton's *Memoir*. It has faulty lines, forced inversions, raises fewer questions than Yeats' poem, finds no original images. Yet it is not unworthy of comparison. It has momentum; has a wholeness of feeling, which is astonishing when it is considered from what conflicting thoughts it is made; has dignity. It uses the names of the dead, as *Easter 1916* does, working from the same Gaelic naming tradition. A curious touch of the humdrum, but therefore of the real, is imparted to it by

*See *Letters from AE*, edited by Alan Denson.

its dictum "You paid the price". The anti-materialists, and AE especially, ridiculed the Saxon method of judging by monetary standards. Yet they often used the test of "paying the price" in a moral and political context. AE had doubted, when he saw the Fenians drilling and heard the underground leaders planning, whether they were ready to match threats with deeds; he had thought them braggarts. In *Salutation* he apologises:

> Life cannot utter words more great
> Than life can meet with sacrifice.
> High words were equalled by high fate.
> You paid the price, you paid the price.

The verses in *Foreign Affairs* are printed as part of an article in which AE surveys Irish politics in his time. They turn on a national pun, a play on the word Rising. The Easter Rising was the Easter Rebellion; it was also the Resurrection of the Messiah:

> Last year at Easter there were faces pale and bright,
> For the Lord had arisen from the grave which is fear.
> Hearts were airy, eyes filled with inner light;
> It was wrought this miracle among the ruins here. . . .

The same politico-religious *double entente* is the basis of the third statement *Michael*, a lengthy poem, eventually included in *The Interpreters* in 1922. *The Interpreters* is a symposium in which the men who have taken leading parts in the Rising (slightly disguised and modernised into "science fiction" terms) explain their motives and hopes. The poet Lavelle—an interesting combination of AE himself and Yeats—shapes this poem in the light of the exchange of views, realising that the Rising, like every revolution, is an effort, inspired by the "oversoul", to realise on earth the perfection of eternity.

The poem has the Wordsworthian title *Michael* and a Wordsworthian content to match (for the Irish of this generation were essentially heirs of Wordsworth). Michael leaves his fisher-cabin home on the Irish coast, where "things delicate and dewy" have

educated him, for the dinginess of Dublin, and toiling his soul
away there

> Within his attic he would fret
> Like a wild creature in a net.

But he meets nationalists who teach him the stories of the Red
Branch and modern nationalist poems—

> And soon with them had Michael read
> The legend of the famous dead,
> From him who with his single sword
> Stayed a great army at the ford,*
> Down to the vagrant poets, those
> Who gave their hearts to the Dark Rose.

He takes part with these friends in the Sacrifice of Easter:

> Thrice on the wheel of time recurred
> The season of the risen Lord
> Since Michael left his home behind
> And faced the chilly Easter wind,
> And saw the twilight waters gleam
> And dreamed an unremembered dream.
> Was it because the Easter time
> With mystic nature was in chime
> That memory was roused from sleep
> Or was deep calling unto deep?
> The lord in man had risen here
> From the dark sepulchre of fear
> Was laughing, gay and undismayed,
> Though on a fragile barricade
> The bullet rang, the death star broke,
> The street waved dizzily in smoke,
> And there the fierce and lovely breath
> Of flame in the grey mist was death.

> Yet Michael felt within him rise
> The rapture that is sacrifice.

*i.e. Cuchulain.

The star that fell over Parnell's grave has now become "the death star", an image for the bullet that killed a rebel in the Post Office, and so produced, in the smoke and rapture of sacrifice, the expected Messiah. In the emotional aftermath of the Rising, the desire for order has given way, the images of the 'nineties have been remembered and refashioned, and Messianism is alive again in AE—momentarily—with something of its original fervour.

In an article written in the *Freeman*, during the period of post-1918 struggle, to appeal to American opinion against Britain, AE uses the Messianic image. Britain, exulting in material power, has tried to crush Irish culture—just as when Christ was crucified, a materialist may have eyed his body on the Cross, "murmuring as he went homeward, 'It will all blow over now' ". But "After the spiritual powers, there is nothing in the world more unconquerable than the spirit of nationality".*

In the New Year of 1922 he was writing hopefully of the new Ireland: "Ireland is intensely interesting, more so than I have found it since I was a boy. The young men are full of possibilities, and I watch them and study their minds and I am full of hope not indeed of an ever peaceful country but for a country with a great many fine personalities."† But though there were glimmers of optimism like this for some time to come, his temper grew dour as he scrutinised the complexion of the new nation. Lady Gregory transcribed into her journal on April 30th, 1922, part of a letter from Lennox Robinson: "AE is very disheartened, wants someone to write a play about how the generations for 700 years fought for the liberation of beautiful Cathleen ni Houlihan, and when they set her free she walked out, a fierce vituperative old hag". A year later in a contribution to the *Freeman* he reported that the Irish revolution had "triumphed solely in externals. Our spiritual, cultural, and intellectual life has not changed for the better. If anything, it has retrograded. . . . The champions of physical force have, I am sure without intent, poisoned the soul of Ireland."‡

*The Freeman, New York, April 28th, 1920.
†See *Letters from AE*, edited by Alan Denson.
‡ The Freeman, July 25th, 1923.

His discouragement deepened during the last thirteen years of his life. On Lady Gregory's death he wrote to Yeats: "The Anglo-Irish were the best Irish but I can see very little future for them as the present belongs to that half-crazy Gaeldom which is growing dominant about us." The late letters to Minanlabain are shot with exasperation, humorously tinctured but real, at the follies of politicians in general and Irish politicians in particular. He hated de Valera's denunciation of the Anglo-Irish Treaty, considered it dishonesty on the national scale, no different in kind than the petty dishonesty he had lashed in this *Homestead* period, as in that Socratic plea to Dillon in 1912:

> There comes a time in the life of the politician rising to power when the exigencies of cause or party seem best served by the suppression of truth. . . . He has to choose between the success of causes which are dear to him, which are perhaps really high and noble causes, and the maintenance of personal integrity. Alas, it is the curse of our public life that men too often choose to maintain causes rather than their own human worth, and they think their country is served thereby, as if any cause was higher than the character of human life in it. . .

While his good sense told him that the new Ireland was no better and no worse than any other autonomous country, as he had foreseen in 1916, he nevertheless heard in his mind the bourdon that maddened Yeats: that Ireland, though seeming to have won liberty, had lost the main fight for purity and dignity. She politicised for her advantage with no more regard for honour than England had shown. She had succumbed like England to commerce; and just as England had "paid the price" for materialism in the obliteration of her countryside and soul, Ireland would pay. Writing moderately since he was writing for a foreign organ, he said in his *Foreign Affairs* article of New Year, 1929: ". . . we are tired of struggle today. The mood which is most widely spread is a half-cynical, but rather cheerful materialism. It manifests itself in efforts to organise agriculture, to create industries, to have peace at all costs." Then, because it was his habit to finish on a hopeful note, he surmised that young writers would introduce a reaction against materialism—but it was a vaguely-worded surmise.

The new Ireland was carrying her responsibilities for the first time. Her mistakes were palpably her own. AE's demands for sanity were more telling than they could be earlier when England carried the odium of Irish difficulties. Criticism comes best from a man who is sharing the difficulties; and AE had known that, and had resolutely stayed at home nearly all his life. As late as 1933 he was promising to stick at it: "I exist in Ireland because it is my duty to leave as many heresies in its literature as possible. The seeds I scatter will come up in the next generation. . . . One's country or one's nation is a brute to be kicked in the ribs." But like other poets, and like Standish O'Grady who had formed the Irish heroic images, he was so appalled by the discrepancy between the Ireland he had promised and the Ireland that he had got, that he preferred to die abroad. One of his late poems sadly states how he has only the memory of symbols, and his own pseudonym, no longer their creative energy:

> The hills have vanished in dark air;
> And night, without an eye, is blind.
> I too am starless. Time has blurred
> The aeons of my life behind.
>
> Oh, what in those dark aeons lay?
> What tumult, beauty and desire?
> I know not, all are lost beyond
> Sunsets of anguish and of fire.

He says that the star is extinct. Was it out all through the last exasperated years? Was that the end of his conception of the Messiah? In the summer of 1931 he tried to rekindle it by setting himself to the writing of a last work, *The Avatars*. He called it a fantasy, but it is rather, like *The Interpreters*, a symposium. The significance of the title is obvious. He had used the word Avatar in the crucial forecasting of the Messiah in the mid-nineties; it was his word for Messiah, being free from religious associations.

implying a man of what he would have called "dilated consciousness", dynamic, kingly, a natural leader—borrowed,
perhaps, from Browning's *Waring*

> O never star
> Was lost here but burns out afar.
> In Vishnu-land what avatar?

In *The Avatars* his experiences of the early 'nineties are remembered* and recapitulated. He describes a poet, a painter, a sculptor,
an old thinker, an anarchist, and others, who have independently
retired to a lonely part of Ireland, dissatisfied with a mechanical
civilisation and anxious to reconsider their relationship with the
world. They have intimations of a joyful personality about to
arise out of the clay. They have, they gradually realise, been called
together as men capable of sensing and describing a new development of the human consciousness. They are the forerunners.
Then the Avatars appear, Aodh and Aoife, a young peasant and
a princess. A cult of joy spreads wherever they go. The civilised
powers thereupon send police or agents, who infiltrate into a
festival and bludgeon them, and they disappear. But their cult
grows through legends and the artistic records of the forerunners.

Despite the weariness that drove him out of Ireland, AE could
not conclude mournfully. His temperament would not allow it.
The Avatars seems to say that though the Irish revolution resulted
in a mechanical, commercial civilisation like any other (this is
implied in the allegory of the bludgeoning of the Avatars by the
police of the world's mechanised states), the Avatars had made
their appearance and spread their new religion or sensibility, and
the work of the forerunners—of Yeats and Synge and AE and
their friends, he means—remained as the record of that appearance
and the nucleus of a rich culture: ". . . impulses springing up

---

*In the remembering some expressions that were obscure in the correspondence of 1896
are illuminated. For example, the letter quoted on page 174, in which AE tells Yeats, after
describing the Avatar's cottage in Donegal or Sligo, *"Do not spread this about"*. Why had
Yeats to observe such secrecy? The narrative of *The Avatars*, where the same cottage is
described with the addition of the epithet "aureoled", shows why: because AE expected
that if the Herods, Walsinghams, and Metternichs of this world learned the details of the
Avatar's whereabouts, they would send their police to bludgeon him.

deeply within us were messages from the gods . . ." But while this final optimistic statement does affirm that Ireland had her Messiah, it also confesses that AE is tired of revolutions that only produce new civilisations, and thus it looks forward to some future revelation which will release man from the burden of building new States and systems of law and ethics. For it is the differentiating characteristic of Aodh and Aoife that they have left no body of doctrine, no ethic; and no civilisation can be reared on their example.

What have they done, then? By their gaiety they have taught men (says AE, using his life-long myth of the soul returning to the heights of its original godhead, strengthened by its knowledge of the depths) to climb the terraces of being. He writes that all Messiahs have taught gaiety, that certainly Christ taught it, but that their disciples have afterwards concealed it and substituted a doctrine of pain.

By naming gaiety as the distinctive Avatar-quality, AE points to the great lacuna in his life and writing. He had the build of a jester, and his friends knew his humorous side, but he published like a sad, solemn, earnest man. He had often noted the failure in himself. In his very moving introduction to *Collected Poems* he said:

> When I first discovered for myself how near was the King in His beauty I thought I would be the singer of the happiest songs. Forgive me, Spirit of my spirit, for this, that I have found it easier to read the mystery told in tears and understood Thee better in sorrow than in joy; that, though I would not, I have made the way seem thorny. . .

In his dedication to *The Avatars* he admitted, too, that he had desired to transmit to the prose the "spiritual gaiety" that he preached, and that it had not come. Although he numbers himself among the forerunners, his work does not quite equal the requirements he sets, nor does the melancholy and tender writing of the earlier part of the Celtic Renaissance. The Irish writing which most has the quality of spiritual gaiety is work with which he was not particularly sympathetic: Synge's *Playboy*, the middle and late work of Joyce.

In his life there were probably shortfallings from the ideal of gaiety. We do not have many facts at present, but such hints as are available point to a problematical dissociation between ideal and achievement. One fragment of evidence is ominous. George Moore had a rare intuition for finding the vulnerable spots in his friends. He rubbed Yeats at the weakest point by reminding him that his origins were middle-class and pretending that the poet's interest in the nobility was disloyalty to his middle-class father (to whom Yeats had so intense an Oedipean attachment). Now although he made AE a hero of *Hail and Farewell*, he also probed a finger into a sore spot. He uttered only a faint innuendo—"John [Eglinton] . . . admonished me to be very careful what I said about AE's home life"—but it was enough to make AE suffer. Because AE was a Moore hero, and because he wrote an oration for his ashes (an oration which was intentionally ambiguous), we often think of him tolerantly reciprocating Moore's friendship. But he did not. The proof is, that almost at the same date as he was composing the noble obituary, he was writing perhaps the most unsaintly words he ever wrote to pillory Moore as a shallow converter of sacred fact into immoral fiction. He published the passage in *The Avatars* four months after Moore's death. Conaire has brooded on the danger that the legend of the *Avatars* will be misrepresented: "There never yet was a fire which did not cast dark shadows of itself. I wonder what dark counterpart of itself the story will create in some obscene souls." A moment later there are footsteps on the threshold. Paul, the artist, finds at the door "a man he knew a little and liked not at all. He was one of the famous story-tellers of the time." In sophisticated, foppish sentences the story-teller explains why he has come to Ireland: "You know I am a creature of this world. I only came to this country looking for local colour, a romantic background for a tale . . ." He is planning a novel turning the Messianic story of Aodh and Aoife into social paradox and typical physical passion: "What a setting for love, these mountains! these woods! How much more

poetical than an hotel! I will send you this greatest of my love
stories when it is printed." And he leaves with "Well, after hail,
it is now farewell." By that valediction, and the allusion to the
story-teller's holiday, AE clearly identifies Moore; and the pages
are a summary condemnation of his motives in coming to Ireland
in 1899 and of what he wrote around Irish Messianism. The pages
are fascinating as further evidence of how Moore made himself
hated, and as further evidence of how those who hated him did
not dare to publish their hate till he was dead (though this *may*
have been due to a queer compassion for his sensitivity). As regards
AE, what it shows is that he had been terribly provoked; usually
he was kindly, and when not kindly he was open and straight;
this oblique rancorous attack proves the depth of the wound
Moore's innuendo had inflicted.

Whatever facts there may be will emerge during the next
twenty-five years and enable us to probe the deeper layers of contradiction in AE. What is certain is that, in place of gaiety, he had
an extraordinary resilience. In every discouragement he found
material for recovery. He is so resilient that it is a little tiring to
meet, after his statement of difficulties, his regular promise of new
glimmers, new sprouts. And unsatisfactory. He who will not
lie long in his calamity will not have much to tell us about it.

It is typical of this habit of optimism, and of the strength of
his prophetic habit, that when he no longer could predict an
Avatar for Ireland he predicted one for America. In 1896 he had
taken hope for the Donegal or Sligo Avatar from the vitality of
United States mysticism, as reported for twenty years by the
theosophists: "America is on fire with mysticism just now and
the new races are breaking the mould of European thought and
psychics abound. Their light reflects itself in Ireland, and the path
of connection has been seen." In his last years, when he had
toured the Union, talked in her universities, advised her federal
agricultural experts on the co-operative movement, he conceived
her as molten with psychic energy and ready for a new Emerson
to reshape her. On the notepaper of the erudite and dignified
Cosmos Club of Washington D.C. he wrote to Joseph O'Neill in

the New Year of 1935: "... this country is reeking with suppressed mysticism. The current literature, the press fill the mind with other images and words. But when one speaks the suppressed mysticism breaks out. It only needs a greater Emerson with more richness and vitality to transfigure the American mentality. But I wonder will America get such a man...." It is AE's indispensable, forty-year-old murmur of "the big man", "our man of destiny". Finn, again! Em, again! It was the recapitulatory delirium of near-death. He re-crossed the Atlantic, illness in his bowels, and died in the summer at Bournemouth, a more genteel town than Parnell's Brighton, but "not specially Irish".

CHAPTER VI

EDMUND JOHN MILLINGTON SYNGE

1871-1909

In the biographical sketches of *A Vision* Yeats brackets Synge
with Rembrandt. Both exaggerate, for "both delight in all that
is wilful, in all that flouts intellectual coherence, and conceive of
the world as if it were an overflowing cauldron". They represent
the Receptive Man, [who] may seem to care for the immoral
and inhuman only, for he will be hostile, or indifferent to
moral as to intellectual summaries . . . if he is Synge, he
takes a malicious pleasure in the contrast between his hero,
whom he discovers through his instinct for comedy, and any
hero in men's minds. Indeed, whether he be Synge or
Rembrandt, he is ready to sacrifice every convention, perhaps
all that men have agreed to reverence, for a startling theme, or
a model one delights in painting; and yet all the while . . .
there is another summary working through bone and nerve.
He is never the mere technician that he seems, though when
you ask his meaning he will have nothing to say, and will say
something irrelevant or childish.

John Synge was born at Newtown Little, near Dublin, on
April 16th, 1871. An amoralist, he had bishops and clergymen
among his ancestors on both sides of the family; and the man who
was to create a national scandal with a play turning on the
parricidal impulses of the Ireland of his time, he grew up without
a father, for John Hatch Synge, a quiet barrister, died on April
13th, 1872. Synge's mother, according to W. R. Rodgers'

introduction to the Penguin edition of the plays, was a devout woman, "of strong character, pungent expression, and pro-nounced Evangelist views", who reared him on "the milk of the Word". Rodgers tells a story of Synge in the Louvre, looking at an old lady asleep: "stopping in front of her, fascinated, he gazed for some time and said to a friend—'Would you not see all our mothers?' ".

From private schools in Dublin and Bray and tuition at home, he entered Trinity College, Dublin, in 1888. He took a modest degree, but won two prizes—for Irish and for Hebrew, a com-bination significant for the Ireland of the 'nineties. It is curious, and perhaps relevant to the special narrow intensity of Synge's mind, that his mother's father, the Rev. Robert Traill, had been a translator of Josephus. From Trinity Synge went to Germany as a music-student, then abandoned that study and strayed, rather like Goldsmith, southwards and into France and Italy. He was in Paris at the end of 1896, and Yeats met him there in December, told him, according to the famous anecdote, that he was wasting himself on European literature, and advised him to go to the Aran Islands. Synge went to Aran, and for six years divided his time between Paris and Ireland, only in 1902 giving up his *garconnière*. The act clearly denoted a choice in favour of his own country, but, although we think of him in terms of that decision and as a man whose work is purely and specifically Irish, I think that he never wholly forgot Europe—he was in Germany again the year before he died—and that it played a greater part in developing his imagination than we usually allow. He was attracted by the obverse of the subject of his writing, by the strangeness of difference, the exotic which also attracted Joyce. He liked, for example, to claim kinship with Lafcadio Hearn, though Hearn was only distantly connected by marriage, and praised inordinately his Japanese *Exotics and Retrospectives;* his reading in that text is affiliated, however tenuously, with the oriental predilections of Yeats and AE and their interest in the eastern religions; and in general it illustrates how varied and exploratory his reading was. He applied himself, up to the time his first two short plays were in typescript, with sombre concentration to many subjects as if he had not found which subject was his. There is a penetrating comment on his reading by his early biographer, Maurice Bourgeois:

> He would delve into all manner of letterpress and read on for hours at a time whether he understood or not. When he tackled a difficult French book, such as Mallarmé's *Divagations* (which he read again and again), he was fairly sure not to understand at all—first, because of his insufficient French, then and chiefly owing to his own peculiar tenebrosity of mind. . . . All the same, during his French period, the sheer strain of reading made books subtly suggestive to him; and he would go on untroubled. At length, by dint of concentration and brooding, the light of intuition would flash upon him; he would gradually emerge from the perpetual blank fog of his mind, and, by some laborious process of defoliation, get to the very gist of the thing—not the objective thing, but the purely subjective impression it made on him, and on him alone.

While the French critic is a little amazed at Synge's "intellectual mistiness" and utter incompetence in the chess of ideas, his paragraph splendidly recognises the validity of the Irishman's special process. It follows naturally from the process that Synge's creative work bears none of the usual prints of the influence of reading: practically no allusions to books or paraphrases from them or stylistic imitations. But we should not argue from that for the irrelevance of the reading. Something must have altered in Synge's mind each time the long application resulted in the flare of subjective understanding; and perhaps his singular barbarous music was made possible by the blending in his mind of the many disparate aesthetic experiences.

I am afraid that Yeats tried to steal some of the credit for Synge's achievement when he circulated the story of how he told him, when urging the first Aran visit, that the islanders had welcomed his own (very brief) disembarkation with "If any gentleman has done a crime, we'll hide him. There was a gentleman that killed his father, and I had him in my own house six months till he got away to America." Yeats wanted it to be concluded from this anecdote that he planted the seed of *The Playboy* in Synge's head at the initial contact. Yeats was so anxious that the Irish literary movement should be remembered as "my movement" that he sometimes improved the facts. We do, however, know that over eighteen months before the meeting with Synge Yeats was consciously "ransacking Ireland for people to set writing at Irish things",* and he probably treated Synge to the same urging he bestowed elsewhere in those years. The difference was that in this case he flushed a genius. And in this case he had not foreseen that he would. A letter written at a further meeting with Synge in Paris two years later—February 14th, 1899—shows that what he expected of Synge was not creative work but scholarship: "He is really a most excellent man. He lives in a little room, which he has furnished himself. He is his own servant. He works very hard and is learning Breton. He will be a very useful scholar." So Yeats expected Synge's contribution to Ireland to come via comparative Celtics. In fact, John Synge's interest in Breton did have repercussions on the Irish literary movement. George Moore, with his quick sense of a new potential, caught a hint from him; wrote the curious conversation with a Breton sailor into *Hail and Farewell;* and went on to compose the Breton scenes of *Héloïse and Abélard* and *Peronnik the Fool.* It is an interesting by-product of Synge's achievement; Yeats had thought he would work wholly, and presumably further, in that direction.

Joyce calls *Riders to the Sea* Synge's first play and says that Synge read it to him in Paris in 1902. Masefield says that *In the Shadow of the Glen* and *Riders to the Sea* were read aloud in Lady Gregory's London drawing-room in January 1903, and that *Riders* had not yet quite found its final form. Presumably the text shown to Joyce was an interim version, for Synge's method was to type one draft after another, as many as fourteen or fifteen, till he was satisfied. The first play to be staged was *The Shadow,*

---

*The Letters of W. B. Yeats, edited by Allan Wade, p.256.

P

in Dublin in October 1903. It was received with applause and hisses; with enthusiasm from English and foreign critics, and the more percipient of the Irish; anger from the majority of the Irish audience. Maud Gonne left the theatre protesting against decadence, and her fierce nationalist friends denounced the author's libel on Irish womanhood. *Riders* was produced in January 1904, *The Well of the Saints* in February 1905, this latter again irritating the public with its insistence on the ugly reality that underlay the Irish illusion:

> . . . I was the like of the little children do be listening to the stories of an old woman, and do be dreaming after it in the dark night that it's in grand old houses of gold they are, with speckled horses to ride, and do be waking again, in a short while, and they destroyed with the cold, and the thatch dripping, maybe, and the starved ass braying in the yard. . . .

The Playboy of the Western World, presented in January 1907, precipitated a hullabaloo that has become a landmark of Irish literary history. Yeats deliberately chose to stir the broil, as will be described in this chapter, and successfully made *The Playboy* a test-case for his dramatic movement. Though the objections were renewed five years later when the Abbey toured America, *The Playboy* was established as one of the major works on its repertoire and new writers were stimulated to attempt drama in the same key.

In 1908 Synge underwent an operation, then travelled to Germany but was recalled by his mother's death. In 1909 he was again in hospital, and neither the incompleteness of his *Deirdre of the Sorrows*, which he was struggling to finish, nor the affection of his fiancée gave him strength to survive. *Deirdre* was, however, sufficiently advanced for a working text to be salvaged, and was presented at the Abbey in January 1910.

Only *Deirdre* is a "literary" work, drawn from the epic cycles which the Irish literary movement had proposed as the central reservoir for Irish drama. The other plays are developed from stories heard in Synge's stay in Aran and his wanderings through the provinces. The stories are in themselves slight, but he has made them the medium of his peculiar transformation of rural Ireland. They show a countryside which is real but suffused with a light that never was on sea or land. Famous for his taciturnity, his inability to give himself in company, he absorbed impressions and folded them into his plays. Passages in the prose-sketches make it clear that long meditation in the open was a part of the formative process. He "lay for a long time on the side of a magnificently wild road under Croagh Martin. . ." He climbed the ridge of an island and "spent much of my time looking at the richness of the Atlantic on one side and the sad or shining greys of Dingle Bay on the other". He was, as he described Christy in *The Playboy*, "a man you'd see stretched the half of the day in the brown ferns with his belly to the sun". Anyone who has tried open-air meditation, or watched others try it, knows that it is hard to continue it long. When Harrisson and Madge and their friends watched holiday-makers at Blackpool in the 'thirties, they found that a man or woman, though at leisure, seldom stays in one place for fifteen minutes. But Synge had dedicated himself to contemplation, and he had the art by nature and by practice; and though it did not give him an abundance of ideas, it gave to the few ideas on which his imagination worked a distinctness and flavour—the flavour of nut or apple, as he liked to say. It did more: the activation of the stories came through that physically lazy, innerly-intent communion with landscape and weather.

In *The Playboy* there is a sentence with an autobiographical colouring, Christy's appeal to Pegeen to think of his loneliness:

> . . . it's a lonesome thing to be passing small towns with the lights shining sideways when the night is down, or going in strange places with a dog noising before you and a dog noising behind, or drawn to the cities where you'd hear a voice kissing and talking deep love in every shadow of the ditch, and you passing on with an empty, hungry stomach failing from your heart.

Yeats wrote in *A Vision:* "In the works of Synge there is much self-pity, ennobled to a pity for all that lived." That speech of Christy's is an obvious case in point. Synge was not always literally lonely. He stayed with the Aran islanders in the close contact that poverty enforces; he travelled with the tinkers; Moore hints that on one journey a servant-girl gave up her life and went with him (but Moore's sentence is wilfully ambiguous, and may simply mean that the girl had thrown in her lot with his tinker-companions). But even in company he was essentially alone, and beauty sharpened his sense of difference and loneliness. In *The Well of the Saints*, in *The Playboy*, and in *Deirdre*, he rebukes the cruelty of beautiful women. To that sense of the searing in beauty Yeats' comment on a self-pity heightened to world-pity also applies. Synge was the mate of loneliness, experiencing its privations and consolations, under the pull of which his mind made the dialogue of expressive, energetic, interacting people.

He became interested at the end of his life in the possibility of writing urban drama, and began collecting the speech of the city streets. Joyce was working in the same direction, and one or two of the *Dubliners* stories had appeared. But the next decade was the period of the real beginning of Irish urban literature. The national sensibility then began to open to the town. AE grew concerned for the city-worker, wrote on the practical problems of the strikes, developed his economic theorising correspondingly. Joyce throughout that decade worked at the Dublin epic, *Ulysses*. But the stage did not represent the town till the town had seen the fighting of the Civil War. Only then did the Shadow of the Glen become the Shadow of a Gunman.

THE REALIST BASIS OF SURREALITY

Exuberance has its interest, and some writers cannot work without emulating nature and ejecting a great deal in order that a little shall seed. Synge's way was the contrary. His five plays are concentrated. They contain scarcely a line that is idle or borrowed or contrived as a bridge to cover a gap where his invention has flagged. They are compact and personal.

Synge came at a crucial moment in the development of the

Irish literary movement and, with Yeats fighting for him, determined its success and at the same time altered its direction. After his death it developed in his way rather than in the way that Yeats, who had recruited him to it, had previously supposed it should. Yet as a practitioner he had little affinity with the movement he joined. He shared the political convictions of the Irish nationalists, but ignored them in his writing. He contemplated people's appetites, not their causes. Yeats has beautifully epitomised his amorality in the well-known story of the scenario he outlined when asked for a play on the Rebellion of '98: it

> ... read like a chapter out of Rabelais. Two women, a Protestant and a Catholic, take refuge in a cave, and there quarrel about religion, abusing the Pope or Queen Elizabeth and Henry VIII, but in low voices, for the one fears to be ravished by the soldiers, the other by the rebels. At last one woman goes out because she would sooner any fate than such wicked company.

He would not endorse the literature of Cathleen ni Houlihan. He was capable, as his papers from the Congested Districts show, of the sanest thinking on practical measures for the amelioration of rural misery, but improvement, hope, liberty, had no place in his writing. He would have no literary truck with Messiahs. The bent of his mind was against the good news of the evangelists. His pleasure was to discover people who flouted the hopes of his friends—so long as they represented, instead, energy—and to overhear and reproduce nonsense, which mocked the thinkers and planners, so long as the nonsense implied energy. It is typical that in one of his reports on the story-tellers of Aran, he enthusiastically quotes the traditional nonsense-ending to a fairy-tale, "gabbled with delighted haste":

> They found the path and I found the puddle. They were drowned, and I was found. If it's all one to me tonight, it wasn't all one to them the next night. Yet, if it wasn't itself, not a thing did they lose but an old back tooth.

Nothing better shows his separation from the literary movement as it stood prior to his entry. Yeats and Lady Gregory listened to peasant talk too, but Yeats claimed that it betokened dignity, and if he had quoted the story-teller he would have selected some phrase of picturesque fancy, and perhaps embellished it. Or Yeats would have reproduced a sentence in which the belief in the supernatural audibly echoed and have veered away from the reality by writing an exegesis. Synge's quotation shows, like so much of his writing, a strong feeling for the pagan elements in peasant life, but he never loses touch with reality by translating quotation into doctrine.

He has offered brief definitions of his aesthetic in his prefaces. But the prefaces are so deliberate, lapidary, that we cannot make much of them. Just a phrase or two can usefully be examined for his intentions, notably the remark in the preface to *The Playboy*: "On the stage one must have reality, and one must have joy." Shall we read this as "reality . . . and *therefore* joy" or "reality . . . and *yet nevertheless* joy"? Given the state of Ireland, Synge must have meant the latter. He did combine reality and joy, or at any rate reality and exhilaration, and knew that he had accomplished a paradox. His immediate seniors had not been able to do it, nor even to conceive of it. When AE first saw the Congested Districts in the west, he was horrified to silence; in 1897, when he had just begun his rural tours for Plunkett, he wrote to Synge from Belmullet in Mayo: "This wild country here has imposed such a melancholy into my blood that I have not had the heart to write to [Yeats] or anybody else if I could help it. I had nothing to say except accounts of the distress here which is a disgrace to humanity and that is not cheerful subject matter for a letter".* Synge was just as aware of the distress of the Districts when he travelled them with Jack Yeats in 1905, and his prose studies contain the dour reality. But he reared *The Playboy* around the villainy of the men of Mayo, and set it not far from Belmullet; and in the play there is no reality in the English novelist's sense of the term, no fact documented and evaluated; there is Synge's kind of reality.

Letters from AE, edited by Alan Denson.

Some critics might judge the word "reality" inapplicable to his drama. There is an obvious sense in which he invests Mayo or the Wicklow glens with a vigour which is the antithesis of the drab reality and a compensation for it. Yeats thought so in the summer of 1904 when, writing from Coole where he, AE, and Synge were guests of Lady Gregory, he described Irish plays as "a cry for a more abundant and a more intense life".* Synge doubled reality into surreality, giving Ireland what she lacked as well as what she showed him. But he did include what she actually showed together with what he imagined for her. His dialogue supplies images of aspirations, couched in what an Egyptian friend of mine used to call "hashish-poetry", and images drawn from harsh fact. It is a direct counterpoising of reality and dream. Christy's famous speech which uses the conventional Gaelic love-image of "the star of knowledge" turns on the contrast of aspiration, in which the Church and the body are confused, and penurious fact:

> Amn't I after seeing the love-light of the star of knowledge shining from her brow, and hearing words would put you thinking on the holy Brigid speaking to the infant saints, and now she'll be turning again, and speaking hard words to me, like an old woman with a spavindy ass she'd have, urging on a hill.

and Widow Quin's retort caps the reality:

> There's poetry talk for a girl you'd see itching and scratching, and she with a stale stink of poteen on her from selling in the shop.

—an Irish portrait that looks forward to Molly Bloom. Synge disperses what we usually imagine as beauty and in its place finds energy. Energy is the quality that we finally count as beauty in him. Yeats wrote of Synge's "harsh, heroical, windswept view of things", and of those three adjectives the most characteristic is "windswept", suggested by Synge's own description of the

*But see the whole of this interesting letter in Allan Wade's edition of *The Letters of W. B. Yeats*, p.436.

exhilarating open and the wind in his teeth like wine. The sensation of Synge *is* harsh and it *is* exhilarating; it is impossible to live long with it, and yet we tell ourselves under its shock that our nerves are so alight that we are living as never otherwise, lifted out of torpor. The shortness of Synge's life was the registration of this difficulty in his kind of beauty.

Christy's exchange with Widow Quin is relatively simple, and often in Synge the pattern of hope against fact is more intricate, an interfluxion of the real and the surreal, a dependence of the real on the surreal to retain vision and energy, and a dependence of the surreal on the real for efficacy; and the real and the surreal operate as drama—not merely as art which happens to be written in dialogue—because the real elements in the combination necessarily predicate stage-business or inflections of the voice. Synge had learned in Aran that a drowned, headless man may be identified by his clothing. Nora in *Riders to the Sea* identifies her brother by counting the stitches in his stocking: "It's the second one of the third pair I knitted, and I put up three-score stitches and I dropped four of them". Her sister counts the stitches to check her. The epic quality has this commonplace domestic reality at its centre; and the conception is a stage-conception; the actresses must play to each other handling the stocking. In the wonderful sequence of smelling the boot in *The Playboy* Synge exploits domestic reality, requires the third dimension of the group-handling of an object, and enhances the tang of the grotesque vital to his best work. The second act opens with the girls of the locality rushing into the shebeen to find Christy. Sara Tansey picks up his boots:

> NELLY Are you thinking them's his boots?
> SARA (*taking them up*) If they are, there should be his father's track on them. Did you never read in the papers the way murdered men do bleed and drip?
> SUSAN Is that blood there, Sara Tansey?
> SARA (*smelling it*) That's bog water, I'm thinking.

This is one of the two dozen masterly stage-strokes in *The Playboy*.

It is at once social realism and farce; it belongs to the special Irish family of olfactory comedy, that extravagant distillation of the unwashed; it is essentially conceived as drama, notates the actresses' business, and requires them to perform as well as speak the combined realism, poetry, lowness, exaltation.

Of course, the recognition of the stitches in *Riders* is neither so rich nor so impure as that *Playboy* episode. It is the realism of compassion, and there are other similar moments in Synge. When Mary Byrne at the close of Act I of *The Tinker's Wedding* says "It's few would listen to an old woman, few but a girl maybe would be in great fear the time her hour was come, or a little child wouldn't be sleeping with the hunger on a cold night", she offers in the last image simply the poverty of Ireland. But in *The Playboy*, which has had such success that the critics like to look elsewhere to praise Synge, for fear of the obvious, but which is his consummate work, the norm is the heterogeneous. A hard compassion goes together with hyperbole, which is a grand exotic flowering, like Christy's account of his father: "he after drinking for weeks, rising up in the red dawn, or before it maybe, and going out into the yard as naked as an ash tree in the moon of May". This is a visualisation of the father as god and object of worship, not formed through a realistic comparison but carved archetypally out of the unconscious by a man who grew up never knowing his father. Breaking momentarily out of the give-and-take of the real and unreal in Synge's special way it is superb. The extravagances are safely anchored in the reality with which they are associated.

The Playboy was denounced by Dublin for its theme of parricide, but the fact is that, while it makes its comedy from audacious, close looks at the Oedipean struggle between father and son, it ends with father and son united. It is a play of the discovery of the unknown father, a father different from the clerkly, studious, charitable men Synge's immediate begetters seem to have been, a figure outwardly stingy and gigantically repressive, but lit at the centre by rough family love. Christy's early speeches show his fear and anger with his father, but the inner warmth. He answers

Michael James when he is asked whether the police want him for larceny:

> CHRISTY (*with a flash of family pride*) And I the son of a strong
> farmer (*with a sudden qualm*), God rest his soul. . .

Just as the movement of Synge's ideas entails stage-business, so it impels the actor to effective shifts of voice. The break in that sentence of Christy's notates a gasp of recollection, a modulation from pride which is nearly but unconsciously love, to remorse which brings love nearer to consciousness.

The dynamic conceiving of speech and action in terms of the performer is common to every able dramatist (though there are not over many of these at the poetic level). But how did Synge acquire it? Shakespeare had to write more than five plays before he acquired it. We first hear Shakespeare notating for voice and action originally, poetically, and with a clarity the actor may not disregard, in *Romeo and Juliet;* it is an inferior play in thought, but it has that special interest in the Shakespearian canon, that the dramatist is, after some practice, suddenly in control of his medium. Synge had the control before he had any professional practice. Certainly he had the advantage of writing with 300 years of British drama behind him, and of careful study of some of the English and French standard plays both in his room and among theatre audiences, and perhaps he had observed experimental plays on the stage in Middle Europe; he is said to have been taken, like Joyce, by Ben Jonson's comedy; but all this is not an explanation, for hundreds of us have read Jonson and Molière without assimilating a single trick. When he actually worked with the players he probably improved his sense of the trade, as Lady Gregory gained hers; but he had written *The Shadow* and *Riders* before that. Nothing could be a simpler trick, but nothing apter or better-handled, than the sequence in Dan Burke's kitchen when Nora, who believes her husband to be dead under the sheet behind her, talks to her lover about him, and the audience sees him rising to the very posture she is describing: ". . . . It's a queer thing to see an old man sitting up there in his bed with no teeth in him, and a rough word in his mouth, and his chin the way it would take the bark from the edge of an oak board you'd have building a door. . . ." Synge meditated three-dimensionally. Most word-makers meditate in the one dimension of the rhythm, they incantate; a few can alternatively, and fewer still can also, meditate in the second dimension of the verbal image; but to be capable of these and the third dimension of action, which sometimes runs with and sometimes contrapuntally against, the verbal image, is reserved for the rare born dramatist. Apply this test to Eliot, and, for all his fine accomplishment in the theatre, he is not a born dramatist; he has only the first two dimensions. Synge was. "How" remains a mystery of family genetics (since he grew out of clergy-men—but there is admittedly a connection between the church service and the drama) and of national genetics (since he grew up in a country that never had a native drama).

We are occasionally told that Synge was a master of construc-tion. It is true that his structures are excellent, especially in that they do not proclaim their excellence. But they are not intricate. Synge knew what he could do and did not attempt more. With appropriateness and clarity he placed a few effects where they could not fail.

Maurice Bourgeois has detailed from the prose-sketches the original country stories which suggested Synge's plays. A good writer takes what is given and uses it as far as he may but divines at a point that he must break away into his self. Synge most decisively alters his stories in their endings. The characteristic Synge ending is a departure. The tinkers untruss the priest and run away from his pagan curse; Nora Burke goes away with the tramp; the blind couple, after a lifetime in their village, leave for the south; Christy and his father leave the wealth and the women of the shebeen. . . . Synge keeps the tone astringent, gives Nora, for example, her prediction of "wheezing with lying down under the Heavens"; but, for all that, these departures for the roadside ditches are his golden journey to Samarkand; and his endings, and the whole trend of his plays, are a hymn to vagrancy. Bourgeois, when he complains of an aesthetic failure in *The*

Tinker's Wedding, and is "inclined to regret that Synge ever penned this immature comedy", is refusing his sympathy to Synge's strongest image, the image of those wandering amoral tinkers whom the orthodox Irish watched with wonder and envy and Synge at last translated into the nation's literature. Synge was, however, not thinking of the nation; Yeats, with his different cast of mind, would later do that when, learning from Synge to write of poverty and joy, he related the tinker epos to Ireland's hopes. Synge was thinking of his private experience and fantasy, celebrating that fragment of his life which he loved best and in which he found the secret of savour and his individual kind of communion with saints (since, it will be remembered, the Thirty-Six Tsaddiqim are among the vagrants).

All the traditions concur that Synge was, as Yeats called him, "that rooted man". He hated the migratory flow from Ireland. All his writing was about Ireland. When Yeats proposed, in order to educate the Dublin audience and lift its level of comprehension, that the Abbey should form a second company to play international drama, Synge for once came out against him with an unmistakable and formal protest. Yet the inner Synge was a migrant, relishing the liberty and apotheoses of eternal tinkerdom. There is no artist who is not a contradiction, and the contradiction in Synge is that it was his pleasure and his source of strength to wander, and synchronously his pleasure to lie on his belly in one place where he belonged. In the same fashion he had, until he found his *métier*, read and composed music and painted discursively and dabbled with several languages, but he had only one *métier*, drama, and within it only five close-textured scenes to weave. He was rooted, but he had to find in travel the centre to which he was dedicated, and he had in all his writings to utter a note that invited his audience to the same roundabout journey to the self.

SYNGE'S OFFENCE

After the hostile reception of *The Well of the Saints* in January 1905, Yeats realised that Synge would provide the ideal ground for a battle with Dublin—for five years' confused struggle with obscurantist criticism had convinced him that a pitched battle was inevitable if the dramatic movement was to continue usefully. In February, in a letter to Quinn, the strategist in him wrote a quasi-military appreciation of the prospects: "We will have a hard fight in Ireland before we get the right for every man to see the world in his own way admitted. Synge is invaluable to us because he has that kind of intense narrow personality which necessarily raises the whole issue. It will be very curious to notice the effect of his new play. He will start next time with many enemies but with many admirers. It will be a fight like that over the first realistic plays of Ibsen".

Despite his foresight Yeats managed in his schizophrenic way to be absent from Ireland for the début of *The Playboy* two years later. Lady Gregory telegraphed "Audience broke up in disorder at the word *shift*", and, while she resolutely kept the play running against organised interruptions, he hurried back to Dublin, and announced that the following Monday the theatre would be open for a full-dress debate of the issue (the public paying for its participation). The poet and his father took the stage to face all comers. Yeats needed, and exploited, the war-cry that guaranteed his patriotism: "The author of *Cathleen ni Houlihan* addresses you". Writing the first biography of Yeats, Joseph Hone reported that night magnificently, utilising the poet's memory of thirty years later:

> My father upon the Abbey stage, before him a raging crowd:
> "This Land of Saints", and then as the applause died out,
> "Of plaster Saints"; his beautiful mischievous head thrown
>   back.

and including Mary Colum's account, an eye-witness narrative though naturally coloured by the devotion she and her fellow-students lavished on Yeats at that time:

> A motley mixture of workmen, students, and bourgeoisie in evening dress filled the theatre, most of them with denunciatory speeches ready to deliver. Yeats took the platform in

full evening dress and faced the crowd. Step by step he interpreted the play, delivering in the process some of his most
complex theories of art, one moment cowing the audience,
the next shouted down by them.... At one moment a student
supporter of his took the platform beside Yeats and made a
remark which caused nearly all of the few women in the
audience to walk out. Myself and another girl student were
the only members of the female sex in sight: we were surrounded by a group of angry males ordering us, if we were
virtuous girls, to leave the theatre. We stood our ground, and
Yeats, who, in spite of his well-publicised dimness of vision,
could always see when it suited him, saw our difficulties from
the platform and sent a couple of theatre attendants to escort
us to the stalls among the men in evening dress, who, however,
did not regard us with a friendly eye either. I never witnessed
a human being fight as Yeats fought that night, nor knew
another with so many weapons in his armory.

Moore, in the volume of *Hail and Farewell* in which he liberates
his most malicious comedy against Yeats, says unequivocally in
tribute to his *Playboy* battle: "if the play had been altered we
should all have been disgraced, and it was Yeats's courage that
saved us in Dublin. He did not argue, he piled affirmation upon
affirmation, and he succeeded in the end. . . ."
The trouble with all defences is that too many lines of defence
are offered. Synge's work was defended, at various times and
places, as: humour, which is an Irish tradition shared by everyone
from tinkers to deacons; true to folk-lore; true to fact. No one
dares to defend art and pleasure as art and pleasure.
But Yeats had calculated his hour, and he chose his debating
tactics rightly for the hour. *The Playboy* went into the tradition
of the Abbey and changed the literary movement. It ended the
interpretation of peasant life in terms of crooning and faery and
supplanted these with violence and gusto; it encouraged the
writers to greater nakedness and daring and the treatment of
motifs that disturbed the conventions; it opened their eyes to the

oddities in their milieu. Now for some years the Abbey was sent a flow of Syngian hyper-realist Irish rural scripts.

Against this work of "the school of Synge" a voice different from the narrow nationalists or the religious sectarians could eventually be heard protesting. AE came out against comedy which, he claimed, grotesquely caricatured the Irish peasant and swung too far to the opposite extreme in reaction against idealisation. In the *Irish Homestead*, August 31st, 1912, he put it: "Our young Irish dramatists, in a spirit of abject national humiliation, try to escape the terrible charge of 'sunburstery' by drawing nearly all their characters from the imbeciles, the half-witted, the knaves, drunkards, shoneens and fools of Ireland." In another attack he made a solitary exception of Padraic Colum: "Mr. Colum's peasants, in the days when they were seen there, seem to us to have been the only real human beings among the many peasants that have trod the boards of the Abbey Theatre." Regarding Synge himself, AE recognised his genius; his lieutenant, Susan Mitchell, mocked *The Playboy's* critics in some of her *Aids to the Immortality of Certain Persons in Ireland;* and he urged Yeats to protect Synge's posthumous papers from the possible censorship of a moral executor. For all this he grew to speak of Synge with a certain aloofness. His judgment in the matter of Synge and post-Syngianisms was perhaps affected by his early separation from the Abbey movement. He felt that he had played a signal part in giving the Abbey its impetus. When the brothers Fay had read the first acts of his *Deirdre* in the *All-Ireland Review*, they waited on him asking leave to perform it, and it was mounted with Yeats' *Cathleen ni Houlihan* at St. Teresa's Hall in 1902. It had displeased Yeats in the reading, but was liked by the audience; and even Yeats mildly changed his mind and allowed it some merit on the stage: "It is thin and faint, but it has the effect of wall-decoration . . . curiously dreamlike and gentle". Its modest success confirmed AE's close association with the formulation and initial conduct of the Abbey. But in 1904 he quarrelled and resigned, telling Yeats "I know you will be considerably relieved by my taking this step and that you have wished it for a long time". He believed that the theatre, left to Yeats and Lady Gregory, took several wrong turns after that. He thought and said that Yeats greatly exaggerated *The Playboy* row for the sake of publicity. Some years after Susan Mitchell published her *Aids*, she called the Abbey—in her book on Moore—a temple that smothered the religion it meant to shelter; I fancy that is an echo of AE's conversation.

Noble minds make mistakes; by and large AE's attitude to the Abbey in general and its peasant comedy in particular was a mistake. Though normally distinguished by his difference from the Irish popular mind, here he slipped into it, betrayed by that overpowerful moral sense which made him prefer everything straight, not warped as poetry is warped. He still felt what he had felt at Belmullet, that the plight of Ireland was too sad for comedy. The fact was, that the plight was sad and serious enough to require comedy—just as Joyce made comedy out of Bloom's relations with Molly to enhance, not conceal, the violence of the problem.

The vibration of a problem of the same order as Joyce's was a cause of Synge's trouble with Dublin. He was attacked by the nationalists for traducing Ireland, an attack which was short-sighted. In the subsequent years more affection accrued to Ireland from Synge's vivacity than from the nationalist legend of Irish dignity and chastity. But the complaint of a supposed political failing in Synge's work was, although framed in genuine anger and therefore in good faith, a pretext. Nationalists and Unionists alike were excited by the throb in Synge, offended by the secret images it stirred in them. It is notable that even Lady Gregory had taken alarm at this aspect of his work, which she called his "bad language". When she first heard *The Playboy* read she objected and called for deletions, and had, or believed she had, Yeats' support. But she was absent from rehearsals and the deletions were not made, and on that she blamed some of the trouble of the first night. In her journal she triumphantly observes that later performances omitted much "bad language", though the printed text retained it. The proof that "language" meant the images the language prompted lies in the famous crux: "shift".

As her telegram to Yeats pointed out, the indignant public seized on that word to illustrate the offensiveness of *The Playboy*. The *Freeman* wrote: "one of the characters makes use of a word that no refined woman would mention, even to herself". The shift had a history behind it; the anti-Parnellites had waved it in the villages in 1891 to stand for Kitty O'Shea and adultery and to drive the Chief away. It had a history in front of it: it became, thanks to 1891 and 1907, a banner of freedom of expression for the next generation; see, for example, how Frank O'Connor made a point of using it:*

> I, the old woman of Beare,
> Once a shining shift would wear,
> Now and since my beauty's fall
> I have scarce a shift at all.

In *The Playboy* it was not really the word itself but the whole image of which it is a suggestive part that shocked the audience:

> It's Pegeen I'm seeking only, and what'd I care if you brought
> me a drift of chosen females, standing in their shifts itself,
> maybe, from this place to the eastern world.

That endless line of waiting girls stirs the loins. The overt intention of the speech is, of course, absurdly pure, for Christy rejects the queue of houris, wants one girl only, and since she will not have him chooses loneliness. These conflicting considerations, the lewd possibility against the romantic purity, make the poetry of the passage. But all the audience realised in 1907 was the throb of the possibility, and they hated it because they responded with desire— and we must respond with desire or we shall not measure the antithetical awfulness of Christy's devotion to Pegeen.

There is the same shock with a group of different constituents in the priest's remark to the tinker and his bride: "To think you'd be putting deceit on me, and telling lies to me, and I going to marry you for a little sum wouldn't marry a child." In addition to the satire on the priest and the conventional comedy of Irish

*Frank O'Connor, *The Wild Bird's Nest*, Cuala Press, Dublin, 1932.

R

bulling, there is the shock in the hint of the child marrying. Synge seldom writes anything that is overtly and merely erotic, but there is the quiver of eroticism under the exaggerated talk. If David H. Greene, in his forthcoming book based on Synge's papers, prints or describes some of the early play which is reputed to have dealt with monastic life and to have had a strongly erotic tinge, we may be able to define the sexual undertow in his writing more exactly. Yet possibly its power is that it remains indefinable, coming so little into view. In Virginia Woolf's favourite metaphor (which she would not have allowed to be relevant to Synge) the fin just lifts from the wave momentarily. Partner to this sexuality which is latent and obscure is a clear look at life; a look that seemed iconoclasm to orthodox Ireland, though no icons were broken; a disinvolved look, freely delighting with an anthropologist's delight that "all things is queer in the world". Synge truly felt that no human freakery was alien to him. His free-mindedness, which did away with the accepted scale of values and postulated a new scale graded according to energy—that was Synge's offence.

And his art was to communicate to audiences, which were then appalled at themselves, the twitching assent of his nerves to human foibles. Several accounts of him report his nervousness. He admits that his toes were always wriggling, "agile as a monkey's". The Breton folklorist, Anatole le Braz, noted a perpetual trembling of his lips. In his daily life he wanted to conceal this mobility; his taciturnity was a cover, and he hoped it would be construed as evidence of a complete immobility and stoicism; he wanted to resemble the Yeatsian Parnellite ideal and impassively contain the inner "mother", the *hysterica passio*. But the incandescence of his nerves showed through. In his plays it is the motive force of the agitated music sustained from the first speech to the last and it is responsible for the sympathetic excitement which the audience suffers. He neither would remit it nor could. He did not know that he was incapable of compromise. He had that one way of writing.

It was an odd consequence of his method of operation that Yeats and AE, who otherwise differed so much, as we have seen, in their view of his kind of art, both began to plead, when they had had time to consider the significance of the troubles at the Abbey, for a new applied intelligence in Irish life. Synge had offered no particular example of intellect in action; out of his tenebrous concentration he had thrown the wild light that jangled the nerves. But to concede the value of his non-intellectual art required a public capacity for discrimination. And the real reason why the writers now resolved that the great absentee from Irish affairs was intellect, was that they had correlated the Synge battle with the battle over the Hugh Lane Gallery and both with the Parnell crisis of 1891. The modern troubles revealed that the public had learned nothing from the death of Parnell, but still sounded shibboleths and feared reality, welcomed mediocrity and shuddered at genius. They decided independently—and on the part of AE as a triumph over his concurrent anti-Abbey prejudice —on a campaign for education.

CAPTIVATING THE ENEMY

Europe accepted Synge with extraordinary speed. Nationalism and the new anthropology alike made his art, based on the primitive and regional, timely. When he was defending *The Playboy* he had argued for it in terms of "the psychic state of the locality" it described. The phrase nicely expresses the correspondence between his art and the studies in the collective which were being pioneered in the first decade of the century. He was exciting because he spoke from a politically-troubled country yet spoke of human conditions, not merely of causes; and because he went to the most primitive margin of Europe and showed the pagan past alive there together with the naivest Christianity. While Ireland was bickering over its new playwright, there were Czech performances of *In the Shadow of the Glen*, German of *The Well of the Saints*, and performances in a number of British cities.

He disliked England, not only because she was the oppressor, but because her land dispirited him—that, said Masefield, was because his knowledge was limited to London and Devon, whereas "England lies further to the north". But his biggest audience at first was in England, and possibly has remained so. We have seen in the case of Lady Gregory, Yeats, and AE, how willingly England read the literary projections of Ireland's passion for freedom from her. English readers took up Synge more rapidly and more enthusiastically even than Mrs. Watts and Newbolt had taken up *Cuchulain of Muirthemne*. Max Beerbohm showed how the reception would go when he reviewed *The Shadow* in 1904: "it illustrates a very odd thing about the Irish people—their utter incapacity to be vulgar." A Synge fervour followed in Oxford and Cambridge. Masefield, with a spice of anti-Oxford animus, noted that Synge "found the life in a man very well worth wonder, even though the man were a fool, or a knave, or just down from Oxford", and both the universities reciprocally found Ireland worth wonder and Synge worth performance, and both had given *The Well of the Saints* by January 1906. Sir Walter Raleigh's view is significant as representing the reaction of an academician of taste and goodwill though of no specially acute sense of the contemporary. In 1905 he had already lit on Synge: "There's a man called Synge", he wrote on December 7th, "a dramatist, who's a jewel. Speaks Irish. Very unlike Yeats; much more *to* him." Five years later he was buying the four volumes of the Collected Works, and fifteen years later he still regarded him as first-rate: "If you want to read a great living English author, read Thomas Hardy, if you want to read an author of twenty times Bernard Shaw's imagination, who combines truth and poetry in dealing with Ireland, read J. M. Synge." In his letter of 1910 mentioning the Collected Works he amused himself by imitating Synge's style: "If I don't be writing to you now, Lady of the House, I never will at all, for I'm in the black trouble of business and the young men to be taught, and you laughing at it all in the banqueting-house on the hill-top".* And certainly part of the attraction of Anglo-Irish writing to England was the new literary convention of peasant Anglo-Irish. Lady Gregory had pleased the Oxford firesides with it in *Cuchulain*, but Synge putting it into dramatic dialogue, which raised its intensity,

*See *Letters of Sir Walter Raleigh 1879–1922*, Methuen, London, vol. II, pp.289, 358, 521.

and adding his masculine extravagance, gave a headier brew. England was beguiled by the pleasures of familiarity and the pleasures of the alien combined in one language, and voiced as dialogue, loving or railing.

When Lady Gregory proudly cited Synge's compliment to her, that *Cuchulain* was his "daily bread", she implicitly claimed precedence in the discovery of that successful medium. She liked to think that she had shown him the way to his style. Synge was, gravely and courteously, participating in the conspiracy of compliment to her. He would have discovered his idiom without her example. They were working independently (independently except for Yeats' initial encouragement to each) to the same purpose. When Lady Gregory went folkloring to Aran, she was a little piqued to find that Synge, whom she did not yet know, was already working there. They both benefitted from their constant movement through the Irish countryside and a common power to listen instead of talk. Nevertheless, it may be that *Cuchulain* helped to *confirm* Synge. Confirmed, he became richer and more forceful than she could be, partly because she had the art to recognise but not to heighten, partly because she was too genteel. People would not speak as rudely in her presence as they would in Synge's, nor, if she heard them, would she have used what she heard. Audacity and a malicious love of shock were needed to raise the idiom from charm to poetry, and Synge had these.

The dialect captivated English readers; but they were also persuaded by the very thing that dismayed Ireland, the free energy. Shaw said in the Preface to *John Bull's Other Island* that the English were the fantasists, the Irish the practical contrivers. Whatever the truth about the inner Englishman, the certainty is that the English feel it difficult to express their fantasy freely and are delighted by every contact with foreign peoples who can freely gesticulate and orate their dreams. Synge offered the spectacle of fantasy boiling and no crust to contain it. That was irresistible.

English Syngophilia changed its complexion when *Deirdre of the Sorrows* began to circulate. The delight in fantasy and energy receded, for a time at least, in favour of melancholy beauty. The change was unfortunate, and Yeats, I am afraid, assisted it, without realising the danger, by his frequent praise of Deirdre, especially in her "Draw a little back with the squabbling of fools". That phrase leads to her suicide. *Deirdre of the Sorrows* has beauty, but a less living beauty than *The Playboy*. Synge always had a sense that Ireland's vividness was passing; it can be detected in the familiar dictum "In Ireland, for a few years more, we have a popular imagination that is fiery . . .", and in his notion that the Gaelic League would temporarily stimulate the provinces but that in the rebound from its failure (Synge expected that!) the emigrant ships to America would be doubly loaded. For the greater part of his short life his writing was the more intense because of the haste that feeling enforced. But in the last play the competition with death was too urgent, the vividness too far spent, and the speeches say not that life is life but that life is ending, Ireland ending. There is a *Götterdämmerung* hue to the frequent repetition of the prophecy that Deirdre will "bring destruction on the world". If Synge could have attempted the same story in his stronger days he would surely have done something different with it, conceivably using in the third act the opportunities for realism provided by the saga version, in which Deirdre survives Naisi for a year as Conchubor's wife before she chooses a gruesome death. In neglecting this cue Synge made his one obeisance to sentimentality. Death, and a fiancée acting his drafts in his hospital room, did that to him. England then associated Synge with Deirdre's death rather than with the vigorous cruelties of Mayo. There is always the temptation in nationalism itself to prefer what seems the noble transfiguration of suicide to rude survival, and it is not surprising if a nation's sympathisers in the enemy country thrill to the noble death instead of to political survival or political success and its mundane aftermath.

Some of the enthusiasm for Synge led to overstatements, like Yeats' comparisons with Aeschylus and Sophocles, and these in turn led to a reaction. There was, early after his death, an English middle-brow reaction which appealed for moderation. Then a highbrow reaction went to the extreme of denying him any greatness. This was in Bloomsbury. According to her diary, Virginia Woolf enjoyed a destructive week-end talk with T. S. Eliot in September 1922; she recorded how he doubted the value of all English poets since Johnson, and caned Joyce, Sacheverell Sitwell, English writers who wrote under the disabling shadow of Dostoievsky, and 'Singe'—so she spelled him. "Singe a fake", Eliot said, or V. W. thought he said. And Eliot had given signs of antipathy for Synge in his *Egoist* contributions four years earlier. Evidently he felt that the Kiltartan diction beguiled the critical judgment from its functions. We would not, he hinted analogically and ungallantly, imagine Irish girls to be so pretty but for the word "Colleen". Eliot approached Irish literature conscious of the warnings of his teacher, Babbitt, who had written:*

> The man who turns away from the masterpieces of this [Greek] tradition to study the "Nibelungenlied", or the "Chanson de Roland" or the Irish sagas is running the risk, even when he is not blinded by national enthusiasm, of impairing his sense of form.

Eliot eventually overcame the prejudice under the spur of a spontaneous admiration for Joyce—for the power, the intellect, and the experimentalism of Joyce. Part of the splendour of Eliot's long championship of Joyce is, in fact, that it was undertaken in despite of his Babitual convictions, was a triumph of instinct over education. Virginia Woolf's prejudices against Ireland proved incorrigible, the more so as they were already grounded in instinct, not doctrine. Leonard Woolf gave interest and support to Ireland through his political journalism, but she, and Bloomsbury as a whole, were the centre of anti-Hibernianism in literature. Her acquaintance, Rupert Brooke, wrote as early as 1911 a satirical expression of his vague and perhaps good-humoured sense of difference from what seemed to him the Celtic vagueness:

The Celt
Moans round with many voices.

*Irving Babbitt, *The Masters of Modern French Criticism*, Boston, 1912, p.25.

and she and her set hardened into antipathy, disliking later realist Celtic work even more than the original moan. We can see why she should dislike literature with an external mission, and Irish literature, even when it was least nationalist, was nationalist enough to incur this charge. But on other counts she might have felt a link with Yeats and with Synge. She shared Yeats' aversion for middle-class English writing. Forster could just as easily have been writing about Yeats as about her when he subsequently spoke of her distaste for "all that has characterised English fiction for good and evil during the last hundred and fifty years—faith in personal relations, recourse to humorous side-shows, insistence on petty social differences. . ."* She shared Synge's a-didacticism. They both distilled pleasure; for them whatever is, is, not necessarily right, but aromatic. But he conveyed the whiff of the one-room cottage with the pig's stall in it, she of flowers in the drawing-room and books on the shelves; and, although she had an occasional nostalgia for virility, she could not stomach his sort of it. She could not forget that she was the daughter of the Dictionary of National Biography and the foster-child of the London Library. She despised and drew away from anything "uneducated", by which she meant not "unschooled" but lacking several generations of education and therefore incapable of velleities and carefully-caught regrets and just-evoked memories (refinements which Eliot satirised in poetry but could not resist as Bloomsbury practised them). By this definition the Irish, although they had an unbroken connection with the eighteenth century, were uneducated.

Late in life Virginia Woolf made an attempt to represent the appeal of Irish nationalism. When she planned *The Years*, which was to document her class in her time, she knew that she could not ignore a force that had evoked so much passion. She drew the picture of the younger sister, Delia, who transfers her family's militant energy from an English to an Irish cause (the elder sister had preferred social welfare and feminism). Delia worships Parnell, goes to Brighton to work for him. But the end of her Celtic

*E. M. Forster on Virginia Woolf, in the *Criterion*, April 1926.

ardour is that she marries an Irishman who is a Unionist. That twist—catching the irony of life in the manner of Hardy—is psychologically accurate; but I detect the overtone of a jeer. Even in the nostalgic context of the much-decried but important and moving *Years*, Virginia Woolf could not wholly forget Bloomsbury's hostility to the Irish. The Irish were equally hostile to Bloomsbury. The reciprocal insensitivity should be analysed one day.

It may have particularly harmed Synge with Bloomsbury that he had been friends with Masefield, whose record of their few London walks and meals together became a standard document in the very scanty archives of Synge. In the 'twenties the Woolfs and Eliot reacted against the public overestimation of Masefield, realising, what the general public did not, that he attempted far more than he could do. He had, however, his own limited but real range, and his most effective writing shared Synge's tang of open-air experience. But Bloomsbury saw no reason to admire an Irishman who had affinities, however superficial, with a Georgian.

SYNGE AND JOYCE

When Joyce was a young man, "proud as Lucifer" according to AE, he treated everything that was shown to him with arrogance. Yet some of the work that he apparently disposed of with superb detachment stayed in his mind and became sympathetic and a touchstone. Gorman says that Joyce picked out faults in *Riders to the Sea* that Paris morning in 1902 when Synge put the typescript in front of him, but he translated it a little later, and fifteen years later listed it among the Celtic dramas to be presented by his English Players in Switzerland and wrote this programme-note:*

> Whether a brief tragedy be possible or not (a point on which Aristotle had some doubts) the ear and the heart mislead one gravely if this brief scene from "poor Aran" be not the work of a tragic poet.

But while *Riders* meant so much to him alike for personal reasons,

*Quoted by Herbert Gorman in *James Joyce*, Farrar and Rinehart, New York, 1939, p.258.

the associations of youth clustering round it, and for its appeal
to the classicist in him whose original preference was for clarity
and economy of form, the Synge work which became the
subject of his emulation was *The Playboy*. Gorman has documented
his agitated reaction when the news of the *Playboy* row reached
him, through an English press report, in Rome. He wrote to his
brother: "The whole affair has upset me. I feel like a man in a
house who hears a row in the street and voices he knows shouting
but can't get up to see what the hell is going on".*

The nearest thing to drama in early Irish literature is the
Colloquy between Ossian and Patrick, a flyting in which the heroic
pagan view of life and the Christian view are compared as Ossian
yields control of Ireland to the "man of croziers". In *Ulysses*, as
Hugh Kenner has pointed out,† Joyce remembers his 1902
meeting with Synge and transforms it "into St. Patrick's meeting
in the forest with the archaic Ossian whom it is his destiny to
supersede". The *Playboy* row was the essential reason why Joyce
chose Synge, rather than, say, Yeats, whose poetry he devotedly
admired, as the man to be superseded. Joyce heard of the Abbey
tumult at the critical moment when he was feeling towards his
future mode, but did not yet see it clear; he was actually about to
write *The Dead* which marks a great advance in his power and
his first assimilation of warmth and nostalgia, yet is still short of
the heterogeneity which would surpass Synge's. The news stirred
excitement and envy at what he had not yet discovered and
Synge had. He was confident that he could do better, could out-
shift Synge by the mere dropping of a letter and fifty variations
on it; and in the result he did go beyond not merely the disputed
word but the whole image it supports. He knew that he could
take the action from the unworldly fringe of Aran into the
populous city where—as Synge himself soon realised—Ireland's
future would, for all the predilections of Yeats and Lady Gregory,
be shaped.

*Ibid., p.188.
†Hugh Kenner, *Dublin's Joyce*, Chatto and Windus, London, 1955, p.356. But Kenner
has dealt summarily with the paragraph and there is much in it that awaits further
explanation.

In the Joyce hierarchy the old master is significant; it is not altogether derogatory if an arrogant young man thinks another artist fit for him to supersede. Synge had characteristics which won Joyce's respect and sense of kinship. He was a solitary. He never compromised. (Yeats, as Joyce points out in *Ulysses* and in *The Day of the Rabblement*, did.) Synge worked with the brutality of Ireland, and with the darkness, for though he made it glitter with lights his material was originally that darkest Belmullet that had disheartened AE. Joyce had chosen darkness and paralysis for his study, and was gradually delving to the fires within it. Synge had looked at the sanctities of Church and sex and seen them new. Joyce was to explore the same way and beyond. Synge had provoked the fury of the rabble, Joyce hoped for the same fury to prove the excellence of his art.

Moreover, Synge was a foil to Joyce's ambition because he was a dramatist. When he started to write he meant to be a fellow-practitioner of Ibsen, then of Jonson. One of the consequences of his wilful exile in countries speaking languages not his own was that he could never fulfil that intention, which can only be developed if a man has a stage constantly at his disposal for trial and can there test his pressures on an audience which knows the nuances of his language. In any case, the cast of his mind was not ultimately dramatic. But he had gifts for the dramatic detail though not for the dramatic whole; and while these do not function when he uses the dramatic form—there he is like a man tongue-tied from excess of desire—they do come into action in his novels. His dramatic devices incorporated into the narratives include, as I shall illustrate in the next chapter, borrowings from Jonson; there may be borrowings from his favourite Ibsen; and there are certainly effects learned from Synge. Among the Syngianisms are the following: absorbing the objective scene into the voice; dramatising the comedy of filth taken from life; marrying comedy with poetry.

The communication of the objective scene through dialogue is a striking skill of Synge's plays. No writer has reproduced pictures of the outer scene so sharply as this egocentric and apparently inward-looking man. It is, of course, common and relatively easy for a sensitive writer to put the thing observed, countryside or town, into descriptive prose, while the action halts and waits on it. Synge puts the country smells, sounds and sights, the streams running between rocks, into his dialogue, so that they belong to the action and go with it, not stop it or obtrude. Joyce recognised this art in Synge and imitated it. He too, in his mature work, never stops to describe. Though writing the prose of the novel, he carries the Irish scene as the dramatist does, through dialogue or the tone and imagery of the monologuist.

In *Dubliners* Joyce is too intense and indignant to write the comedy of filth. There are hints of it, not consummated. The same is still approximately true of *A Portrait of the Artist*. The student breaking wind, for example, is realism, but not yet comic realism. It took a great deal of meditation before he could equal Sara Tansey smelling the shoe. That was how he had to go, by way of Sara to reach his more violent comedy of ravished holyhead. Synge had drawn Sara and her natural nostrils from Irish reality. Perhaps the prototype of the scene can be identified in the anecdote that Synge enjoyed telling Masefield, that one night when he lodged in a country cabin, he asked for a basin to wash, and was given a wooden box well-smoothed with much use, and in the morning was roused by a call from his host: "Have you washed yourself yet? Herself is wanting the box to make up the bread in?" Synge worked, and Joyce, more industriously but with the same stomachy relish, set himself to work, to transform Irish fact. Everything that made the Heraclitans like AE miserable, they transformed, not merely by word-play but first in their understanding, into comedy: they metamorphosed alcohol, prostitution, jobbery, reek. The vital point, however, is that their comedy is not an oscillation from anger to the other extreme. They married comedy and poetry, so that the comedy is in touch with what mourns in man. Synge showed how this could be done, and he made his demonstration when it was urgently necessary. The early Abbey experiments in drama tended to separate poetry and comedy. The fault was initially Yeats'. He was up, he later acknowledged, at "the high window" of an esoteric dramatic verse. Lady Gregory felt that from his rarification "ear and mind crave ease and unbending" and tentatively sketched lower and simpler comedies; and Yeats saw the point and made attempts with his own at comedies with only a trace of poetry. Without a theory to prompt him, on his instinct, Synge saw that the splitting of the genres was unhealthy. He corrected it with his hetergeneous form, and Joyce took that over for *Ulysses* and *Finnegans Wake*, plunging deeper into the dark than Synge could go, though Synge was not lacking in audacity—only Synge perished quickly in the struggle, and Joyce was tenacious, paying for his discoveries with parts of his body but, like Captain Carpenter, riding determinedly.

In the essays describing Synge's pilgrimages through Ireland there are a dozen things that could have, and may have, been suggestive to Joyce. Did Joyce read Synge's sentences on the Ceathair Aluinn, the Four Comely Ones, from whose island cemetery the Saint fetched the holy water that cures blindness (and Joyce was combatting blindness when he conceived the Four)? Did he read the description of the Inishmaan girls washing their flannels in the surf—"Their red bodices and white tapering legs make them as beautiful as tropical sea-birds"—and remember it in *A Portrait*, or was his distant encounter with the girl on the Liffey estuary real and so strong that it needed no reinforcement? Did he read in the Wicklow sketches the Enniskerry balladsinger's jingle

> Botheration
> Take the nation,
> Calculation,
> In the stable,
> Cain and Abel,
> Tower of Babel,
> And the Battle of Waterloo

which is a resumé of *Finnegans Wake*? There are other possible points of contact; but I have come across nothing that proves that

Joyce read Synge's travel prose. Mulligan in *Ulysses* derides the "pampooties" that are several times described in the Aran papers, but very likely Joyce could turn that joke without the help of a text. However, Joyceans may know of a link. The *Complete Works* of Synge were among the books that Joyce retained after the 1938-9 sale of his library, but that was the Random House edition of 1935, and its retention proves only his affection for the works and the memories surrounding them.

CHAPTER VII

JAMES AUGUSTINE JOYCE

1882-1941

EVERY ambitious bookseller hopes to discover a copy of the lost pamphlet *Et Tu, Healy*. Joyce was nine when Parnell was destroyed. He wrote a poem of passion for the leader and denunciation of Healy, prototype of a figure he was to see, or imagine he saw, throughout his own life, the friend who begins as the *fidus Achates* but becomes the traitor. His father, a man upheld among crumbling finances by an extraordinary sense of caste, and drawn by a temperamental affinity towards Parnell's amoral despotism, had the poem printed.

In the Christmas-dinner scene of *A Portrait of the Artist*—which led H. G. Wells in his early review in the *New Republic*, in March 1917, to compare his art with Sterne's—Joyce has told of the charge laid on him to remember Parnell's fall and riven Ireland:

—O, he'll remember all this when he grows up, said Dante hotly—the language he heard against God and religion and priests in his own home.
—Let him remember too, cried Mr. Casey to her from across the table, the language with which the priests and the priests' pawns broke Parnell's heart and hounded him into his grave. Let him remember that too when he grows up.

He wrote it into the world's memory. In all his work there is an enquiry into the actual circumstances of Parnell's rise and fall, and a brooding on their implications and the legend that Ireland made of them.

Joyce was born at Dublin in 1882. His family was Catholic; his great-grandfather on his father's side was a cousin of Daniel O'Connell. He was educated at Catholic schools and the Catholic University College, Dublin. Under the university syllabus he studied Italian, and in his leisure he learned Norwegian to read Ibsen. Ibsen seemed to him to have chastised and stirred a country as narrow as Ireland and to have become a world-master through his attack on a local conscience. He wanted to do as much, and thought that he would have to imitate Ibsen's exile in Italy, Mohammed's flight to Medina, as the essential de-restricting preliminary. He had a conviction, justified in the result, that in Europe he would see Ireland in perspective, document her more significantly under the stimulus of continental movements. *Ulysses* bears a trace of a complementary hope of carrying a message from Ireland to Europe—"Missionary to Europe after fiery Columbanus". It is recorded in the tone of ridicule; yet he accomplished that too.

His first sortie was to Paris in November 1902. He had hoped to study medicine but found that impossible, and spent the winter reading Ben Jonson in the Bibliothèque Nationale and speculating on aesthetics in the light of the dicta of Aristotle and Aquinas. In the spring of 1903 he was called home to his dying mother. In June 1904 he met Nora Barnacle, "deadleaf brown with quick-silver appliqués", and left for Europe with her in October. He spent the rest of his life on the Continent, except for a brief 1909–10 attempt to establish a Dublin cinema for four continental enterprisers, and a summer holiday in Dublin and Galway in 1912.

He had made his first draft of an autobiography by the beginning of 1904—a part of which was posthumously published as *Stephen Hero*, a clear, bare, self-centred account of his student life. Deliberately seeking to put aside its solipsism and to translate the criticism of his society into objective representations of it, he worked at his stories, *Dubliners*. One or two were published in the *Irish Homestead*, most were ready for book-publication by

1905, but the resistance of publishers and printers (who, like the professional readers of Hardy's first novel, smelled mischief) was not overcome, despite contracts, until 1914. A small volume of quasi-Jacobean lyrics, *Chamber Music*, had appeared in 1907. It caught the attention of Pound, who wrote to Joyce in 1913 for permission to use "I hear an army charging" in the *Imagist Anthology*, and discovered in the correspondence that Joyce had *A Portrait* in manuscript. As an adviser to the *Egoist* Pound recommended this autobiography to the editor; it was printed as a serial from February 1914 to September 1915. At the end of 1916 Ben Huebsch in New York published it in book form. The play *Exiles*, which Joyce had written in 1914–15, was published in 1918; the author worked devotedly to obtain performances. There were several near-misses. In England Bernard Shaw intervened to have it cancelled from the Stage Society's programme. It was produced in a German translation in Munich in 1919, but withdrawn at once, and, though it has since been occasionally attempted on both sides of the Atlantic, has only a meagre theatre-history.

As early as 1906, when he was in Rome, an idea for a story to be called *Ulysses*, with a Dublin advertisement canvasser called Mr. Hunter as its hero, was in his mind. He started work on the novel *Ulysses* in 1914. Offered the early chapters at the outset of 1918, the editor of the *Little Review*, Margaret Anderson, called to her assistant Jane Heap "This is the most beautiful thing we'll ever have to publish".* Beginning March that year, twenty-three instalments were published before the Society for the Suppression of Vice interfered. In London the *Egoist* printed five instalments between January and December 1919. The *Egoist's* editor, Miss Harriet Weaver (whose assistant from 1917 to 1919 was T. S. Eliot) tried to persuade the Woolfs to undertake book-publication through their private Hogarth Press; Virginia refused to see the point and showed the bulky manuscript to her visitors as a joke— but at the end of her life remembered, as a historical moment,

---

*See Magalaner and Kain, *Joyce, the Man, the Work, the Reputation,* New York University Press, New York, 1956, p.162.

R

how one guest, Katherine Mansfield, gradually stopped smiling as she turned over the pages and said "But there's something in this". The book was published in Paris in 1922. Joyce began to rough out sketches for a new work, setting various themes in motion, waiting patiently till he could establish connections between them, then rewriting and complicating the texture of the book. The process took sixteen years: *Finnegans Wake* was published simultaneously in England and America in 1939. There had in the meantime been further short poems, *Pomes Penyeach* in 1927, and a gathering, *Collected Poems*, in 1936.

Until Pound came to his help in 1913 Joyce had worked only from his belief in himself, meeting discouragement everywhere. The next eight years were still a period of struggle, though support was now coming. After *Ulysses* had appeared, he was recognised as a master, and disciples resorted to him in Paris. In the *Stephen Hero* draft he had predicted the high "cost of being exceptional". The cost of twenty years of lonely individuality and the constant necessity of looking inward was a series of maladies of the eye, operations, and semi-blindness. There may be a sense in which he chose his affliction in emulation of Homer and Milton, but there evidently had to be a devastating affliction. Campbell and Robinson, the authors of the pioneer *Skeleton Key to Finnegans Wake*, noted his usage of Prometheus, Jason, and Jacob ". . . the hero who wrests symbols of life substance from an older dispensation. Often as in the case of Prometheus (and H.C.E.), atonement is exacted." Joyce felt that he had performed in literature and for Ireland the Promethean function, and as proof he paid the penalty. Moreover, in the intensity of his concentration he generated a psychic field which disturbed those around him, especially his daughter, whom he loved as passionately as an over-developed intellect must love an *anima*-figure.

THE ARTIST AS HERO

Like Yeats he was militantly ambitious from the start. His patterns at first were dramatic adventurers: Hamilton Rowan, Napoleon, Marshal Browne, the Count of Monte Cristo. The events of 1891–2 and his father's tears for Parnell established the "dead king" as his model. Then he felt the appeal of the Jesuit soldier-saints. When he reacted in his teens from a precocious patronage of the Dublin brothels in favour of an extreme religious phase, it seemed that he might enter the priesthood. He had an intuition of the priest as hero. He rejected it because it meant community, the loss of distinction in equality of duty—and "the pride of his spirit . . . had always made him conceive himself as a being apart in every order". His decision against the Church was confirmed when he saw a girl wading on the beach; he had been looking for a sign of the potentialities of the secular life, and she supplied it, suggesting "the gates of all the ways of error and glory"; with an image of a flower "glimmering and trembling, trembling and unfolding" he authorised himself to live the artist as hero.

A passage in *Stephen Hero* describes the insufficiency to the near-adult of the political versions of heroism:

> the temptation which Satan was allowed to dangle before the eyes of Jesus . . . is, in reality, the most ineffectual temptation to offer any man of genius . . . for Jesus the kingdom of this world must have been a very empty phrase indeed—at least when he had outgrown a romantic youth. ≪Satan, really, is the romantic youth of Jesus re-appearing for a moment. I had a romantic youth,≫ too, when I thought it must be a grand thing to be a material Messias: that was the will of my father who will never be in heaven. But now such a thought arises in my mind only in moments of great physical weakness.*

The artist is a hero because he sees what mediocrity cannot see and dares to report it. That opinion Joyce retained all his life. At the period of *Stephen Hero* he also thought—but it is debatable and must be considered later how far he retained it—that the greatest artist is a Messiah, whose reports will change his people. When at the age of twenty-four he argued with Grant Richards

*Theodore Spencer, who edited *Stephen Hero*, (New Directions, Norfolk, Conn., 1944,) used the notation ≪ ≫ to enclose phrases that Joyce had scored out.

for the printing of an uncensored text of *Dubliners* he insisted
that the function of the stories, which any mitigation of them
would dislocate, was to change the Irish by mirroring their
deformities:

> ... I believe that in composing my chapter of moral history
> in exactly the way I have composed it I have taken the first
> step towards the spiritual liberation of my country

and again

> It is not my fault [i.e. it is Dublin's which he has described
> naturalistically] that the odour of ashpits and old weeds and
> offal hangs round my stories. I seriously believe that you will
> retard the course of civilisation in Ireland by preventing the
> Irish people from having one good look at themselves in my
> nicely polished glass.*

He rather grimly urged a claim to be doing something not done
before.

George Moore, however, had already made a bid in the same
direction, three bids. Joyce may possibly not have read *A Drama
in Muslin* or *Parnell and his Island*, but he certainly knew *The Untilled Field*. *Dubliners* is another *Untilled Field*, closely connecting
with it at two points: they both attack the dirt of Ireland, and the
ignorance they make it represent; and they both catch a Russian
quality, which Moore had deliberately borrowed from Turgenev,
and which Joyce now borrowed from Moore. Joyce knew the
resemblance, but disregarded it; for Moore was nearer to him
than any other writer, Catholic, knowledgeable about Ireland,
ready to cry unpleasant facts aloud; and Joyce was jealous at the
likeness, and guarded against any suggestion that Moore had
anticipated him. He did not want to have an Irish Catholic
precursor. He saw to it, to justify his claims, that he did the work
of reporting his country more closely and energetically than
Moore could. Moore had made his tales, despite their realism,
artistic in a shapely Paterian sense. While Joyce's stories have an

---

Letters of James Joyce, edited Stuart Gilbert, London, Faber and Faber, 1957, pp.62–4.

extraordinary art, it is carefully hidden, and he contrived an outer effect of what he perfectly called "scrupulous meanness". Moore openly abused his audience. Joyce, without uttering a word of abuse in his own voice, described the facts and let them speak and smell* their meaning. As the stories *were* tighter and harder than Moore's, who was in any case now working a different mode, Joyce was perhaps entitled to talk like a pioneer.

In 1901 he had announced his independence of the Irish literary movement. At that date the literary movement was as near as it ever was to be, to the simple-minded political wing of nationalism. Joyce's nationalist friends lived, he thought, in make-believe: they talked about Irish chastity, whereas he regarded the Irish peasant as *le grand masturbateur;* they talked about the importance of Gaelic, which he regarded as a blunt instrument; they raved against commercial England's materialism, while he argued that the Irish peasant was rapacious as the Yorkshire peasant and that the first result of Irish political success would be the bolstering of Irish commerce.† He was amazed in 1901 to hear the senior men of the Irish literary movement talking like student politicians. Yeats and Moore were paying lip-service to Gaelic, although they could not use it; Yeats, Lady Gregory and AE were lauding the spirituality and imagination of the bog; and he was afraid that the dramatisation of the early epic-cycles, just beginning, would flatter the Irishman into complacency rather than show him his own responsibility for his problems. He wrote a denunciation of

---

*Note the place of smell in the Irish writing of this critical period. George Moore had maliciously said Yeats had no olfactory sense, meaning he was not Irish enough. Yeats was jolted. He had been cultivating a very special olfactory sensitivity; in reading Henry More he had discovered how that seventeenth-century philosopher distilled fine perfumes from his body, and had been concentrating to do it too. But this was an escape from real Ireland. So (as the mutual taunting of the Irish writers was usually dynamic) he proceeded, very slowly but effectively, to develop a realist nostril. See the formidable late epigram, *A Stick of Incense.*

†A passage in George Borach's *Conversations with James Joyce* (translated by Joseph Prescott in *College English*, vol. XV, no. 6. March 1954), reveals how Joyce interpreted Odysseus in his own image. "Odysseus didn't want to go off to Troy: he knew that the official reason for the war, the dissemination of the culture of Hellas, was only a pretext for the Greek merchants, who were seeking new markets." Change "war" to "revolution" and "Hellas" to "Ireland" and you have Joyce exposing current ideals (after Ibsen's example). He was not against Ireland's commercial development: he subsequently made that clear: he was against the promotion of it under sentimental trappings, and the self-deception that made that possible.

the process as an article for his college magazine, and when the authorities pitched it out published it in pamphlet. *The Day of the Rabblement* contends that the Yeatsians had properly begun their work in Dublin as a mission against the tawdry and vulgar, but "after the first encounter"—he means the struggle over *The Countess Cathleen*—"surrendered to the popular will". He quoted Giordano Bruno against them: "No man, said the Nolan, can be a lover of the true or the good unless he abhors the multitude; and the artist, though he may employ the crowd, is very careful to isolate himself".* If Joyce had been born six years later and had been in college during the *Playboy* row, which capsized Yeats' dream of a popular theatre, he might have had to adopt a different position towards the Abbey; unless, perhaps, in any context he would have found causes to quarrel and take an independent path, since that was his real determination.

Joyce was confirmed in his isolationism when he read Jonson in the winter 1902–3. He stiffened himself to repeat Jonson's contemptuous battle with the audience, to live the challenge of the Apologeticall Dialogue:

> if I proue the pleasure of but one,
> So he iudicious be; He shall b'alone
> A Theatre unto me: Once, I'll say,
> To strike the eare of time, in those fresh straines,
> As shall, beside the cunning of their ground,
> Giue cause to some of wonder, some despight,
> And unto more, despaire, to imitate their sound.
> I, that spend halfe my nights, and all my dayes,
> Here in a cell, to get a darke, pale face,
> To come forth worth the iuy, or the bayes,
> And in this age can hope no other grace—
> Leaue me. There's something come into my thought,
> That must, and shall be sung, high, and aloofe,
> Safe from the wolues black iawe, and the dull asses hoofe.

*Yeats may have been strengthened in his readiness to fight the audience by Joyce's pamphlet and his conduct as an uncompromising isolationist. It has been noted on an earlier page how wonderfully Yeats could learn from a younger man. If Joyce's rather priggish reprimand annoyed him on first reading, events soon showed its validity.

After 1907 Yeats made the same passage his touchstone, incorporated it into the great sonnet at the end of *Responsibilities*, and thought of it when he abandoned hope of the popular stage of Shakespeare or Sophocles and turned to a select chamber audience.

In *Dubliners* Joyce intended to teach the Irish masters a lesson by doing what they were not yet doing: showing the reality of Ireland rather than the hallucinations. One story, *A Mother*, pivots on this very issue of the self-deceptions of nationalism. Mrs. Kearney's daughter is called Kathleen. "When the Irish Revival began to be appreciable Mrs. Kearney determined to take advantage of her daughter's name and brought an Irish teacher to the house." The assistant secretary of the *Eire Abu* Society is called Mr. Holohan. He invites Kathleen to appear as pianist in a series of concerts which his society will give in the Antient Concert Rooms (where Yeats had launched the national dramatic movement with *The Countess Cathleen*). Mrs. Kearney is ready to show off her daughter's accomplishments, but insists on a contract for an eight-guinea fee in advance. The fee is unpaid, Mrs. Kearney says "She won't go on without her money", and she doesn't go on. Mrs. Kearney orders her family home:

> As she passed through the doorway, she stopped and glared into Mr. Holohan's face.
> "I'm not done with you yet," she said.
> "But I'm done with you," said Mr. Holohan.
> Kathleen followed her mother meekly. Mr. Holohan began to pace up and down the room, in order to cool himself for he felt his skin on fire.
> "That's a nice lady!" he said. "O, she's a nice lady."

The story is a chain of sneers: at the middle-class fashionability of Gaelic, no more serious than a decorative vogue; at the artificiality of the concert arrangements; at the commercialism of spiritual Ireland epitomised in Mrs. Kearney's insistence on contract and fee; and the points are summed up in the choice of names. Joyce is playing on the sentimental name of Ireland, Cathleen ni Houlihan, and especially on the recent resurgence of her image through Yeats' popular playlet. He splits Kathleen off from Holohan, and puts them at loggerheads over a miserable fee.

Sometimes the symbols in *Dubliners* tell of light struggling to illuminate the corrupt darkness of the city. Little Chandler, as his name shows, is a potential source of a little light in Dublin. But he is easily snuffed out. Lights flicker, darkness supervenes: that is, deliberately, the overall effect. If we give too much attention to the symbols, we may lose it. In the contrapuntal play of symbols and a Zola-esque naturalism—and by 1903 Joyce knew at least *Au Bonheur des Dames* and described it admiringly as "an epic for drapers"—it is essential that the naturalistic reportage prevail and leave its dead taste with the reader.

Joyce felt a certain contrition at the bleak picture. His biographer, Gorman, reports how, in the late summer of 1906, he wrote to his brother:

Sometimes thinking of Ireland, it seems to me that I have been unnecessarily harsh. I have reproduced (in *Dubliners*, at least) none of the attractions of the city. . . . I have not reproduced its ingenuous insularity and its hospitality. . . . I have not been just to its beauty. . .*

Next year he set out to compensate by writing a final story for the volume, *The Dead*, and reproduced in it something he loved, the hospitality, music and warmth of late-Victorian Ireland. But that very story implied in the outcome a still deeper paralysis. A paralysis, however, that could be overcome when Joyce had gone deeper still into it and discovered the problems beneath it; and he did that in *Ulysses*, whereupon he also was able to do justice to the vigour in Dublin.

A Portrait of the Artist as a Young Man pursues the purposes of *Dubliners* but adds to them, and it represents a change in technique and a step-back in time so that Joyce may explain himself. The autobiographical elements in *Dubliners* were severely controlled into objective documents of public corruption. In *A Portrait* the autobiography is overt and dominates the narrative. In *Ulysses*

*See Herbert Gorman, *James Joyce*, Farrar and Rinehart, New York, 1939, p.170.

and *Finnegans Wake* it is combined with non-autobiographical material so that the critic and the subjects of his criticism are shown and explained simultaneously and equally. Joyce had so complete a conviction of his heroic stature that it seemed natural to him from the start that he should write his story. He thought, what Moore was soon to lay down as a principle, that an autobiography is a perfectly possible form for a sacred book. The last pages of *A Portrait* frankly claim a Messianic mission. He conceives his friend Cranley as John the Baptist. He goes, like Mohammed, into exile "to forge in the smithy of my soul the uncreated conscience of my race". By writing his own story he says three things to the Irish: let me show you how backward you look to me; let me show you how I have fortified and sharpened myself, imitate me; see how I have sacrificed myself for you. If the name Daedalus is a claim of intellect and creativeness, the name Stephen is a claim of a sacrificial Christ-function. In the Irish celebration of St. Stephen's Day, a wren was killed and carried about the town hung on a stick. The theme of the crucified king of the birds later runs through *Finnegans Wake* as one of the mutating motifs, Joyce examining his early claim from all angles favourable and adverse. In *A Portrait* the claims are simple and arrogant.

Joyce was arrogant because everyone around him was paying service to shibboleths, behind which he saw barbarism. *A Portrait* continues the exposure of facts begun in *Dubliners*, but drops naturalism for symbols. He wants to show Ireland as primitive, blind, groping, and chooses the symbols of a bat; a dull stare of terror in the eyes, the terror of soul of a starving village under curfew; a pregnant wife, half-undressed, inviting a stranger into her empty cottage—"a type of her race and of his own, a batlike soul waking to the consciousness of itself in darkness and secrecy and loneliness and, through the eyes and voice and gesture of a woman without guile, calling the stranger to her bed". He is told of an old man in a mountain cabin in the west who says "Ah, there must be terrible queer creatures at the latter end of the world", and is horrified by the exhibition of peasant ignorance: "I fear him. I fear his redrimmed horny eyes. It is with him I must struggle all through this night till day come, till he or I lie dead, gripping him by the sinewy throat till . . . Till what? Till he yield to me? No, I mean him no harm." His readers are meant to adopt these images from his mental life into their own. They are dynamic; they are to be worked on by the "active imagination"; the dramas they describe have more than one possible outcome; Joyce thinks Ireland can determine her future by brooding on them as he does.

AE in his early solitary wanderings used to disinter characters like the old man of the mountain cabin. He usually made them say something magnificent. To Joyce their wittering is horrible. AE may perhaps lie behind this red-eyed old man who commits him to a night-long struggle. Joyce's attitude to AE was always odd. He wrote of him as the absurd and pontifical opposite of Stephen, yet the fact is that there were similarities between the young Joyce and the AE of fifteen years earlier. Just as AE had searched for the sound which represented "the most primeval thought" and read the theosophists and oriental scriptures for clues, Joyce "read Blake and Rimbaud on the values of the letters and even permuted and combined the five vowels to construct cries for primitive emotions".* Just as AE dramatised for himself the primitive vegetable world, Joyce "doubled backwards into the past of humanity and caught glimpses of emergent art as one might have a vision of the pleiosaurus emerging from his ocean of slime". A good deal that seems bad-mannered in Joyce's attitude to AE is clearer when a fundamental resemblance underneath the younger man's greater erudition and agility is taken into account. Joyce made a call at AE's for a conversation. He conducted the talk with the pride of Lucifer; but it was Stephen in search of a father. Detecting a kinship, he could not resist a tributary visit, though he promptly shied away from the older man's heavy, vague manner. He borrowed money from him but would not repay it. He wanted to be recognised by AE, and when he was insufficiently recognised, and then condemned by

*Stephen Hero, edited by Theodore Spencer, p.32. The next quotation is a cancelled passage from p.37 of the same book.

the drear moralist in the poet for taking Nora away to Europe, he blasted him. He could only be a rebellious son.

COMPLEX STRUCTURES

The *Stephen Hero* draft, the foundation on which *A Portrait* was raised, contains much non-symbolic plain argumentation about the shortcomings of Ireland and her nationalist ideology, very little of which was retained in *A Portrait*, not because Joyce had changed his opinions but because he had decided to jettison the scaffolding by which he had reared his symbols. In his early career he valued clarity. To sculpt clear outlines, free of jagged fringes, obscurities and uncertainties; to eliminate distractions and shape the residue into concord; that was his first consideration during his twenties and early thirties. That was the process that produced the poems of *Chamber Music* and the paragraphs of *A Portrait*. At the beginning of *Ulysses* there are passages that still derive from it. The early passage that describes the *Rosevean* coming up the Liffey is beautiful, but too beautiful; its over-perfection, though intended to write a period to Part I, disturbs. The extension of Joyce's art lay through the abdication of autonomous perfection in favour of complex structures within which no part need be self-explanatory. During heavy composition of *Ulysses* Joyce observed "I fear I have little imagination". If imagination means inventing, this is right; his art was to organise with exacting intricacy. That was what he had learned in the school of old Aquinas. His complex structures were conceived in the image of the Catholic Church, and while he was attacking the Church for impeding the enlightenment of Ireland he was building *Ulysses* in its image. Then he went on to extend his power of complication from other antique sources. *Finnegans Wake* is Cabbalistic in its techniques, oriental in its convolution and involution.

One of the Joycean paradoxes is that though he consistently wrote autobiography and worked from himself outwards, he found it difficult to release his personal feelings. The formality of his daily life, a formality by which he insulated himself from the world, has been documented by his acquaintances. For his feelings to come through into his writings he had to concentrate on organisational problems. In *Ulysses* he set himself a series of puzzles: to devise a plot which would run parallel with the plot of the *Odyssey*, detail equated with detail; to make each chapter represent (through its incidents, tempo, tone and vocabulary) a colour, a part of the anatomy, a technic; to effect a steady convergence of his major characters and themes. T. S. Eliot wrote in an early comment that feelings matter most in Joyce. "Crudity and egoism", he said, are the hallmark of Irish writers but are "justified by exploitation to the point of greatness, in the later work of Mr. James Joyce. Mr. Joyce's mind is subtle, erudite, even massive; but it is not like Stendhal's an instrument continually tempering and purifying emotion; it operates within the medium, the superb current of his feelings". It is true that the feelings are grand and matter most; it is also true that nothing tempers them; but we must add, what Eliot could not yet see or say in that 1919 comment but acknowledged later, that they are contained by maximally formal writing, and they rush powerfully because forced through its grilles.*

Joyce's complexity was a necessity to him, and it doubled the force of his feelings by channelling them; and he found an additional purpose for it in *Ulysses*—he proffered it as a decoy. His material was drawn from living people who must be protected. He contrived his writing so that it should compel the attention of serious readers but yield its meaning to them only after a generation of fascinated playing among the outerworks of the technique. The first generation of critics enjoyed the tabulation of his tricks, and read the novel more as if it were the Greek than the Dublin *Odyssey*. But the Dublin reality and Joyce's feelings about it matter more. He made out of his private problems a story which integrated them with the national problems of Ireland, and permanent problems of man. What is most amazing in the end is not the ingenuity which the critics love (by which, for example, Joyce breakfasts Bloom on kidneys, because in the Old Testament the kidneys were associated with the

*Eliot was reviewing Yeats' *The Cutting of an Agate* in the *Athenaeum*, July 4th, 1919.

heart as the seat of the emotions), but the power which makes Stephen and Bloom so important to us that we think with them for days after a reading, trying to understand some phrase they throw up in their introspecting—as if the mystery of human experience lay in their memories, and if we could draw the cloud away we should know more about the human drama than ever before.

At the beginning of *Ulysses* there is a scatter of overt biography to connect the novel with *A Portrait*. *A Portrait* finished with Stephen leaving for Paris. Now back in Dublin Stephen recollects the events of the Paris winter. To those critics who have denied that Stephen is Joyce it must be answered that these recollections are nothing unless they are autobiography, and that they are a kind of autobiography conspicuously absent from *A Portrait*: there everything showed the artist's heroism, here Joyce realises that he can only describe the artist properly by admitting his debits too—his dirt, fears, guilt. And by describing the artist's subject-matter, the common man and the common woman. *Ulysses* essentially operates like *Six Characters in Search of an Author*: in both works the finished result is the story of the discovery of the materials used for it and combines the making and the made. Pirandello's play was ready, like Joyce's book, in 1921. Gide used the same procedure for *Les Faux-Monnayeurs*—published in 1925, but the first entry in the journal for it is dated June 17th, 1919. The dates suggest that none of these writers depended on the precedent of another, but that the mirroring, self-documenting form is a symptom of the time.

One of Joyce's most brilliant strokes was to make his Irish common man Jewish. He saw that this would amplify the range of allusion. The Jew as an exile and wanderer represented the life he had chosen and man moving through the incertitude of the void. Again, as indicated in the first chapter of this book, it was an Irish convention in Joyce's time and his father's to compare the Irish and Jewish destinies. The purpose of the comparison was to promise Ireland escape from the house of bondage and a feast of liberation. Behind it lay a mythical connection, such as other western peoples cherish in their legends, between the early Irish and the Near East. In Douglas Hyde's *Literary History of Ireland* Joyce had come across a passage which stimulated his ingenuity. Hyde describes how the founder of the modern Irish race, Milesius, son of Breogan, traced his genealogy through twenty-two Gaelic names and thirteen Hebrew names "passing through Japhet and ending in Adam". The Irish were an Israeli tribe who had wandered from Scythia (where their king Ferrius Farsa, evidently a man of Joyce's disposition, had inaugurated a great language school) across Europe through Spain into Ireland. The names of his brothers who helped him to subdue the country were recorded in Irish topography: "Slieve Cualam in Wicklow—now hideously and absurdly called the Great Sugar Loaf!—is named from Cuala, another son of Breogan; Slieve Bladhma, or Bloom, is called from another son of the same; and from yet another is named the Plain of Muirthemni. . . ." * Joyce makes Bloom say, when he hears the schoolchildren at their lessons, "At their joggerfry. Mine. Slieve Bloom". Of the possible names offered by Hyde's narrative Joyce preferred this partly because it is a common Jewish name all over Europe, more because of the meaning "flower" which he exploits repeatedly (and, as a tribute to the nature of woman, renews in *Finnegans Wake*). Molly's history also owes something to Hyde. She had lived in Spain, has Moorish beauty. Bloom and Molly between them represent the racial and religious tangle of Ireland. Bloom was the child of a Hungarian Jew; was brought up nominally Protestant (his father a famine-convert who still retained his faith and ritual); married a Catholic wife; and in love with her Mediterranean beauty was in love with his ancestral self.

Settling in Europe Joyce had met Jewish intellectuals, had been welcomed as their counterpart in his exilic intellectuality, and had learned in contact with their families something of Jewish ideals and ways. He had not always learned accurately, as curious errors perpetuated in the text of *Ulysses* show;† but he had learned

*Douglas Hyde, *A Literary History of Ireland*, 1899, p.48.
†Perhaps the most striking (except that few seem to have been struck by it) is "Agendath Netaim". Joseph Prescott has pointed out others in his *Notes on Ulysses* in the *Modern Language Quarterly*, XIII (1952).

avidly, with an appreciation of the warmth of the tradition opening to him. Before he met the reality of Jewish life he had already
felt drawn to it. In his early Ibsen article of 1899 there is a reference
to the Semite as "a lover of righteousness". Here Joyce identifies
himself with a standard Irish literary view, which one can hear
again in, for example, AE's *The National Being:* "The cry of ancient
Israel for righteousness rings out above all other passions, and its
laws are essentially the laws of a people who desired that morality
should prevail." Joyce still had this in mind when he spoke to
Budgen of the value of Bloom's "justice and reasonableness".*
But side by side with this austere respect grew an exotic and violently
sensuous delight, such as the nineteenth- and early twentieth-
century French writers found in *la muse juive*. In *Dubliners* one or
two Jewish figures, too little developed to be classified as characters, haunt the fringes of the stories. As Joyce came nearer to them,
he invested them with a quality not unlike that knowledge of
lust which Yeats recognised in tinker and beggarman. When the
teen-age Joyce strayed, by the skill of his feet, into the brothel-
area of Dublin, he wondered "whether he had strayed into the
quarter of the Jews"—

> Women and girls dressed in long vivid gowns traversed the
> street from house to house. They were leisurely and perfumed.
> A trembling seized him and his eyes grew dim. The yellow
> gasflames arose before his troubled vision against the vapoury
> sky, burning as if before an altar. Before the doors and in the
> lighted halls groups were gathered arrayed as for some rite.
> He was in another world: he had awakened from a slumber
> of centuries.

This is the kernel of the oriental images that riot through *Ulysses:*
the Turkish girls in yashmaks; the hammam; the Turkish
prostitutes who do their work between graves; Stephen's dream
of the Baghdad street, the melon, and the red carpet; Molly's
Moorish memories; the plantations of Jaffa and Tiberias.

The pure calf-love of Joyce's boyhood had been described in

*Frank Budgen, *The Making of Ulysses*, 1934, pp.115–6.

the setting of "Araby", and the girl he loved then was called "Mangan's sister", a description clarified by a paragraph in his article on Clarence Mangan:

> East and West meet in that personality (we know how): images interweave there like soft luminous scarves and words ring like brilliant mail, and whether the song is of Ireland or of Istambol it has the same refrain, a prayer that peace may come again to her who has lost her peace, the moonwhite pearl of his soul, Ameen. . . . How the East is laid under tribute for her and must bring all its treasures to her feet.

"Mangan's sister" is the Orient, the East that complements the West of his mind. All the poets of the Irish literary movement, with Mangan as their forerunner, asked the Orient to give them something: AE asked for authority for his intuitions, Yeats for the trappings of a system, Joyce for the polar opposite of his intellect. A part of Bloom's birthright is the eastern capacity for the sensuous. But Joyce scrupulously keeps in view that another part of his birthright is the demand that justice prevail.

And the expectation of a Messiah is in him from birth. The Jewish people is the Messianic people par excellence, still waiting for the king to be given: "Yes, says J. J., and every male that's born they think it may be their Messiah. And every Jew is in a tall state of excitement, I believe, till he knows if he's a father or a mother." *Ulysses* is agog with Messianic prediction and incident, beginning with Buck Mulligan's Ballad of the Joking Jesus, whose mother's a Jew, whose father's a bird;* through the advertising of the pseudo-Messiah from Zion, Illinois; through the brothel-delirium in which Bloom hears himself hailed as Dublin's Mayor and Israel's king; to the midnight talk when the cabman promises "One morning you would open the paper . . . and read, *Return of Parnell*". Bloom had been at different times a Parnellite and an

---

*Note that Yeats had read the "Ballad" in the early serialised version of *Ulysses* before he wrote his famous *Leda and the Swan*—another case where he took a hint from the younger man. But both Joyce and Yeats had derived their conception of the divine bird-progenitor not so much from Christian nor Hellenic sources, but Celtic. Mrs. Clapp at Montana State University has pointed out to me the important role of the birds in the genesis of the hero Cuchulain.

activist of the Irish underground, translating his Messianism, in the late nineteenth-century manner, into revolution for the "material Messias" that Stephen Hero outgrew. In his mellowing age Bloom is moving towards pacifism and simplifying his hope to a comfortable home—a domesticated last illusion.

Stephen is still offering himself as a Messiah in the form of a master-writer. The claim is implicit in a deliberate mistake which he filters into his exposition of Shakespeare to the literary coterie at the National Library. He tells his listeners that Shakespeare was born under the omen of a new star and that it shone over him when he walked back from Shottery and Ann Hathaway's arms. But he knows, as W. E. Schutte has pointed out in *Joyce and Shakespeare*, that the new star over delta in Cassiopeia was visible from 1572 to 1574, and Joyce makes him think his correction in these terms: "Don't tell them he was nine years old when it was quenched". By attributing the appearance of the star to Shakespeare's birth Stephen wants his listeners to think that a star of Bethlehem always greets a master-artist, and to remember the star that fell over Parnell's grave and associate it with him; and Joyce phrases the mental correction to remind the reader that the star fell over Parnell's grave when he was nine, just as the firedrake faded when Shakespeare was nine. Is the double-play too adroit to be serious? Perhaps. But Joyce is often numerological, superstitious in accordance with his mediaeval, cabbalistic make-up. There is no question that he is serious in the Circe episode where Stephen anathematises the deserting Lynch as "Judas"—which means that Stephen is Christ.

During his Dublin fieldwork to gather material for his comprehensive biography of Joyce, Richard Ellmann gathered a story that explains the "Judas" cry and illuminates *Exiles* and *Ulysses*. J. F. Byrne (Cranley of *A Portrait*) had already told in *Silent Years* of a crisis in 1909 when Joyce came to his home, 7 Eccles Street, and "wept and groaned and gesticulated in futile impotence as he sobbed out to me the thing that had occurred".* He had not

*J. F. Byrne, *Silent Years*, Farrar, Straus and Young, New York, 1953, p.156 (and see p.167 for his insistence on the mystery).

S

disclosed "the thing", but some pages later hinted that it was one of the mysteries behind *Ulysses*. Ellmann learned that* during the 1909 visit to Ireland Joyce met his former friend Cosgrave—i.e. Lynch—who claimed to have slept with Nora. Joyce was not a cuckold, Ellmann points out, but in great agitation he believed that he was. He staggered to Cranley for help, wrote agonised letters to Nora. His brother Stanislaus came to the rescue, sending word that Cosgrave had told him, on the very night the incident occurred, that a pass at Nora had failed. Joyce was glad to take the explanation and bought a present for Nora and pretended the matter was over; but *Exiles* and *Ulysses* show that he continued for ten years to brood on the charge. He was amazed at the pain he suffered, evidently acted and re-enacted all the possibilities in his mind, reconsidered the literature of adultery in the light of his plunge into the feelings of the cuckold. He reviewed the whole Parnell story, for whereas he had identified himself as a young man with the hero Parnell he now had a vision of himself as the miserable O'Shea. Kitty O'Shea published her two-volume story of Parnell in May 1914,† and he urgently read it in the hope of discovering there the psychology of woman, dispenser of pleasure or pain. The last of the notes with which he prepared himself for *Exiles* shows that this line of exploration was negative: "first, because Parnell was tongue-tied and secondly because she was an Englishwoman. Her manner of writing is not Irish—nay, her manner of loving is not Irish. The character of O'Shea is much more typical of Ireland." That O'Shea sentence is significant. At the time of *A Portrait* he had imagined Ireland as a pregnant woman beckoning a young man to adultery. Now he complemented the image: Ireland was also the acquiescent O'Shea. He noted that while the cuckold in the art of earlier epochs was a figure of fun, the sympathy of a modern audience lay with him rather than the gallant, but that no modern writer knew how to

*Ellmann reported the story, with much revealing Dublin information, in the *Kenyon Review*, vol. XVI, no. 3 (Summer 1954). In the next paragraphs I am working from his article and the article in which Empson followed up his disclosure.

†Katherine O'Shea, *Charles Stewart Parnell. His Love-Story and Political Life*, 2 vols. Cassell, London, 1914 (May 19th). Instalments had been published in the Press prior to this date.

avoid hesitancy and suffering in the presentation of him.

That last observation is the first intuition of a character who, for all that he is a cuckold, is positive, rounded, vital. Joyce created him in Bloom. In *Exiles* he discussed the issue in terms of the conflicts of intellectuals, and the result was utterly hesitant and moribund. His artist protagonist Richard evidently thinks of himself as a liberal intellectual, but his every inflection discloses a struggle between a desired liberality and a prevalent conservatism. The young Joyce had flaunted a disregard of conventional morality, and practised it in taking Nora to Europe, but there was a conservative side to him. A correction in the draft of *Stephen Hero* illustrates it. Describing his unacceptable proposition to Emma, he writes of his notion of free love: "He was not sufficiently doctrinaire to wish to have his theory put to the test by a general «revulsion» revolution of society but he could not believe that his theory was utterly impracticable." He intended to write "revolution", but wrote "revulsion", the unconscious conservative protesting against his liberal programme; then he saw his error and corrected it. Discovering these contradictions under the thrust of the 1909 crisis Joyce attempts an exploration of them through Richard.

Richard desperately wants the fidelity of Bertha, yet masochistically dallies with images of her contact with his friend, which are the more pricking because they bring a sensitivity to his friend's body as well as his wife's. He forces himself to present her with the opportunity for adultery. His friend finally avows "I failed. She is yours. . . ." The audience does not know whether or not it is the truth, and Joyce's notes insist that the closing sequences of the play must all sustain the uncertainty: "The doubt which clouds the end of the play must be conveyed to the audience not only through Richard's questions to both but also from the dialogue between Robert and Bertha." It is clear that, though all assurances regarding Nora were accepted so that life might continue, the inner Joyce clung to doubt. The deliberate uncertainty of *Exiles* represented Joyce's ambivalence, and perhaps he thought it a clever theatrical stroke to keep the question and drama alive in the audience when they left the theatre. But it was unsatisfactory; his art could take him further than the mere stalemate representation of his problem; could, if pressed hard enough, with his organising brought to bear and with fertilisingly rank Dublin for its setting and Dubliners for its character, probe the depths of the problem and re-arrange his attitude to life. So, after the digression of *Exiles*, he returned to his engrained Irish themes, and the problem of cuckolding woman and cuckold man was, through interaction, solved in the following way.

THE COMEDY OF MOLLY

The *Odyssey* is the story of an unfaithful man and a faithful woman, and its use as frame of reference might seem to imply that Joyce had determined to prove Nora's fidelity. So might the quotations from *Cymbeline*, another story of virtue. But the technique is ironic. He had found a nice Irish inversion of Homer in Lady Gregory's *Jackdaw*, in which, knowledgeable of course about the ways of purdah-enclosed women, a village Irishman says that Penelope wasted the substance of the house during Ulysses' absence: ". . . . Ulysses that came back from a journey and sent no word before him but skipped in unknown to all but the house-dog to see was his wife minding the place, or was she, as she was, scattering his means". He also had in memory the famous Irish tradition, that the nation's servitude began with the adultery of Dervorgilla. He denies the virtue of poor Penelope. The only Penelope he recognises is Penelope Rich, whose notorious appetite, he suggests unhistorically but deliberately, may have afforded a niche even to Shakespeare.

Studying what Shakespeare had done with Ulysses he had re-read *Troilus and Cressida*. That sent him further back to Chaucer's Cressida, as he lets us know when he uses Chaucer's "quopping" for Bloom's troubled heart-beat at the sight of the fancy adulterer, Boylan. Imogen had arisen in his mind as guarantor of Nora's loyalty, but she was not dynamic enough to stand up against the figure of Cressida. And Joyce had an innate sympathy for Thersites' illusion-stripping. Wars and lechery! As an alternative to the feeble doubt of *Exiles* he decided to take the position of safety that Thersites offers, and that in the still more powerful play *King Lear* Edgar recommends: the lowest point of fortune. If he accepted the assumption that all women lie, he had drawn a bound to his suffering.

As he worked on the plan of *Ulysses* an extraordinary transformation took place. That acceptance of infidelity was, for all its rock-bottom security, as negative as suicide. Now it changed to a positive intuition of pulsation, sympathy, the pleasure of the world. Joyce saw that he could never have had the love of Nora, the moment at Howth Head on June 16th, 1904, when "kissed, she kissed me", but for what he was puritanically regarding as the lapsability of woman. And if there was an Ur-Molly who had taken him to bed, as Empson thinks possible, he could not have benefited from her help but for blessed lapsability. Bloom suffers but from the loss of his son and the consequent breakdown of his relations with Molly, rather than from her conduct. In fact, he loves her vitality, and it is some compensation for the decline of his own enjoyment of her if he can make others admire and enjoy her. Joyce ends by loving her vitality, too, giving her the last chapter with its repeated affirmation. He made it clear to Budgen that the last chapter is the celebration of a woman's body, and that the affirmative yes is the place of love. To that delight he came from his puritanical and conservative suffering.

The critics and readers of our time have found Molly's chapter one of the great experiences of literature, so completely it accords with their twentieth-century desire to de-mechanize, renew contact with the earth and the rhythms of nature. J. Mitchell Morse, protesting against the deification of Molly, has listed a great many details from *Ulysses* to show that she is drab, lazy, sterile—all that in our current view the goddess earth should not be. By making her what we want her, he says, we "myth the point". His case* is beautifully argued; yet I think the whole momentum of *Ulysses* is against it. Molly's sexuality *is* positive;

---

*J. Mitchell Morse, *Molly Bloom Revisited*, in *The James Joyce Miscellany*, second series University of Southern Illinois).

Joyce himself praised her as Bloom's "passport to eternity"; and Gorman has given the text* of the *Molly Brannigan* parody which Joyce wrote when a dream of separation from her had made him anxious lest his grip on the positive, real world should falter:

> My left eye is wake and his neighbour full of water, man
> I cannot see the lass I limned for Ireland's gamest daughter,
>   man,
> When I hear her lovers tumbling in their thousands for to
>   court her, man,
>   If I were sure I'd not be seen I'd sit down and cry.
> May you live, may you love like this gaily spinning earth
>   of ours,
> And every morn a gallous sun awake you to fresh wealth
>   of gold,
> But if I cling like a child to the clouds that are your
>   petticoats,
>   O Molly, handsome Molly, sure you won't let me die.

This appeal is unmistakable. And even without it there is a decisive piece of evidence that Joyce acknowledged through Molly the triumph and beauty of amoral nature: he repeats the *Ulysses* account of woman in *Finnegans Wake* and hearkens back to Molly's kiss on Howth Head and integrates it with the kiss of freedom that earned the name "Nora of the Kiss" for the heroine of a nineteenth-century Irish play. J. S. Atherton, whose superb studies of the materials used in *Finnegans Wake* have been increasingly clarifying its organisation, showed† in 1949 that Joyce expected his readers to recognise a system of allusions to Dion Boucicault's play *Arrah na Pogue*—"Nora of the Kiss". That romantic Nora's foster-brother was lying in Wicklow gaol waiting to be hung. She carried a letter, the plan for his escape, in her mouth and passed it to him with a kiss. On June 16th, 1904, the date of the action of *Ulysses*, Joyce and the real Nora had bought seedcake before they climbed Howth Hill, and, when they lay

*Herbert Gorman, *James Joyce*, Farrar and Rinehart, New York, 1939, pp.282–3.
†J. S. Atherton in *Notes and Queries*, CXCIV 20, (October 1st, 1949).

kissing for the first time, Nora had given a bite of the cake from her mouth to his. Bloom remembers it as if it had happened with Molly: "Ravished over her I lay, full lips full open, kissed her mouth. Yum. Softly she gave me in my mouth the seedcake warm and chewed. Mawkish pulp her mouth had mumbled sweet and sour with spittle. Joy: I ate it: joy." As Joyce wrote the story for *Ulysses*, it was a secularisation of the Mass: Molly's kiss was for Bloom, Nora's was for him, the bread of life. In *Finnegans Wake*, more than ever convinced that a woman's kiss is the key to free-dom, he transubstantiated his memory in twelve allusions to Boucicault's Nora, and ultimately, giving the final word to a woman as he had in *Ulysses*, he turned it into the great wind of death and rebirth which "Jumpst shootst throbbst into me mouth like a bogue and arrohs!"

I must quote one more among the many critics whose researches are building the background against which Joyce is to be read. Adaline Glasheen discovered* that Joyce had read *The Dis-sociation of a Personality* by the American psychologist Morton Prince, who, analysing a patient, located four personalities in her, one of them the essence of uninhibited womanly pleasure and merriment in sex. It is not clear from Mrs. Glasheen's report, perhaps it is at present not known, when Joyce read the book. He drew on it in *Finnegans Wake* for the letter from Boston. It either helped him to learn in the writing of *Ulysses*, or, more probably, confirmed what he had found alone by grappling with *Ulysses*, that "there is no expression of man's sexual energy that can displease the essential woman". This, says Mrs. Glasheen, "was apparently the great revelation of Joyce's life. . . . Molly and Anna Livia . . . stand outside the moral and psychological schemes that man erects to his torment."

We only have to be careful not to let our delight in his delight blur the fact that his form is comedy—not to re-sanctify what he secularised. The saner side of Joyce sometimes revolted at the thought of spinning *Ulysses* out of his fear that a friend might have

*See Adaline Glasheen, "Finnegans Wake and the Girls from Boston, Mass." in the *Hudson Review*, Spring 1954.

known his wife. It was real and necessary, but also ludicrous. He inserted into the novel a caricature of himself writing it. This is Daniel Breen, to whom on the morning of June 16th the mail has delivered a postcard with the two letters u.p. He reads it as a slur on his sanity, and, drawn like a figure from a Jonsonian comedy, he spends the day stamping the town in bath-slippers, dragging his wife behind him, looking for a lawyer to sue for £10,000 damages. It has always been suspected that Joyce is mocking his litigation against the British officials in Switzerland resulting from his theatrical adventures in 1918. He may be; but much more he is saying: "All this fantastic to-do, 300,000 words, because someone pretends he's been u.p. Nora". He had trained himself on Jonson, but he was a greater, or at any rate a more consistently great, comic master than Jonson. Jonson was, not always but by preference, the satirist, the man who, recognising that life is absurd, wants to change it. But satire is only a part of comedy. Joyce writes the comedy in which life is shown to be absurd but absurdity to be the very bloom of life.

But in converting his suffering into an excited pleasure in the adulterous disposition of things, had he not lost his occupation as Messiah? The young Joyce had had a mission much more like Jonson's. He had described Ireland in order to horrify and change her. It now appeared that the woman who called the stranger to her bed was doing nature's work. He could not ask her to change. He could only find a tongue for her and for the tongue-tied Parnell and O'Shea.

There is a good deal in *Ulysses* that still wears the penumbra of the receding desire for change. The Cyclops chapter describes the nationalist Citizen, a braggart, a hypocrite (he grabbed the holding of an evicted tenant), a toper. The last point, and the whole public-house setting, pivots on the 1915 fracas, already described in the AE chapter, in which the Irish M.P.s confused nationalism with the defence of the drink-trade. The British are ridiculed for their major industry, thrones of alabaster; the Irish for their equally unspiritual product, spirits. The Oxen of the Sun chapter goes on to describe alcoholism as a cause and symptom of

Irish non-productivity* (it is, in the metaphor of the chapter, one
of the ways the Irish run mad and slay the oxen of the life-giving
sun); and it attacks the impossibilising of possible souls through
contraception. But these gestures at world-changing are residual;
and the comic tone of the Cyclops chapter has, over all, the
flavour of relish rather than satire.

It is true, however, that the sharpness of the cry "Judas" and
other painful notes remain. *Ulysses* is, after all, a story of the
making of the work made. Out of this agony, says Joyce, in
effect, I arrived at pleasure. The political Messianism of Bloom and
the artistic Messianism of Stephen remain there similarly, as part
of the history: beliefs shed, plus the story of the shedding of them.
Stephen certainly thought he was Christ. And, as Joyce, reading
Hail and Farewell before he completed *Ulysses*, had lit on Moore's
claim to be Siegfried, Stephen called his ashplant *Nothung*—
Sigmund's, or Parnell's, sword, which Moore had offered to
re-forge—and used it to shatter the drear light of the Dublin
brothel. Stephen's hopes, Bloom's delirious fantasy that he is
crowned, blesses the world, is crucified, harrows hell, sees
Armageddon, rises again—all these are recorded as the imagery
that, under various metamorphoses, accompanies the good man
through life until he makes the decision not to change but to

---

*Compare AE's argument, quoted on page 194 above, that a year's abstention from
alcohol would "release a blaze of productivity" in Ireland. J. Mitchell Morse suggested
to me, when we discussed this one morning, that Joyce may have been thinking of the
meagre productivity of his student period of whoring and pub-crawling. On the other
hand, it cannot be said that Joyce was slow in his writing. He had an enormous amount
in manuscript before he was thirty.

Of course, the anti-contraception theme is more important in the Oxen of the Sun
chapter than its final breakdown in alcoholism. Notice the several effects that Joyce gets
from the scene where Alec Bannon arrives, describes his intensive flirtation with Milly,
and proposes to invest a sovereign in a capote. It (a) fulfils Bloom's expectation that sooner
or later his daughter will be seduced; (b) shows that Milly will go through the same
pattern as Molly, since it is the pattern of life; (c) condemns the Manichaeism, which, as
noticed several times in this book, intermittently shot to the surface from the lower
deeps of the Irish (whom we normally think of as vigorous, though Joyce thought of them
as paralysed); (d) attacks Joyce's rival artist-Messiah, Moore, who had often run to
Manichaeism, and nihilistically offered himself to Ireland, at the climax of *Hail and Farewell*,
as Messianic evangelist of contraception. (Therefore Joyce's favourite *double entendre* for
Moore; "lecturer on French letters to the youth of Ireland"—i.e. evangelist of French
culture and rubber. In 1929 Moore made a good-tempered riposte by sending Joyce a
copy of *The Brook Kerith* inscribed "To James Joyce, whose great book 'Ulysses' I am
reading in French with much admiration".)

accept. It is explicitly stated that Bloom makes that decision. When he reaches the point at which Odysseus killed the suitors, he triumphs by killing pain and anger and hope of change: he accepts the apathy of the stars and the satisfaction of adipose posterior female hemispheres. So the occupation of Messiah is, according to the record, abdicated. But by the very making of the record itself it is in a measure retained, for the story of the pain and the delirium is the story of Gethsemane, a crucifixion, and a resurrection; and the publication of the story shows that Joyce still believes in the artist's mission.

HE PROPHETS MOST . . .

In the introduction to *Irish Fairy and Folk Tales* Yeats records ". . . in the old days many tales were to be heard at wakes. But the priests have set their face against wakes." That is one reason why Joyce makes his last book a wake: to defy the priests, and to enjoy the tale-telling. He also wants to raise the dead with the wine of the country, as, the ballad said happened at Finnegan's wake. Again, the title is a call to the epic hero Finn MacCool: "Finn again Wake!". So for his last, complex-perplex-duplex-stuplex* book he takes up the Messianic theme again.

When he had been engaged in the writing for over four years and had twelve in front of him, he dreamed an image of his creative procedure and its result: "I was looking at a Turk seated in a bazaar. He had a framework on his knees and on one side he had a jumble of all shades of red and yellow skeins and on the other a jumble of greens and blue of all shades. He was picking from right and left very calmly and weaving away".† The Anatolian rug, woven of the split rainbow, recalls the Mangan essay, the Turkish allusions in *Ulysses*, the Moorish touches in Molly, and how the Near East meant sensuality and pleasure to him and developed his creativity as he explored sensuality. It illuminates his technique; in the same letter he says "I have woven

*See *Letters*, edited by Stuart Gilbert, p.222.
†Ibid., p.261.

into the printed text (of *Anna Livia Plurabelle*) another 152 river-names. . . ." It represents the final design of *Finnegans Wake*, tiny scatters and larger medallia interrelating in a congruous whole, border lying outside border.

The autobiography in *Finnegans Wake* includes a review of the writing and reception of *Ulysses*—"a dodecanesian baedeker of the every-tale-a-treat-in-itself variety". The discussions of *Ulysses* are written from an apparently hostile standpoint in mock reproduction of the criticisms to which Joyce had heard it subjected; but above the parodies sounds the tone of elation. Evidently Joyce never suffered that recoil which made Forster think, as he closed the manuscript, that *Passage to India* was a failure. He was sure that *Ulysses* was a major achievement. Committing himself to his new book, he felt uncertain in the early stages of writing how the discrepant themes he was handling would synthesise, and even in the late stages uncertain of the total intent; but "It certainly means something", though he was not sure what; and he was satisfied of its importance. His greatest anxiety was that ill-health might prevent its completion. James Stephens promised to see it through to the end if the need arose, and came to him for briefing. But Joyce had a tenacious hold on life in defence of his books, and stayed the distance till publication.

He had grown up in the shadow of a crime and a fall. The year of his birth, 1882, had been the year of the assassination of Lord Frederick Cavendish in Phoenix Park. His family life had jolted to the fall of Parnell. He had seen the fall of an Irish genius in England, Oscar Wilde—a fall the full impact of which scholarship has not yet described, but which can already be measured, by such accounts as Rickett's in *Self Portrait* and the letter from Gordon Bottomley which he prints there, as the overturning of all values. In Paris he had seen the later phases of the Dreyfus affair. The Wilde and Dreyfus convulsions had taught Gide, in correction of an earlier entry in his journal, "Malheur à celui par qui le scandale arrive—mais il faut que le scandale arrive". Did not Parnell and Wilde together show Joyce that disaster is a regular function of greatness? Their catastrophes were present to him at that early date when he warned himself of the high cost of being exceptional. His pride was balanced by a guilty anticipation of danger. In *Ulysses* he records instances; he wants to give the facts self-critically and confessionally; but he keeps them brief, as in this Paris recollection: "Yes, used to carry punched tickets to prove an alibi if they arrested you for murder somewhere". Evidently whenever his eye caught a press report of a crime bloody enough, he expected the police to haul him in, and compulsively established his alibis. When we read *Ulysses* we are probably intended to connect these guilt-thoughts with the drowned man, in whom (we know from his "Full fathom five" association) he sees his rejected father, and to suppose that once Stephen realises that he has found his real father in the Common Man his guilt will clear or come under control. But for all Joyce's mastery of design, the book ends with this thread left loose. His concern with Eve's* role in the Fall had distracted him from Adam. *Ulysses* completed, he went back to labour at Adam's problem.

As soon as he began work he realised that he was setting out to do what, in his brash days of 1904, he had boasted to Eglinton could easily be done: rewrite *Paradise Lost*. Milton had examined the Fall, to justify God's ways to man. The scriptures of the great religions had done the same, and so perhaps all epics—"What theme had Homer but original sin?" Yeats had asked. Joyce planned to incorporate scriptures and epics; nursery rhymes, ballads; popular theatre and popular songs (this group constituting the scriptures that the masses, giving a superficial obedience to the Church, serve on their pulses); books that he admired as demonstrations of the artist in action or the Irishman in action; books that he did not admire but which were rivals to his as the sacred books of Ireland (a striking case was Yeats' *Vision*, which also presented a theory of cyclical history, and did it solemnly with pseudo-mathematics, inviting his rude parodies), or criticised

*Note that when he describes Eve in *The Wake* he footnotes "I have one just like that to home".

his, or were held up by critics as superior to his (Gogarty had said, for example, that he would never capture ". . . the Attic note. The note of Swinburne", so he made a point of creating the white death and the ruddy birth and writing passages with the rhythms of the best of Swinburne). He took material from these originals and parodied or converted it with erudition, insight, humour, and with a sense of at least equality. Not that he was wanting in reverence for other men's achievement; his letters attest a full-developed respect; but he genuinely thought himself the equal of the highest. It is fascinating to follow in the exegesis of a critic like Atherton how, for example, he welded the Koran into *Finnegans Wake*, making himself the equal of Mohammed, Messenger of God.★ He swallowed the competing revelations to produce the panoramic sacred book which his Irish forerunners had promised.

Possessed by that extraordinary memory which has character-ised many artists in our time, he offered in *Finnegans Wake* to make good all his early bragging. When the young Joyce said that the Irish material had never come under a shaping hand, he implied that a master could make of them something more than the collective had. Now he carried Irish epic and Irish history into his work, to show what could be done. He made, however, only little use of Cuchulain, the preferred hero of the literary movement. It was pleasing to him to differ from the movement, and he had good reasons beside for choosing Finn MacCool in substitute: Alfred Nutt had in 1900 published an account of Cuchulain calling him "The Irish Achilles", but Joyce preferred the wise Ulysses, and Finn had touched the salmon of wisdom; Finn's name coincided with Finnegan's of the Ballad of the Wake; Finn was connected with the locale of his personal memories and writing, since "his head is the Head of Howth, his feet stick up in Phoenix Park, his body supports the city of Dublin";† Finn had an un-faithful wife, Grania, a woman of strength and vitality whom he

★J. S. Atherton in *Comparative Literature*, (Eugene: University of Oregon) VI, pp.240–55.

†Adaline Glasheen, *A Census of Finnegans Wake*, Northwestern University Press, Evanston, 1956, p.38.

pursued and eventually recovered. There is a sequence of thirteen pages at the beginning of Section vi of Book I which describes Finn MacCool, the avatar, in his wonderful violence and absurdity; and in a hundred mutations, including possibly a mutation into the enemy-figure Magrath, he appears throughout the story. It was an illusion on Joyce's part to think that by using the Irish epic material as the concomitant of non-Irish, universal material he gave it of necessity finer artistic shape than his predecessors or made it more significant to the world. We have seen that the very narrowness and provinciality of Synge gave his plays, modern and epic, a power of immediate penetration into the world's sympathy. Nevertheless, Joyce accomplished something different from his predecessors: remaking the Finn MacCool myth with that comprehensive quasi-philosophical brooding that leads to the special poetry of epic, he made modern Dublin, its fantasy and paralysis, its dirt, gossip, guilt, and protests, more intelligible and more interesting. He threw light into corners long dark, showed the past lurking there.

Moreover, concerned at once nostalgically and angrily with both the creativeness and the failings of his Church, he added from the early and mediaeval history of Ireland to the characters and type-events through which the modern Irish writers and audience struggle with their nation's destiny. He had been looking at the Book of Kells, and used that and its illuminator. He had long been attracted by the figure of St. Patrick, now he made something of him. Intrigued by the possibility that St. Kevin might just possibly have been born in the numerologically significant year 566,* and by the fact that Kev rhymes with Dev (which facilitated a name play with De Valera), and above all by the fact that his Irish name Coemghen gave an irresistible eye-association with the key-phrase "Come again" and its cyclical and resurrection implications, he renewed in the mind of Ireland and established in the imagination of the world the idyll of St. Kevin's seven solitary

*See attempts at explaining the numbers in various critics, including Campbell and Robinson, *A Skeleton Key to Finnegans Wake*, and John V. Kelleher in the *Analyst*, Northwestern University, No. X.

years among the sources of the Liffey at Glendalough. Apart from
Catholic history, he worked into the book many minor Irish
characters, some of them discreditable but colourful, some of them
contributors in one small way or another to the cause of civilisation. A nation depends best on its few great figures for the dynamic
projection of its character—in the case of England on the Wife of
Bath, Troilus, Bottom, Falstaff, Hamlet, Brutus (and it will be
noticed that they do not have to be born native to have a native
meaning)—but the array of minor figures gives valuable support.
Ireland's major figures, I suppose, are Cuchulain, Esther Waters,
Moore and Martyn, St. Joan, the Playboy, Bloom and Molly,
H.C.E. and Anna Livia; Joyce produced more of these than any
other writer, and he also produced incontestably more of the
supporting figures.

Finnegans Wake is a congeries of riddles. Mrs. Glasheen has
pointed out the seriousness of the riddling: the book "is a model of
our universe which is mysterious as a whole and in its parts.
Joyce is, therefore, mysterious in his turn. . . . It was conceived as
obscurity; it was executed as obscurity; it is about obscurity."*
This is beautifully put, but we must add that the things that human
beings do to each other can be alarmingly clear although very
mysterious and confusing, and often the incidents of the *Wake*
are correspondingly clear—just as moments of a chaotic dream are
insistently precise, although inscrutable. In *Ulysses* Stephen had
deplored history as "a nightmare from which I am trying to
awake". Joyce now goes into the nightmare, as a more rewarding,
at least a more informative, procedure than trying to break from
it. In fact, part of the human problem, he now realises, is that we
are all trying to awaken from history, convinced that there is a
more lucid and agreeable morning; that is our Messianic myth,
and he calls its imagined dawn "the great day of the messicals".
With "Messiah" that last word commentatingly combines
"Mass", "mess", and "testicles" in the two meanings of "balder-
dash" and " vigour of procreation".

When the Four Apostles (who may also be, inter alios, four

*Adaline Glasheen, op. cit. p.xvi.

literary predecessors, perhaps Lady Gregory, AE,* Yeats, Moore)
hold their seance over the recumbent Yawn, they elicit a con-
catenation of apocalyptic and atavistic voices from Wagner,
Mohammed, the hounds of the Yeats poems and hound-man
Cuchulain, the *Irish Times*, Parnell; and it seems that the great day
is breaking. But does it come? Almost everything in *Finnegans
Wake* both does and doesn't. Campbell and Robinson in their
pioneer *Skeleton Key* very well put it "Always seek in a Joycean
expression an antimony or contradiction".† In the Messianic context he coins the word "anteproresurrectionism". He asks "Whur
that inclining and talkin about the messiah so cloover?" He
describes "the whole thugogmagog", which is to be wound up
with a Magnificent Transformation scene—a scene that will be
delightful but the whole performance only pantomime. He has his
Irish politician throwing "jehovial oyeglances". He shouts "Ecce
Hogros Chrisman". Perhaps in accordance with the demands of
his technique we must be content to leave the Messianic and all
major questions open or in oscillation—a word which Joyce would
surely have glossed by combining it with osculation. My impression, however, is that he believes that the dream is reality and
eternity and that there is no waking, only repetition. Perhaps

---

*Note that, as AE was the dourest, most official Messianist of the literary movement,
Joyce goes to him to borrow a number of Messianic properties for the *Wake*. He uses, for
example, the Waves of Fohla (see page 177 above), though I think he makes them, in all
but one place, four instead of three, so as to augment his quadrilateral or "four-part cycle"
groups. At one point he concertinas Parnell's cry, "Do not throw me to the wolves"
with "Fohla", writing "Call Wolfhound! Wolf of the sea. Folchu! Folchu!" He then
comments "That folklore's straight from the ass his mouth".
   That might make AE the donkey. But I rather suppose that the donkey, which after
all carried Christ into Jerusalem, is too important for any one individual to merit the
honour of identification. Joyce may intend it to represent Ireland. (Compare Yeats' rather
different, simple and violent, use of the donkey at the last plop of his Messianic trajectory.
See page 158 above).
   †It may be that the system of contradictions in *The Wake* is founded, not as it would
appear on the philosophers and their dialectic, but on Joyce's ineradicable neurotic uncertainty over the cuckoldry charge of 1909. He writes, for example, of "arrah of the
lacessive poghue", where poghue means more than a kiss and lacessive means "liberating"
because it includes the word "keys" but also means "injurious". I am not sure but what,
among the plural implications of the title *Finnegans Wake*, we have the following:
Boucicault in *The Shaughraun* (which Joyce could have seen in Dublin in that crucial
summer of 1904) had used the theme of the mock-dead man at his own wake, and Synge
had used it to carry the folk theme of the husband trapping his faithless wife; with these
precedents in mind Joyce may, in the very title as well as in the dominant technique, be
recapitulating his old dilemma. "She did–she didn't–she did–she didn't."

the following sequence may be abstracted, though it has as little value as any other abstraction from a work of art which says much only as long as it uses its own words and order:

(a) *The millennium is always expected. We must take the expectation of the day of peace and universal welfare as a regular component of the pattern of life.*

Joyce supports his narrative with Messiahs and millennialists who are everywhere remembered and with obscure millennialists who are almost forgotten, and with mutations of millennium-promising tags (such as "Off to Philadelphia in the morning", which points to the day when men will love each other like brothers—but we know from the struggle between Shem and Shaun how brothers love).

(b) *The men who offer themselves as Messiahs are often mere exploiters of the common illusion.*

Shaun-Jaun is the typical fake-Messiah. He combines all the gentlemen whom Joyce disliked or wanted to deflate. Hugh Kenner has shown the demagogic De Valera in him,[*] and we may add traces of bad critics like Shane Leslie and posturers like Yeats and Shaw (in their special roles as public men, not as writers). When the Leapyear Girls weep him and lay him to rest with Good Friday celebrations Joyce is exposing the ineptitude with which the public interprets its hopes. The Girls cry "Peace" in a score of languages. Explaining the episode to Miss Weaver Joyce reminded her that in 1918 the word "Peace" was sighed round the world like that, and he pointed out that when his sequence finishes in English "O peace", it means "enough of that nonsense".[†]

(c) *When an exceptional man offers himself to the public, his originality will cause his downfall; he will be betrayed and crucified; and the drama will satisfy the public, and it will appear that a momen-*

---

[*]Hugh Kenner, *Dublin's Joyce*, Chatto and Windus, London, 1955, pp.357-9.
[†]See *Letters*, edited by Stuart Gilbert, p.264. I fancy that Jaun's visit to the girls' school may owe something to Yeats' poem *Among Schoolchildren*—Joyce being delighted (for all his admiration of the poems) by the picture of the Senator rolling his vain and agedly-virile eye in the schoolroom—a massacre of the innocents.

T

tous change has occurred; but that is an illusion, too, for all that has happened is a renewal of the process.

This is one effect of the repeated Parnell allusions: the continued play on the Piggot charges; the echoes of the fight in the Committee-Room and the last campaign through Ireland, and the mutated appeals "Do not throw me to the wolves" and "When you sell, get my price". Joyce urged Miss Weaver to read the biography of Parnell to follow his drafts. Yet I am bound to add that the inference I have drawn under (c) depends on the correlation of the allusions with Joyce's earlier statements. If we read *Finnegans Wake* in isolation (which perhaps is impossible, and certainly unlikely to occur) we cannot draw the inference from the tone of the allusions, which are blended with the "D'ye ken John Peel" halloo of the hunt of life. And this leads to

(d) *Whether fake or failed, and even though an illusion, every Messiah does something for a people. He increases the entertainment which is the nourishment of life.*

The nightmare is the reality. Morning, the hunt, Philadelphia, the awakening, are all a dream within that dream. But they make it entertaining and therefore tolerable.

In one of his mock-annotations to Book II, Section ii, Joyce glosses "noland's browne jesus" (which we may read "Dublin's contemporary Messiah" or "Messiahs then and now" or "the Messiah who has never come to any land") with "What a lubberly whide elephant for the men-in-the-straits". The Messiah is a white elephant, a fraud on the public. But at the outset of the story we were told that at the crucial date 1132 "Men like to ants or emmets wondern upon a groot hwide whallfisk which lay in a Runnel. Blubby wares upat Ublanium". John V. Kelleher has shown that the shoal of big fish cast ashore in 1331 relieved a famine. So even a whide elephant may be a hwide whale and an answer to a need.

(e) *In fact, since life is entertaining why should it be changed? Why wake up (even though the title of the book can include an impera-*

tive)? The round of illusions produces "lots of fun at Finnegans Wake".

Bloom had acquiesced in the pattern of the universe. Joyce goes further now, appears to extol "the best of all possible worlds". It is an extraordinary conclusion for the man who began as a rebel and authoritarian castigator of all his associates. It is an extraordinary conclusion for the man who told Miss Weaver, at the very time he was perfecting it, that "there are moments and hours when I have nothing in my heart but rage and despair, a blind man's rage and despair".* He turned his rage into energy, and sometimes he turned his despair into nostalgia, and that results in the singular interpenetration of tones of comedy and beauty. His claim for the universe, once reduced to a claim, lies outside the sympathy of the modern reader; but in the reading he keeps our sympathy by the variety of his dramatisation of all the dreams, inner and outer.

A book which works on the universal scale is bound to suffer the limitation of illimitability. Where everything is an epiphany, nothing is. Although the great works of literature that describe the cosmos are admirable, we often turn away to something narrower, trivially passionate. *Finnegans Wake* may in the end be read as well as praised by virtue of the points at which it fails in its world-view: where the rage has not been wholly refined, where the edge of the despair still cuts. The overtly autobiographical passages have sometimes been criticised as embarrassing. They are all the more alive for that. If we think of *Paradise Lost*, our first memory is likely to be "Seasons return, but not to me returns . . .", or a passage equally autobiographical or incidental which questions as much as justifies God's ways. With *Finnegans Wake* we are likely to think of the autobiography: how he would be a farsoonerite; how he created alchemistically from his own dung (he surely remembered how Yeats had compared him with Ezekiel); how he locked himself in his room on Unity Sunday, "his cheeks and trousers changing colour every time a gat croaked".

*Letter of May 1st, 1935, in *Letters*, edited by Stuart Gilbert, p.367.

His references to *Ulysses*, I have said a little earlier, are elated; but his account of his conduct is not; it is free from defiance, is still self-interested, but is genuinely self-critical. He does not rebut charges, he confesses them. Among his aphorisms, for example, is this: "He prophets most who bilks the best". It confesses his record of dependence—from the youthful application to Lady Gregory for his Paris fare, to the later substantial help given unasked by generous admirers. Other weaknesses are confessed, at least one of them surprising.* The autobiographical sections of the book may be his act of contrition. But the confession is also a claim. "He prophets most" claims the excellence of his prophecy. Like Parnell he is a failed rather than a fake Messiah.

Though domestic autobiography may be the book's ultimate claim on readers, Joyce knew that it could not be its first. People will accept nostalgia, feminine beauty, before they will accept masculine. He had the same predilection himself, he loved the breeder better than the male. His masculinity was a triumph over his facility. He was far-sighted and worldly enough to exploit that. The first part of *Finnegans Wake* he released was the river chapter, *Anna Livia Plurabelle*. In both his masterpieces he gave the last chapter to the woman's voice. But he knew precisely what he was saying when he said of *Ulysses* that the last chapter was Bloom's passport to eternity. He meant not only that she had given him life when she kissed the cake, or the keys, from her mouth into his, but also that the audience would first receive the book in admiration of the sensuous writing for the soprano, but the real immortality would lie with the man whom they would come to know, more slowly, through her; they would continue to listen to him, always discovering something new, when they were sated with her chapter. In *Finnegans Wake*, similarly, the washerwomen or Anna Liffey's last chapter must be the first revelation of the power of the book, but it must lead on and back to the male study, and that will be durable—and she knows that and begs "mememormee" (but even here there is an echo of a man's voice, Hamlet's father's).

Apart from particular passages, there is one other thing that

*See *Finnegans Wake*, p.186, 27–8.

always stays with a reader of *Paradise Lost:* the cadences and momentum, what we call, by a rather awkward metaphor, the music. Joyce like Milton was a gifted musician; like Milton he wrote with a momentum or music prefiguring the writing. Until we are possessed as he was by the "sing-song" of the river-name chapter or by the tumbling-barrel music we are perhaps not yet reading the *Wake.* But though his mind worked for this purpose like Milton's, he did not like Milton invent a new music. His delicate ear and the concentration with which he applied it gave him an exceptional power of representation and imitation: he astonishingly notated the music of the world. But when he was not documenting sounds, when he turned from that to the melody and rhythms of literature, he tended to imitate what he loved best, the warm bubble and lilt of nineteenth-century light music for the drawing-room and popular stage, or of nursery rhyme, limerick, rude ballad, or poetic bravura. This he does magnificently; the fact that we do not care for them as much as he did does not mean that they are not worth caring for; in fact, a by-product of his literature will be the transmission of them to another age which will appreciate them more. But it is questionable whether he anywhere speaks with a distinctive new melody. Eliot put it that he has no voice of his own, which may not be quite true, for under his parodies and mimicry we can just detect his feminine note and his masculine note, but they never are elaborated into music. Yeats, without a note of music in him in the musician's understanding of the word, developed his own new melody in the lyricist's understanding of that. Joyce, I think, recognised his deficiency and in the *Wake* successfully made it good: bringing his organising skill to bear, he used Wagner's recurring motifs and gave a new force to the device by the bold metamorphoses (possible when you use words instead of tunes); and he constructed the whole book as a counterpoint of ear effects against eye effects. It was an astonishing feat in a near-blind writer, demanding an intense inner visualisation. The polyphony, exasperating and rich, was his original contribution to the music of literature. I say original even though he had predecessors in jabberwocky. They followed their fantasy, he filtered everything through his intellect. What he planned as counterpoint of ear and eye is also in the result counterpoint of fantasy and intellect.

CULMINATION WITH THE RABBLEMENT

In *Finnegans Wake* Joyce has dropped the justifying notions of an artist's function by the support of which he first separated himself from Dublin and chose to work in isolation. He had justified his first stories as holding up the mirror so that those who found themselves dirty should wash. In the *Wake* there are traces of *The Water Babies*, but I doubt whether Joyce is urging its Victorian lesson: "Those who wish to be clean, clean they shall be". He is only including it in the pleasant conflicting motley of life. In *Ivy Day* and *Ulysses* he connected Dublin's drink trade with its paralysis; the *Wake* rings with the name of Guinness only to help the whirligig turn. As a student he had modelled himself on Ibsen, and his first critical publication had been the review of *When We Dead Awaken*, a title that completely fitted his mission to rouse Ireland from deathlike paralysis to intellectual awareness and vigour (at least, we may phrase the objective for him this way, though the *Portrait* image of the red-eyed moron shows that he baulked when it came to stating an objective). In *Finnegans Wake* Ireland is not to be awakened, its phantasmagoric history, past and present, *is* vital as it is syung, and though the huntsmen ride hallooing "to waken the dead" the chase is its own object and justification. When his critic in the *Wake* accuses his books of adding to the misery of the world, he retorts that on the contrary he has made the Irish stew merrier. Yet though he abandoned reformism, he clung to the last to one student belief: that the artist is exceptional, "a god in the manger". During the composition of *Ulysses* and *Finnegans Wake* he noted, with a superstitious exaltation, that when he wrote a living person into his book the man died; it happened only two or three times, but he elevated it to a principle. When all other forms of Messianism had been subdued in him, he still announced the inspiration of his profession. It is notable how he stressed the importance of according the proprieties to the memory of artists, even those he had earlier denigrated: he sent a wreath to Moore's funeral, and was angry when news came that Irish literary men in London had not attended the ceremony. His attitude arose from identification: he did as he would be done by. By far the first concern with him was that an artist should do his work and let the world howl, but a strong second concern was that the discerning part of the world set the rest of the world an example of recognition and respect of the artist. And late in life, buttressed by achievement, he could admit what he had once tried to disregard, that Moore was the beginning of the contemporary tradition which he crowned.

Joyce was the culmination of the Irish literary movement. He had observed it with distaste in 1900, criticised the senility of the folk-art it praised, scorned the shapelessness of the epics it revived, denounced its submission to the rabblement. He had disliked and feared involvement in it or its political counterpart, had removed himself from its influence, and wrote to efface it by doing differently and better. His achievement, however, was built on it; he took up and completed its work.

Back home from Paris in 1903 he had read Yeats in the September issue of *Samhain:*

> I have always been of Verhaeren opinion [sic] that a master-piece is a portion of the conscience of mankind. . . . Every generation of men of letters has been called immoral by the pulpit or the newspaper, and it has been precisely when that generation has been illuminating some obscure corner of the conscience that the cry against it has been more confident. . . .

He immediately took up that thesis. And similarly wherever his disdainful gaze rested, he found something to his purpose. In AE's theosophical activities he found much to satirise but also the metempsychosis axis of *Ulysses* and its later development in the *Wake*. He assimilated the oriental interests of the movement to his art, relating the oriental theme to the Irish context more closely and clearly than any other writer. He took up the Messianism of Yeats and AE, and Moore's version of it, displayed its place in the Dublin drama and the world's, deflated it only after the fullest exploration; he disclosed its orgiastic accompaniments of hope and despair, saw them as part of the comedy and pleasure of living. He hesitated over the use of the heroic legends, but at last accepted that heritage, too, and interpreted it. The *Wake* prolongs his derisive attack on his forerunners but is the best tribute to them.

Of course, he completed their work by amalgamating with it what they were less equipped and sometimes unwilling to infuse: images and discipline from Europe past and present: from Greece, Italy, Norway. But the centre of his works, as of theirs, is Ireland. They had meant to make the world see the dignity and charm of Ireland. He began by telling of her indignity, but gradually broadened to take in all she had, a licentious vitality which the others had omitted until Synge's experiments. Going far beyond Synge, he detailed her oddest oddities and produced the Irish *Comédie Humaine* that Yeats once thought of but could not even design, still less write; it is curious how Yeats and Joyce each had skills beyond the other. By the unflattering completeness of his picture Joyce did more to make the world Ireland-conscious than the dignity-mongering and charm-mongering had done (though they had done something). Readers of Joyce everywhere are today ransacking the Irish press, chronicles, Blue books, directories, soaking themselves for his sake in the Irish epos. As he foresaw this he wryly allowed Shaun to accuse him of "rightdown lowbrown schisthematic robblement", which means, among other meanings, that he had travelled with the literary movement, though more systematically, to the market-place and rabblement. So he had assisted in the national act of hibernianising. But that is in the nature of literature: the man who criticises country, tribe, family, self most intimately and analytically, does most to make it loved.

Driven by a determination to prove himself above mediocrity, he wrote the epic of the mediocre, incorporating the popular and the banal because they fascinated him, not because he courted popularity. A characteristic of his art is to use popular conventions and codes, ideals, language and toys, in a form accessible only to those who have otherwise turned away from them. Eliot took up the Symons-Moore investigation of the music-hall, and then of the popular stage, in the hope that by mating his thought, the thought of the exceptional man of conscience, with a popular form he could speak to a larger audience. In a superior sense of the term this *was* courting popularity. The younger English poets of the 'thirties did the same thing when they studied jazz and the dance-hall and borrowed lyric-forms there. Joyce out of his passion for the popular drew it into his intricate designs, careless whether it found an immediate audience or not, though confident that this very indifference to any order but his own would eventually assure a fit audience.

In an article sent to the *Boston Pilot* in 1891 Yeats detected an appetite for immediate results, "fatal to great work", as the bane of Irish writing. "It will leave us", he suggested, "with the approach of more orderly and successful times". Without successful times to help him, obedient to his nature, but helped by observation, however critical, of the trial and error and gradual advance of his immediate predecessors, Joyce expelled it from Irish work.

CHAPTER VIII

IRISH AND ENGLISH

An Irish priest in Pittsburgh, where I finish this book, tells me that though the Irish now recognise Joyce as a great writer, they refuse to take him "too seriously". If so, it is a way of dodging what he tried to say to them. He intended, certainly at the beginning of his life when he wrote as a new Ben Jonson, to make a moralist's impact on his people. But there is a respect in which their reception is right. He did not want the Irish to receive the moral with a long face. He assumed the contrary, that they would only understand his viewpoint if they read him farcically.

Outside Ireland we many of us, especially in the universities, read him and his predecessors with long faces. As a corrective to our reverence, it would be healthy if we shifted with the Dubliners to the farcical level. In fact we shall probably be rewarded with an epiphany when we stop over-epiphanising. The record of the posturing, the rivalry, the recriminations, and the intermittent generosity of the men who wrote the Anglo-Irish literature of this great period is rich in entertainment: George Moore registering "The Society for Irish Folk-Lore" as the imprint for his salacious last books; Yeats murmuring all over America "What a pity Moore never had an affair with a lady, always with women of his own class"; Gogarty wetting Synge's front door and Joyce commemorating it. Anglo-Irish literature signified at the outset a protest against the Stage Irishman, and look at it from one side and it does appear his very antithesis, an aristocratic, despotic, paternalist, Parnellite figure; but look at it from the other side, and it is Stage Irish buffoonery for the delectation of all time. The reader

who works at it from this side is sure of some pleasant evenings—
and also some critical advantages: he will be clearer about the
shortcomings of AE who divorced his comedy from his vision;
clearer about Yeats, who, having a great deal of comedy available
to him, made poetic statements not so much exclusive of it as
above it (as in the poem "Speech after long silence", where his
mind has thrust up through regret, pain and sweetness, comic
wisdom, to a peak from which he sees the tableland of life);
clearer why Synge and Joyce, comic practitioners, say more, and
to more people, than the rich-minded Yeats.

But this comic literature is political literature. The two types
go together. Tragedy deals with the irremediable in life, comedy
with the remediable and therefore with the potentially political—
and this holds even when the politicians and their politics need
the remedy. The florescence of this literature we have been
reviewing came when a political catastrophe exposed the nasty
comedy of English and Irish politics alike. It was not less comic
because the protagonist, Parnell, had scarcely a grain of humour
at his disposal. Only a sadistic pleasure once at the gloom on the
face of the boy who had waited an hour with his horse while he
rambled with Mrs. O'Shea; only an exultation when he had cowed
his party into accepting something he wanted and they didn't.
He loved to read *Alice in Wonderland* while he lay in hiding from
the Government; never smiled in reading it; called it "a curious
book". He was, to a caricaturist extreme, the frigid Englishman
of the world's imagination. Through his image the Irish paradox-
ically proceeded to fight out, indignantly and farcically, the
reorientation of their politics.

That does not mean that if there had been no Parnell there
would have been no literary movement. As everybody knows,
some of its characteristics were already visible when his Parliamentary career was only beginning. In the 'eighties the young
Yeats and AE were occupied with Celtic legend, cottage tales,
country ballads, and the anti-commercial protest, inherited from
mid-nineteenth-century nationalism and "Young Ireland". Even
themes that might at first sight seem specifically post-Parnell are

not entirely so: that enquiry into sex, which made Bernard Shaw wonder why the three most "obscene" writers of his day were Irish, had begun at least as early as 1886 when George Moore, his natural proddery stimulated by his reading of contemporary French literature, had published the *Drama in Muslin*. The value of despotic leadership might be thought a thesis obviously derived from Parnell, but Standish O'Grady was already independently preaching it in the 'eighties.

But although the exploration of almost all the themes had begun, the Parnell crisis *was* decisively formative. It ended simple idealism. It forced a review of assumptions. It showed that Irish freedom meant an anti-Irish as well as an anti-English fight. Just as Ricketts in England said after the Wilde case that he could never trust the English again, so the Irish now regarded their public with a hitherto unknown doubt, and became quick to interpret the further experiences which reinforced it. Because Parnell had fallen over a sexual issue, Moore's experimental enquiries into the Irish "purdah" grew into the messianically orgiastic celebrations of Synge, Joyce, and the later Yeats. In the martyrological passions and public guilt of the end of 1891 the Irish Messianic legends were remade and the themes of the national literature coalesced and were remade. But remade slowly. It took ten years for the Messianic theme to grow, traceable only through the help of journals and letters, and emerge in literature. And not remade in a permanent, settled shape, but still changing in the light of the Irish experiences during thirty-five revolutionary years and then the first years of independence and responsibility.

The ten-year time-lag is notable. I do not know whether such a delay is to be regarded as the rule for the assimilation of a public problem into literature, or whether it occurred in Ireland because there was no writer already mature enough though still ardent enough, to evaluate the situation more rapidly. Parnell's fall came at the moment when Yeats, AE, and Katharine Tynan were adapting from adolescence. The shock matured them, but it first arrested their maturity—it was such a reversal of their expectations of their country, such a jagged split down the national experience.

The poetry of AE and Yeats up to 1901 has, with much beauty, the tone of protracted adolescence, a sign of the temporary paralysis under which they began to knead new intentions and a new outlook on politics and the public. It is part of their interest and excellence that they pushed out of their silence not by forgetting the incident which had shocked them but by remembering and using it, accepting their function as the memory of the people. They insisted—when they, gradually, saw that they must—that it be taken as typical, an essential indication of the virtues and faults of the Irish people, and a lesson to their captains and deliverers.

The first writer actually to use Parnell neat in his work had been scarcely more than a child in 1891. Joyce had the experience in his viscera at nine years old and it grew with him organically. In *Ivy Day in the Committee Room* in 1905 he insisted on the legendary Parnell despotism: "He was the only man that could keep that bag of cats in order. 'Down, ye dogs! Lie down, ye curs!' That's the way he treated them." This story shows that Joyce had a clearer view of the Parnell legend than his literary seniors, and used it in literature before them. But his use of it did not shape their view for them. *Ivy Day* did not reach print till the delayed *Dubliners* appeared in 1914. Lady Gregory's *Deliverer*, studying Parnell through Moses, had been produced at the Abbey in 1911. Yeats had addressed his Hugh Lane poem to Parnell's "unquiet" shade in September 1913. But *Dubliners* once published, and the *Portrait of the Artist*, with its "My dead king" cry of grief, published two years later, Yeats was undoubtedly stimulated by Joyce's incisive treatment to the sharpening of his own image of Parnell. It is possible that he could not have developed to the different and individual incision of *The Words upon the Windowpane* without the help of reading the early Joyce.

In the development of the Parnell legend among the writers the strangest thing is their reception of Katharine O'Shea's biography in May 1914. We have seen how Joyce seized it immediately,[*] desperate for information on the mind of adultery. I do not know how soon Yeats read it—his 1914 letters have survived as scantily

[*]See above, p.264.

as Joyce's, apparently—but he certainly read it: the story of the storm-swept Brighton Pier, retold in *A Vision*, comes from it; and his bitter late epigram, hard as if it were granite from Parnell's Arklow quarries, is cut from it:

> Parnell came down the road, he said to a cheering man
> 'Ireland shall get her freedom and you still break stone'.

Yeats had, I take it, been brooding on the story Mrs. O'Shea twice tells, that Parnell, who hated social gatherings, loved to talk to labouring-men met on the road or at brick-kilns, men with hammers or picks in their hands. Joyce and Yeats, then, both hard minds and impatient with ineptitude, had read a book in which there are passages soft to the point of ineptitude. And, having worked for many years with an heroic view of Parnell, they found passages that undermined the view. Roger Casement evidences the kind of reaction an Irishman could have on reading Mrs. O'Shea's book: he told Wilfred Blunt in May 1914 that "if the revelations had been made two years ago there would have been no statue of Parnell today in the streets of Dublin".*

I must not overstate the revelatory quality of the book, though Casement's remark encourages overstatement. Some of the peculiar limitations of Parnell had long been recognised. The old J. B. Yeats, for instance, had known and disliked his cultural shortages. His early, sympathetic biographer, R. Barry O'Brien, working from the hearsay legend and crystallising it, had acknowledged them. How the legend stood two years before Mrs. O'Shea published can be defined closely. On May 16th, 1912, Joyce's article, *L'Ombra di Parnell*, appeared in the *Piccolo della Sera*, Trieste. There are signs that it was a good deal influenced by O'Brien, but O'Brien remembered (for a date is given wrongly). These are the points Joyce makes:

> Parnell: led his people, like Moses, from the house of bondage
> (*casa di vergogna*) to the borders of the Promised Land;
> was *bleso* (stuttering—i.e. tongue-tied, but compare
> H.C.E. in the *Wake*); of delicate physique; ignorant of

*Wilfred Scawen Blunt, *My Diaries*, vol. II, Knopf, New York, 1923, p.425.

Irish history; a speaker who lacked eloquence, poetry, or humour; of a frigid courtesy which separated him from his colleagues; a protestant of patrician descent; and—*per colmo di sciagura*—spoke with a distinctly English accent.

Joyce tells the anecdotes of Parnell's acceptance of Dublin's "tribute" cheque without a word of thanks; of his contemptuous treatment of meetings; of his disregard of the cheers of the Commons, for which Gladstone characterised him "an intellectual phenomenon".

A touch of the Saxon in Parnell and some of his lacunae are admitted there. But all centres on the figure of the despot. O'Brien and the talking Irish had agreed on the despotic side of the legend, and avowed the foibles that supported it. But Kitty O'Shea, while adding more evidence of the same kind, brought evidence of other foibles as well.

Her two volumes stress Parnell's English temperament; that he offered Ireland her welfare like a foreign despot, contemptuous of his Irish colleagues; that he manipulated public opinion ruthlessly, and portrayed himself a martyr while he lived easily. When he was in Kilmainham Prison and the party propaganda was announcing his sufferings and hunger, he had—so he tells Kitty, either fibbing to keep her spirits up, or because it was true—good accommodation, care, conversation, exercise, and "chops or grilled turkey or eggs and bacon for breakfast, soup and chops for luncheon, and joint and vegetables, etc., for dinner, and sometimes oysters". His horse was called President, the name of the horse he gave Kitty, Dictator. He called Kitty his Queen, or Queenie, she called him "my King". Did Joyce blench when he read their exchanges of "my Queen" and "my King"? He had already written the Christmas-dinner scene. He must have been disturbed, thinking that if Kitty's pages seized the public memory, they might tinge Mr. Casey's "Poor Parnell! . . . my dead king!" with their absurdity. As for the love-passages, the only possible evasion was to suppose that she composed Parnell's rhetoric when she assembled the book: "For good or ill, I am your husband, your love, your children, your all. And I will give my life to Ireland, but to you I give my love, whether it be your heaven or your hell. It is destiny. When I first looked into your eyes I knew." No wonder Joyce scribbled into his *Exiles* notes that she was English and he was tongue-tied.

The Irish public did not tear down the statue. They did not think an Englishwoman's book that important. Their politicians had blamed Mrs. O'Shea, over drinks and dinner-tables for twenty years, for the aspects of Parnell they found hard to swallow, and they were able to continue to blame her, and to remain unmoved by the disclosures of "a woman who was no better than she should be". The carelessness of public and politicians at the 1914 stage of the game is not astonishing. What about the writers? They did not go back on their view of Parnell. They advanced their view, building into it material Mrs. O'Shea provided.

Yeats disregarded everything in her book that did not under-write his conception of a powerful, dictatorial Parnell. Had he ever been pressed on the subject of Mrs. O'Shea, I believe he would have said of her, as he said of a very different woman, Hazel Lavery, that her life was a ballad-singer's tale, and he would have found significant that at two crucial stages of Irish history these two women, one English, one American, were the channels of communication between the aggressive Irish leadership and the British Cabinet. But what captured his interest in her narrative to the exclusion of her loving or anything else she did, was her description of a problem Parnell faced in Ireland, analogous, he saw with excitement, to one of his own. Parnell believed that he had personally mobilised hatred and energy, and, according to Mrs. O'Shea, he

> stood appalled at the intensity of the passion of hate that he had loosed, and no one but he—and I with him—knew the awful strength of that force of destruction that was only held in subservience by the sheer dominance of his will. He replied to my pleadings [when she tried to induce him to a policy of

reconciliation with the British Government!]: "Yes, I hold
them now with my back to the wall, but if I turn to the
Government I turn my back to them—and then—?"*
Yeats thought that his plays, especially *Cathleen ni Houlihan*, had
released a new quota of violent energy. In the knowledge of the
parallel he could not forsake the Parnell legend. Rather he must
try to develop Parnell's power to hold and guide the passions. In
1914 (the political developments, unknown to him, already
beyond his holding) he was imaginatively exercising his power of
control by working with the theory of passion contained under
the cover of an impassive Mask. The O'Shea fragments that helped
him were: the notes for the speech pulped in Parnell's hand, and
the nailmarks in his palm, when he had addressed the House; the
chair held, when a picture ominously crashed down from the
dining-room wall, an inch off the floor "in a grip that showed his
knuckles white"; "that low, broken monotone, that with him
always betokened intense feeling strongly held in check". These,
and the Brighton Pier passage, proved the majesty of Parnell's
control. They were in Yeats' mind and he attempted to work to
them during his senatorial and polemical career in the 'twenties,
and when he retired disappointed but experienced he re-grouped
them in the 'thirties to form his model of the ideal dictator.

Yeats' dictator contemptuously holds down the "rabble" and
never explains; he deliberately mystifies his followers, in accordance with Parnell's discovery that "what was lost by a speech not
made [i.e. when he missed a platform engagement on an impulse
and stayed at home with Kitty] was amply compensated for by
the deepened impression of his mystery and power gained by the
people"; he strikes down the human obstacles in his path; he
believes and acts what Parnell told Kitty: "some of these Irish folk
are genuine in their belief that forms and creeds can govern life
and men; perhaps they are right so far as they can experience life.
But I am not as they, for they are among the world's children.
I am a man, and I have told these children what they want, and
they clamour for it. If they will let me, I will get it for them."

*Mrs. O'Shea's *Charles Stewart Parnell*.

V

Shakespearian paternalist after Coriolanus, eighteenth-century oligarch after Pope and Swift, Yeats' dictator is a perfected Parnell.

Joyce read Mrs. O'Shea differently. Ten years earlier he had been thinking of Parnell as the more-than-human master of the bag of cats, and had modelled his threshold of manhood behaviour on Parnell's arrogance. Now Kitty showed him that there was a human silliness in Parnell, too, and much simplicity. From now on he slowly amended his picture of himself, and his conduct, to match. Kitty showed Parnell courteous and grave. The late Joyce grew courteous and grave. Kitty said "one of the greatest charms of Parnell's personality was the extraordinary simplicity of his outlook on ordinary life allied to the extremely subtle trend of his intellect." Joyce said "My thought is always simple. . ."*

But it is not what he absorbed into his private behaviour that matters, for he was his least vivid character, but what he absorbed into his novels. There are passages in *Ulysses* that have been either suggested by Mrs. O'Shea's version of Parnell or enriched by it. The little acrostic sent by Bloom to woo "Miss Marion Tweedy" has usually been related to a love-letter jingle sent by a schoolgirl admirer to the schoolboy Joyce. Stanislaus Joyce avers it, and should know, but his evidence often sounds thin to this reader, whose belief is that Joyce was more effectively influenced by an O'Shea anecdote of marvellous ineptitude: Parnell was gardening and she watching, when he suddenly told her that he was a

*I suspect that Joyce's first notion, after reflecting on Mrs. O'Shea's book, was to write a conversational narrative that would embody, stylistically, the "simplicity" of Parnell's relationship with her. When he says in the *Letters* that he wrote part of the *Nostos* of *Ulysses* several years before 1920, does he not mean that after the reading in 1914 he rapidly sketched *Eumaeus*? He used there the setting of a midnight coffee-stall because he had been struck by Mrs. O'Shea's tale of talking to Parnell at a coffee-stall at St. Pancras after a night-long sitting of the Commons; he used Bloom's thoughts of Parnell, and the O'Shea story of Parnell's hat dropped in the newspaper-office fight, for an important section of it; and he wrote with a deliberately simple and sententious prolixity. Later he saw that, valuable as *Eumaeus* would be in the design of *Ulysses*, it was too elementary a reaction to the Parnell stimulus. He went on to understand "simple" as "basic and humane", not "sententious", and to translate the "subtlety", which balanced Parnell's simplicity, into the complex structures native to himself.

Note the different stylistic lesson which Yeats drew from Mrs. O'Shea. He observed Parnell's remark "that most Irishmen spoilt things by over-elaboration". It confirmed him in his endeavour towards a naked style.

poet, a better one than his ancestor Tom Parnell, and threw down his spade and scribbled seven lines for her:

I was forced to confess that I agreed with him, as I do now, that it was, and is, as good as, and better to me than, any of Thomas Parnell's stuff, or "the stuff" of any poet who ever graced the world with song. This is it:

> The grass shall cease to grow,
> The river's stream to run,
> The stars shall ponder in their course,
> No more shall shine the sun;
> The moon shall never wane or grow,
> The tide shall cease to ebb and flow,
> Ere I shall cease to love you.
>
> CHAS. PARNELL.

Parnell's experience was used for Bloom. And it is striking that very little is transferred from Parnell to Stephen Daedalus, even though Stephen carries the ashplant Nothung in emulation of Moore's Siegfried who is son of Parnell; but much is transferred to Bloom. Having learned the underlying humanity in Parnell, Joyce blended his human traits into his Great Common Man, the anti-type of Yeats' dictator.

Bloom's kindness to women is Parnell's. The association of Bloom with flowers derives—with some changes—from Mrs. O'Shea's stories about Parnell and flowers: his love of white roses, his habit of picking flowers with the stalks too short. . . Bloom's scientific and technical hobbies resemble Parnell's: "Parnell had so many hobbies and interests in his home life that it is difficult to enumerate them all. He once said rather wearily that if he had not 'taken off his coat' in the Irish cause and for the Irish people he could have been always happy at home working at things so much more congenial to him." Parnell took up book-keeping to check his agent's accounts; he spent hours in architectural drawing, walked about the new Brighton station blue-printing it so that he could erect a cattle-shed like it at Avondale; he invested time and money inventing copper stabilisers for ships; he assayed quartz from his quarries, at his private furnace extracted gold for a ring for Kitty, realised enough to line her ring; and in particular, from the moment when he casually picked a book by Sir Robert Ball from her shelves, became interested in astronomy, taught first by her, then going ahead of her with his own study. Bloom has Sir Robert Ball's *Story of the Heavens* on his two shelves; his devotion to astronomy is connected with the leading motif in *Ulysses*, the motif of the Great Star and the apathetic multitude of the stars. As he works this sky material, Joyce significantly separates from Parnell. Parnell gave up astronomy: "He said it was all too immense and absorbing to think about in a life that was primarily concerned with politics." In the contemplation of the stars Bloom accepts the mutual cannibalism of this world; he makes, in effect, a decision against politics, against the struggle to restrain cannibalism and amend the human order.

Joyce used Mrs. O'Shea's picture of herself, naturally, to add details to his adulterous Molly. A branch of Captain O'Shea's family was established in Madrid, and the couple lived there early in their married life; she records that since that stay she has "always thought that the admixture of Irish and Spanish blood is most charming in result". That, together with the Milesian story, helped to form the Irish-Spanish Molly. More striking, Joyce drew courage from Mrs. O'Shea's picture of herself to describe himself as Stephen. Her father spent his last illness in a great bed that Queen Elizabeth had once slept in, and she watched his last days, sleeping on a sofa at its foot. As he died she and her uncle prayed. "When we came to 'Thy will be done' I was too choked with sobs to repeat, or to feel it, but my uncle was insistent, and a faint smile passed over my father's face as he tried to press his fingers in my hand." Reading this, and recoiling from it, Joyce saw how to use his terrible memories of his mother's death. He invented the *non serviam* demonstration: "to think of your mother begging you with her last breath to kneel down and pray for her. And you refused." He could at least have simulated the prayer, goes on Mulligan, since he is "the loveliest mummer of them all". Kitty

O'Shea had used, two chapters before the death-bed scene, the epigraph "Ah, well, we're mummers all!"

The book was still in his mind, if further back in the recesses, when he wrote *Finnegans Wake*. There are allusions to the bed Elizabeth slept in, partly as an item in the museum of history, more to betoken a parental death-bed. The hunting-scenes from Mrs. O'Shea become part of the *D'ye ken John Peel* system of imagery. Parnell's hobby of extracting gold from Arklow quartz reappears transmuted into the alchemical system of imagery. His passion for cricket, and her indulgence in laying out a pitch for him at Eltham, suggests the cricket imagery.

The *Wake* involves, of course, more of the Parnell legend than Kitty's book supplies. To carry the theme of the humanness of a leader, the hatred of those he leads for signs of their own weaknesses in him (compare the mood of the British public at the time of the abdication in 1936), and their scotching of him, he used most conspicuously hints at Parnell's most famous speeches, at the struggle with *The Times* and Piggot, and at the divorce scandal (and in the references to the popular play, *The Royal Divorce*, does he not imply, inter alia, a comparison of the Parnell fall and the 1936 abdication?). But the reading of Kitty O'Shea at the time when he was so sensitive to the voice of Eve-the-knowledgeable had given him the vital impetus. Perhaps it even helped him to conceive the world-view of the *Wake*. Describing the outlook from the windows of the house she and Parnell finally took, 10, Walsingham Terrace, Brighton, she said that at sunset the harbour and Shoreham and the church at Aldrington against the Downs "were touched with a pearly mist of light that lifted them far out of the prosaic ugliness we knew by the blank light of midday. Parnell used to say to me as we walked away to the golden harbour, 'Is it really like this, my Queen, or as we see it at noon?' I could only reply that it was both—the both that made life at once so interesting and so difficult."

Other critics have discerned seeds of the *Wake* elsewhere; notably Arthur W. Litz has pointed to Joyce's intuition, in *Ulysses*, of the world of the blind boy; and I suppose diverse

V*

impressions congregated to shape Joyce's last technique; but among them I would include this passage, especially since it describes the view from the room where Parnell died.

But although he built so effectively with its materials, the record shows that *Charles Stewart Parnell. His Love Story and Political Life* did cause Joyce disappointment at first contact. He was repulsed by the English voice of Kitty, and the silence of Parnell which was an English silence. The lady constantly reminds the reader that Parnell was English by all his education and behaviour. He was psychologically English, had the execrable taste to love an Englishwoman, had a superstitious aversion from the colour green; and any freedom that he brought to Ireland in his personalist way would be an English gift.

Perhaps Joyce, the expatriate who could identify himself with Ibsen's situation in—and out of—Norway and with the Jewish situation in exile, was better fitted than any other green-Irishman to understand Parnell's passion against the English kind and culture. He did understand; how well, his retention of Parnell as hero shows; though this also shows his deliberate loyalty to the memory of his father's emotion at the Parnell crash. Nevertheless, he had, in 1914, been struck by the alien element in Parnell, and the temporary depression that it brought had consequences. It made him speculate what, if Parnell was fundamentally an English politician, might be a model Irish politician. In *Ulysses* he did not act on the speculations; he still found Irish comic vitalism more absurd than admirable: irresistibly interesting, since he shared it, but absurd and satire-provoking. He jeered at his father, still alive, as "all too Irish". When he wrote *Finnegans Wake* he had changed, taken up his 1914 conjectures, and celebrated his father's fantasy, his all-too-Irishness. And as the corollary he celebrated Ireland's old politician, Daniel O'Connell. There had been premonitory references to him in earlier Joyce, for he was a kinsman of the family on his father's side, he lived in the family's talk, and Joyce was actively aware of him long before he recognised how to use him. Now in the *Wake* Joyce retained Parnell as the leader whom a people betrays; placed beside him O'Connell, the leader who betrays a people while he helps and helps while he betrays, all too Irish and echt Irisch, the walking paradox of a liberator best described by one of his opponents, John Mitchel in the *Jail Journal*:

> . . . wonderful, mighty, jovial, and mean old man! with silver tongue and smile of witchery, and heart of melting ruth!— lying tongue! smile of treachery! heart of unfathomable fraud! What a royal, yet vulgar soul! with the keen eye and potent swoop of a generous eagle of Cairn Tual—with the base servility of a hound, and the cold cruelty of a spider! Think of his speech for John Magee, the most powerful forensic achievement since before Demosthenes—and then think of the 'gorgeous and gossamer' theory of moral and peaceful agitation, the most astounding *organon* of public swindling since first man bethought him of obtaining money under false pretences. And after one has thought of all this, and more, what then can a man *say*? what but pray that Irish earth may lie light on O'Connell's breast—and that the good God who knew how to create so wondrous a creature may have mercy on his soul.*

At the beginning of this book I wrote of Lady Gregory's peasant-friend in the mountain-pass and his Messianic tale about O'Connell; then about Yeats and the planning of his campaign after the model of O'Connell's campaigning; but after that O'Connell diminished in the literary perspective. Now at the end in Joyce he suddenly returns in full size, Parnell's contrary but his equal. The magnificent Daniel is the Stage Irishman carried to the extreme, more dramatic than any Abbey fantasy. Joyce finds that, although Mitchel broke off with no more to say, there *is* something more to say about him: to show him heroic in his duplicity and representative of Ireland although the caricaturist extreme.

Joyce accepts and loves O'Connell for his father's sake—not merely because the two men were blood-kin but because they

*John Mitchel, op. cit., p.141.

resembled one another in temperament and conduct. Joyce's father was another O'Connell. I have not yet convinced myself whether Joyce had already seen that in the first drafting of the *Wake*, or whether he realised it and incorporated it only after his father's death at the close of 1931. Certainly the *Wake* references to the bed Elizabeth slept in, still looking back to Mrs. O'Shea's book, finally speak of his father's death-bed, not his mother's. Joyce is thus the more completely identified with Mrs. O'Shea, for she, as we have seen, was writing of her father's death. In the years after 1931 Joyce was haunted and delighted by the memory of his father. We know from the *Letters*, thin as they are, of one of his fantasies concerning the dead John Joyce. In 1937 he received news that a steamer, the *John Joyce*, was carrying pleasure-makers on cruises of Dublin Bay. Just as in *Ulysses* he had represented a locomotive puffing out of Westland Row Station with the onomatopoeic "Yooka .... Yook .... Ook", he now represented the steamer's chug, or whistle, with "ook ook". When he writes "And ook ook, fanky! All the charicatures in the drama!" he is thanking the costumed players assembled on the stage for the final curtain, and maybe moving off like a train as they did at the end of Cocteau's *Wedding-Party on the Eiffel Tower* (performed in Paris when the *Wake* was begun there, but possibly more familiar to Joyce through performance on the B.B.C.), but he is also thanking his father, the steamboat-man for all the fantastic personalities of the Irish story—since his father was their impersonator and mimic, had opened Joyce's ears to them, was a summary of them.

De Valera, also a Stage Irishman though not so vital a one as O'Connell, has been shown by Hugh Kenner to be a figure in *Finnegans Wake*. Kenner finds Joyce's version of De Valera hostile. The man who had decided to accept and enjoy O'Connell, should have accepted De Valera too. But it was difficult for Joyce to extend to a living politician, and one who was his exact contemporary, the tolerance he extended to a forerunner of his father. There is a breakdown of consistency, as much acrimony as humour in the picture of De Valera, and a trace of the satire that calls for change. Yet I find the *Wake* treatment of even De Valera gentle. Compare it with Yeats' bitter last poems and AE's late statements on Ireland; there we hear unmistakable anger. We have seen AE, who had meant never to quit Ireland, finally quitting Ireland to die. Joyce had never been sanguine of changes in Ireland; he could not be disappointed, as his predecessors were, and as men after him were.

★

Ireland had—as Thomas Davis had long ago feared, and AE repeatedly warned—been made safe for commerce. Not for ideas. Scarcely a flicker of enlightenment showed in the Irish body politic in the years of freedom. An apologist might argue that after a quarter of a century of trial and error the Abbey Theatre had full houses when O'Casey's plays of the nationalist agony were put on. But even then, with the keener, fuller audiences, educated by their writers, to help, the old opposition to the poet's or dramatist's truth were not ended. The same heresy-hunting that caused *The Countess Cathleen* scandal, the self-hating puritanism that caused *The Shadow of the Glen* and *The Playboy* scandals, persisted. O'Casey had to meet difficulties as thorny as Synge's: protests from the players against his language; deletions, by managers in provincial houses, of lines that trespassed on religion or sex. Most striking of all, Yeats himself was brought down at the end by Irish orthodoxy and timidity. Since 1899 he had won round after round at the Abbey, usually in the interest of other writers. In the last round he was defeated over his own plays. The *Herne's Egg* "disturbed the Abbey board until I withdrew it". *Purgatory* got by the management and had a successful staging, but the usual "tribal dance and the drums" of the Press and the clerics sounded against it.

What seemed most depressing to an observer like AE was that no improvement had been brought about in the level of public life. None of that intellect for which he had been writing for twenty years had developed. On December 12th, 1932, he wrote a letter to the *Irish Times*, attempted to counter Irish chauvinism with arguments for the value of crossed strains, complained against the bankruptcy of public life: even in religion, he said, the island of saints had produced nothing, no mighty saints. Then (with recollections of the Eucharist Congress of that summer, which also reverberates in the *Wake*) he wrote:

> We can, of course, with our talent for organisation, get a million people on their knees before an altar in the Park; but did there come out of all that piety a single vision, a song, a music, any visible sign that the sacrifice was accepted and the fiery tongues had descended? Our politicians who attended went back unaffected by all those sanctities to renew in the Dail, with even intensified bitterness, the manners of the public-house, degrading our public life as I never before remember it being so degraded since the Parnell split by personal abuse".*

The Irish had learned nearly nothing from their great men. They did not and do not want freedom any more than the English (no longer in the villa, where Moore pilloried them, but the semi-detached) want it. Perhaps the Irish want it less than any other western people. Today they have the most oppressive censorship in the world. According to a letter in *The Times Literary Supplement* on February 10th, 1956, it bans 1,000 books a year.

Still, were the old men, Yeats and AE, justified in their final pessimism? Yeats by his passionate rhetoric and AE by his sober concern pull us into identification with their point of view, so that we assent when they imply that it was useless to have worked for so shallow an Ireland, and worse than useless to have asked the world to admire an Ireland which, when they saw her born, they themselves could not admire. There are two reasons for thinking that they were over-severe. The first is that if the new Ireland was defective, so is every other country. The nationalist dream of an oppressed people is a fine dream, and not least fine in that it

*See *Letters from AE*, edited by Alan Denson.

prompts an active demand for a country that will be better—more moral or more honourable or more intelligent or more just, according to the predominant local nomenclature—than the patently defective older nations. But the dream is no more likely to be realised than the male dream of a faithful Penelope. Not even the new Israel with its special advantages, nor the new Czechoslovakia of 1919 which had the dreaming of Smetana, Dvorak, and Janaček behind it, came perfect out of the caul. In politics, as in domestic life, the result is always less than the dream. It is open to a man to rage at imperfection and to continue to press for something superior, or to reconcile himself with it as Joyce reconciled himself with Mrs. Bloom and O'Connell. Literature is capable of either of these functions: to protest and castigate, keeping the image of perfection bright, insisting that it still be the target; or to subtilise our insight into the world as it is, and thereby to produce so vivid a pleasure in its mechanisms that the question of changing it is forgotten.

The fact that the Anglo-Irish movement did create a literature that, considerable in volume, varied in kind, exercised both these functions, is the second reason for thinking that its pessimism was exaggerated if not wholly unnecessary. A national literary movement may in the end itself be the Messiah it proclaims. It is the best and most complete embodiment of the vitality that comes out of the mountain and stands in the smoking Post Office. The Anglo-Irish movement produced work that bites into the memory, that insists on the voice singing it, that mobilises the archetypes; that is tragic; that is comic at the intellectual level and at the level of legpulls and cockpulls; that criticises; that politicises sometimes socratically and sometimes inflammatorily; that is at once elemental and civilised; that contradicts itself, so that its programmes may be disregarded, as all programmes should be, in favour of something else that it postulates, a *temper* by which to live.

The literature of the Irish rejection of England is in English instead of Gaelic. The nationalist writers conferred a superb gift on the enemy they drove out. This was just: after all, England had assisted them to make their art for Ireland. They had worked with the experiments and findings of the whole of English literature behind them; they had discovered how to express themselves by reading not only Standish O'Grady and Douglas Hyde, but Blake, Shakespeare, Nashe, Ben Jonson, Spenser, Chaucer, the *Agenbite of Inwit*, and Dame Julian of Norwich. They had adapted their conqueror's vocabulary, images, rhymes, and rhythms to their own foreign tradition, but they had themselves been changed in exploring and changing them. Some of the knowledge and power, a tinge of the characteristic liberal and civic passions, by which English writers have struggled against themselves, had seeped into them and blended permanently with their rage and pride and cold intellect. Above all, they had learned more about their nationalism through England. In the nineteenth century English literature and the English political platforms alike were channels for the quick communication of the Continental nationalisms. Paris also, it is true, taught Ireland the ideals and methods of the Continental freedom movements (and the Irish who learned in Paris helped, between 1880 and 1914, in communicating to London what Paris was doing); and America taught them much through Emerson and Whitman, who were standard reading with them in the 'eighties and 'nineties. But England taught them most. The passion of English poets and novelists for the independence movements in Greece, Hungary, Poland, and especially for Italy— that English passion leaped through the medium of the common language into Ireland and taught the Irish military underground its tactics, the politicians their best appeals, the Irish poets their trade. In return Ireland donated this massive new segment, alien yet harmonious, to English literature.

Is it graceless in an Englishman, whose country wronged Ireland, to speak of this debt? I think it is; yet the principle that follows from it may justify the bad manners. A curious and important feature of nationalism is that, while it announces a whole-hearted concentration of interest on the native virtues of its people, it actually amplifies and leavens those virtues by borrowings from abroad, and especially by borrowings from the enemy and overlord whom it is engaged to expel. So Ireland learned even from England. So Ireland's most successful leader, not least successful in his fall and crucifixion from which he was reborn as a potent myth, had an English education and temperament. So his legatee, Patrick Pearse, had an English father and an Irish mother. Ireland borrowed from England above all, and then from France, America, Italy, from Herder in Germany, from Bishop Grundtvig in Denmark, from Ibsen in Norway, from the Russian prose of the soil. Joyce's self-imposed mission to Europe and his colloquy with the world's tongues were the ultimate expression of that process.

This is not to belittle the Anglo-Irish achievement, but to give the proper credit to the writers for their courage and success in working (not each of them, but between them) at home *and* abroad and thus providing their people with an amalgam, something never available before. As theorists Yeats and his friends had often chanted their doubts of the value of a "web . . . woven of threads . . . spun in many lands", but as makers they daringly produced that very thing, and it was brilliant.

Does not the realisation that the new Ireland must be created not only out of its old self, but also out of the enemy and the stranger, lie behind a dream of Yeats which is quoted, from his unpublished private papers, by A. Norman Jeffares in *W. B. Yeats: Man and Poet* (page 157):

> Woke Monday morning having dreamed in early morning that I was in Dublin and wanted to go to England, but in a trireme. I proposed this to an assembly of people, members of the Abbey and some fashionable young men. . . . The project had to be given up and I surprised myself by doing this without regret but said: "One has a thousand ideas and only one or two are carried out. Yet I am right. One cannot understand the Odyssey if one has not sailed in a trireme." Was it all a symbol of the Abbey's lack of capital?

Yeats' last sentence is not to be accepted as the interpretation of the dream, but as an association which helps towards the interpretation. The Abbey Theatre stands for Ireland, her arts and intellect, her future. Capital stands for energy. The Abbey had, of course, been floated in the first instance by capital lent from England; later it would move on its own, but that help from the enemy's obverse, liberal side had been vital* The dream reminds Yeats that for the realisation of a new Ireland energy from abroad must be added to her local resources to complete her assets. Accordingly her writers must accept their meed of exile, the twenty years' absence of Ulysses in war and wandering. It is also and equally true, and the dream clarifies this point just as much as the other, that they must accept their share of life at home with its narrowness and frictions and sense of the hearth. At the moment of this dream—Professor Jeffares has not given a date, but it appears to be before 1914—Yeats recognises that his place is still in Ireland; but the dream insists, and Yeats is to accept this and obey it, that the journey of exile must later be made.

Exile was not the paramount, but it was an essential, feature of the Anglo-Irish literary movement: it was partly a way of re-enacting the wild-goose history of the Irish and so giving the new nation a knowledge of itself, and it was partly a way of teaching humanity to the nation by bringing home a knowledge of the outer world. The nation did not let itself be taught, remained as duncish as any other; but it was free; and, thanks to six authors in search of a character, who turned out to be Parnell at one side of the looking-glass, O'Connell at the other, it had its Sacred Book.

*See Rex Pogson: *Miss Horniman and the Gaiety Theatre Manchester* (Rockliff, 1952).

INDEX

INDEX

Breogan, 260
Bridges, Robert, 98
Brighton, 3, 44, 211, 238, 292, 295, 297, 299
Brittany, 80
Brod, 69
Brook Kerith, The, 34, 65, 72, 73-6, 79-80, 271
Brooke, Rupert, 237
Browne, Marshal, 248
Brown, Dr. Malcolm, x, 33, 35
Browning, Robert, 207
Bruno, Giordano, 252
Budgen, Frank, 261, 267
Buffalo, ix
Bunyan, John, 17
Burke, 151
Burran Mountains, 59-60, 62, 64
Butt, Isaac, 122
Byrne, J. F., 9, 263-4
Byzantium, 147ff.
Byzantium, 148

CADBURY, 191
Calderon, 125
Cambridge, 234
Camden Town (Flecker), 38; (Innes), 38
Campbell, Harry, x, 248, 276n., 278
Campbell, Mrs. Patrick, 146
Canavans, The, 86, 100
Candle of Vision, The, 182
Canterbury, 191
Canterbury, Archbishop of, 191
Cape Horn, 80
Carlisle, 194n.
Carlyle, Thomas, 171
Carrington, G. E., 129n., 187n.
Carra, Lough, 32
Carroll, Lewis, 289
Casement, Sir Roger, 139, 292
Cathleen ni Houlihan, 101, 107, 127, 128, 149, 227, 229, 295
Cavendish, Lord Frederick, 273
Caves du Vatican, Les, 65
Ceathair Aluinn, 243
Celibates, 48
Celtic Twilight, The, 17, 87, 112, 145n., 167
Census of Finnegans Wake, A, 275
Certain Noble Plays of Japan, 138n.
Chamber Music, 247, 257
Chamberlain, Austen, 193
Charlemagne, 8
Charles Stewart Parnell, His Love-Story and Political Life, 264n., 292-300
Chaucer, 87, 266, 306
Chelsea Pensioners reading the Gazette of the Battle of Waterloo, The, 43
Chesterfield, Lord, 153
City Girl, A, 38

Clapp, Mrs. Mary B., x, 266n.
Cleared, 187
Cocteau, 302
Colindale, x
College English, 251n.
Collected Poems (AE), 175, 201, 208; (Joyce), 248; (Yeats), 136
Colloquy between Ossian and Patrick, 240
Colman and Guaire, 100
Colum, Mary, 53n., 88, 227-8
Colum, Padraic, 229
Columba, St., 4, 23
Comparative Literature, x
Complete Works (Synge), 234, 244
Confessions of a Young Man, The, 33, 35, 36, 37, 38, 39, 44, 47, 49, 50, 52, 55, 56, 60
Congested Districts, the, 220
Connolly, 160
Consuelo, 118
Conversations with James Joyce, 251n.
Coole, 83, 85, 87, 120, 124, 153, 154-5, 221
Cooper, Douglas, 35-6
Cork, 193
Cosgrave, 158
Countess Cathleen, The, 86, 113, 125-6, 252, 253, 303
Crazy Jane on the Mountain, 161
Cregoostha, the, 99
Criterion, 143, 147, 155, 238n.
Croagh Martin, 217
Cross of Cong, 59
Cuala, 260
Cuchulain, 26-9, 30, 95, 102, 181, 199, 203n., 262n., 275, 277, 278
Cuchulain of Muirthemne, 85, 94-5, 96-7, 101, 102, 149, 161, 234, 235
Cutting of an Agate, The, 258n.
Cymbeline, 266
Cytherea, 36

Daily Express (Dublin), 26, 58
Daphnis and Chloë, 34
David Reubeni, 69
Davies, 5
Davis, Thomas, 41, 151, 303
Davitt, Michael, 33, 98
Day of the Rabblement, The, 241, 252
De Valera, Eamon, 158, 205, 276, 279, 302-3
Dead Sea, 73
Dead, The, 137n., 240, 254
Death of Cuchulain, The, 158, 159-60
Deirdre, 28, 106, 160, 181, 236
Deirdre of the Sorrows, 216-17, 218, 229, 235-6
Deliverer, The, 25, 86, 90, 91, 121, 291
Demosthenes, 301

INDEX

Denson, Alan, x, 11n., 20n., 53n., 166n., 170n., 171, 174, 200, 201, 204, 220n., 304n.
Derby Day (Frith), 43, 44, 45
Dervorgilla, 105, 140-1, 266
Dhoya, 112
Diarmuid, 140-1
Dillon, John, 98, 185-7, 189, 190, 205
Dingle Bay, 217
Disappearing Castle, The, 47n.
Disenchantment, 55
Dissociation of a Personality, The, 269
Divagations, 214
Divine Vision, The, 139n., 181
Dodds, E. R., 168n., 171, 174
Donini, Dr. Filippo, x
Donne, John, 155
Double Debt to Yeats, A (B.B.C. talk), 114-15
Dragon, The, 86
Drama in Muslin, A, 35, 52-5, 61, 70, 250, 290
Dramatis Personae, 51, 85, 104, 127
Dreaming of the Bones, The, 140, 141, 152
Dreyfus affair, 273
Dryden, 57
Dublin, 1, 3-4, 8, 10, 16, 22, 24, 25, 26, 28, 34, 53n., 54, 59, 62, 63, 64, 66, 67, 69, 73, 80, 90, 91, 96, 107, 109, 110, 112, 116, 121, 125-7, 129, 130, 131-2, 139-43, 147, 166, 169, 171, 180, 185, 188, 191, 194, 197, 200ff., 212, 213, 216, 218, 223, 226ff., 246, 247, 249-50, 252, 254, 258, 259, 261, 263, 266, 268-72, 275, 278n., 280, 284, 285-6, 292, 293, 302, 307-8
Dublin University Review, 112
Dubliners, 218, 242, 246, 250, 253-4, 255, 261, 291
Dublin's Joyce, 240n., 279n.
Duffy, Gavan, 24, 117, 151
Dujardin, Edouard, 57
Dunciad, The, 57
Dvořák, 305

Early, Biddy, 98, 139
Earth Breath, The, 97, 166, 175
Easter 1916, 139, 150, 201
Easter Rising, the, 29-31, 80, 86, 114, 138n., 139-43, 150, 199-201, 218, 305
Edward VII, 125
Eglington, John, 17, 26, 51, 66, 68, 96, 126, 134, 138n., 139, 167, 168, 169, 172-3, 174n., 182, 199, 201, 209, 274
Egoist, The, 53, 237, 247
Egypt, 6, 24, 65, 73, 90, 91, 99, 139, 156
Eliot, T. S., 23, 38-9, 40, 43, 44, 57, 147, 153, 165, 171, 225, 237, 238, 239, 247, 258, 283, 287

Elizabeth I, 109, 219, 298, 299
Ellis, Edwin J., 11, 112, 155
Ellis, W. Ashton, 25-6
Ellis-Fermor, Professor, 86
Ellmann, Richard, ix, 12, 13, 16, 121n., 122, 125, 174, 263-4
Eltham, 299
Emerson, 172, 178, 210, 211, 306
Emmet, Robert, 15, 140
Empson, 264n., 267
English Players, the, 239
Enniskerry, 243
Ervine, St. John, 4
Essenes, the, 75
Esther Waters, 33, 37-8, 41, 42, 44, 45-7, 48, 56, 60, 75, 78, 79, 81
Et Tu, Healy, 245
Eugenics Society, 163
Eumaeus, 296n.
Eve, 274
Evelyn Innes, 35, 52, 56-7, 61, 62, 67, 80, 170n.
Evelyn Sun (New York), 19n.
Exiles, 104, 247, 263, 264, 265-6, 267, 294
Exotics and Retrospectives, 213
Ezekiel, 155, 281

Fairy and Folk Tales of the Irish Peasantry, 111
Farr, Florence, 12, 113, 120
Faust, 18
Faux-Monnayeurs, Les, 259
Fay brothers, 229
Fenians, the, 5, 10-11, 88, 173
Ferguson, 5
Ferrius Farsa, 260
Fielding, Henry, 57
Finnegans Wake, 26, 43n., 57, 243, 248, 255, 257, 260, 268, 269, 272-86, 299, 300, 302-3, 304
"Finnegans Wake and the Girls from Boston, Mass.", 269n.
Fisherman, The, 136-8
First World War, 190ff., 199
Fitzgerald, 15
Flecker, 38
Florian Geyer, 101
Flowers of Passion, 33
Foreign Affairs (U.S.A.), 201, 202, 205-6
Forster, E. M., 50, 66, 110, 156, 239, 273
Fortnightly, 187n.
Four Comely Ones, 243
Four Quartets, 57
Fox, 17
Frampton, Mrs. Jean, x
Free Church Council, 191
Freeman's Journal, 196, 204

INDEX

INDEX

INDEX

Morocco, 6
Morris, William, 22, 102, 163, 176
Morse, Dr. J. Mitchell, x, 267, 271n.
Morte d'Arthur, 85
Mosada, 112, 113
Moses, 24, 25, 75, 86, 121, 291
Mother, A, 253-4
Mourn—and then Onward, 121
Mr. Gregory's Letter-Box, 6, 84, 106
Mrs. Warren's Profession, 79
Muirthemni, Plain of, 260
Mummer's Wife, A, 33, 37, 41-2, 51, 56
Munich, 247
Municipal Gallery Revisited, The, 150, 163
My Diaries (Blunt), 292n.

NAPOLEON, 116, 117, 248
Nashe, 306
National Being, The, 26, 261
National Gallery, London, 84
National League, 1
National Liberal Federation, 1-2
Neander, 169
Nehru, 24
New Being, A, 181
New Republic, 245
New York, x, 39, 247
Newbolt, Henry, 97, 234
News for the Delphic Oracle, 163
Newtown Little, 212
Nibelungenlied, 85
Nineteenth Century, 90, 96n., 106
Noh plays, 138, 140
North, Violet (Mrs. G. W. Russell), 166
Nostos, 296n.
Notes and Queries, 268n.
Notes on Ulysses, 260n.
Nutt, Alfred, 275

O'BRIEN, R. BARRY, 152n., 292
O'Brien, William, 193, 195
O'Casey, Sean, 23, 86-7, 108, 303
O'Connell, Daniel, 4, 6-8, 24, 90, 117, 131,
    246, 300-2, 305, 308
O'Connor, Frank, 22, 231
O'Daly, 132
O'Duffy, 158
Odysseus, 25, 251n., 272
Odyssey, 258, 266, 272
O'Faolain, Sean, 143
O'Flaherty, 157
O'Grady, Standish, 4, 27, 28, 127-8, 154,
    206, 290, 306
O'Growney, Father Eugene, 93
O'Hagan, 97n.
O'Higgins, Kevin, 156-7, 158

O'Higginn, 132
O'Leary, 2
Oil and Blood, 148
On an Irish Hill, 176
On Baile's Strand, 159
*On Behalf of Some Irishmen not Followers of
    Tradition*, 182
*On Hearing that the Students of our New
    University have joined the Agitation
    against Immoral Literature*, 131
On the Border, 162, 163-4
O'Neill, Joseph, 210
"Open Letter to Lady Gregory", 150
Oscott, 32
O'Shea, Captain, 1, 298
O'Shea, Mrs. Kitty, 1, 3, 231, 264, 270,
    289, 291, 292-300, 302
Ossian, 240
Our Irish Theatre, 19n., 66n., 85n.
Oxford, 234

PAGAN POEMS, 33
Paid on Both Sides, 103
Pairc-na-Lee, 157
Palestine, 65, 72-3
Paracelsus, 11
Paradise Lost, 274, 281, 283
Paris, 32-3, 35ff., 40, 41, 52, 112, 135, 213,
    215, 246, 248, 259, 285, 302, 306
Parnell and His Island, 52, 250
Parnell, Charles Stewart, ix, 1-6, 8, 9,
    14-16, 27, 30, 33, 55, 56, 68, 86, 87,
    90, 91, 98, 106-7, 121-2, 130, 132, 133,
    137, 138, 150, 151, 153-4, 157-8, 173,
    185, 187, 204, 211, 231, 232, 233, 238,
    245, 249, 262, 264, 270, 273-4, 278n.,
    280, 282, 288, 289-90, 291-300, 301,
    304, 308
Parnell Commission, 187
Parnell's Funeral, 14, 122, 125, 157-8
Parnell, Mrs. 138
Parnell, Thomas, 297
Passage to India, 273
Pater, 40, 61, 250
Patrick, St., 240, 276
Paul, St., 34, 67, 74
Pearse, Patrick, 29, 160, 307
Peer Gynt, 26
Perfect Wagnerite, The, 26
Peronnik the Fool, 34, 215
Perspectives of Criticism, 22n.
Persse, Adelaide, 88
Persse, Dudley, 83
Philadelphia, 280
Phoenix Park murders, 187-8, 273
Piccolo della Sera, x, 3, 292
Piggot, 280, 299
Pilgrim's Progress, The, 17

315

INDEX

317

INDEX

Ulysses, 20, 23, 24, 26, 43n., 49, 155, 198, 218, 240, 241, 243, 244, 246, 247-8, 254, 257, 258-9, 260, 261, 262, 263, 267-72, 273, 274, 277, 282, 284, 285, 296-7, 300, 302
Un Jardin sur l'Oronte
Under Milk Wood, 99
Under Saturn, 111, 112
United Ireland, 121
University College, Dublin, 113, 246
Untilled Field, The, 61, 66, 77, 250

Vale, 34, 55, 67, 70-1, 82
Valley of the Black Pig, The, 13
Vanessa, 45, 152
Variorum Yeats, 115
Venice, 91, 119
Vernon, Diana, 120
Veronica's Napkin, 148
Victoria, Queen, 104, 174, 198
Vikings, The, 101
Virgil, 76
Vision, A, 18, 104, 137, 144-5, 146, 155, 212, 217, 274, 292
Visions and Beliefs in the West of Ireland, 85
Vizetelly, 51

Wade, Allan, 12, 89n., 126, 130n., 173n., 180n., 215n., 221n.
Wagner, 25-6, 56-8, 66-9, 75, 78, 278, 283
Waite, Arthur Edward, 11, 17, 18
Wales, 99
Wanderings of Oisin and Other Poems, The, 5, 112
Waring, 207
Warner, Rex, 153n.
Washington, D.C., 210
Waste Land, The, 39, 43n., 44, 57
Water Babies, The, 284
Watts, Mrs., 97, 234
W. B. Yeats, Man and Poet, 145n., 307
Weaver, Harriet, 247, 279, 280, 281
Wedding Gown, The, 62
Wedding-Party on the Eiffel Tower, The, 302
Weekes, Charles, 53n., 167, 199, 204
Well of All Healing, The, 139n.
Well of the Saints, The, 216, 218, 226, 233, 234
Wells, H. G., 44, 184, 245
When We Dead Awaken, 284
Where Angels Fear to Tread, 50
White Cockade, The, 86

Whitman, Walt, 171, 306
Wild Bird's Nest, Poems from the Irish, The, 22, 231n.
Wilde, Oscar, 273-4, 290
Wilkie, Sir David, 43
Wind among the Reeds, The, 114, 120, 123
Winding Stair, The, 148
Woman Young and Old, A, 154
Woolf, Leonard, 237, 247
Woolf, Virginia, 38, 51, 87, 232, 237-9, 247-8
Words upon the Windowpane, The, 45, 47, 49, 152, 159, 163, 291
Wordsworth, 102, 171, 202
World's Work, 185, 186

Yale Review, 101n.
Years, The, 238-9
Yeats, Anne, 163
Yeats, Elizabeth, 117
Yeats, George, 163
Yeats, J. B., 110, 115-16, 117, 121-2, 149, 200, 220, 227, 292
Yeats, Mrs. J. B., 110
Yeats, Mrs. W. B., 111, 114, 143-4
Yeats, W. B., ix, x, 2, 5, 7, 9, 10, 11-16, 17-18, 20, 23, 25-6, 27-8, 30-1, 32, 33, 34, 40, 44, 47, 49, 51, 52, 53n., 56, 60, 61, 62, 66, 76, 80, 83, 84-6, 87, 88-9, 90, 92, 93, 97, 97-8, 99, 100, 101, 103-5, 106, 108, 109, 110-64, 165, 166, 167, 168, 169, 170, 171, 173, 174, 175, 176, 178, 180, 181, 187, 188, 198, 199, 200, 201, 202, 205, 207, 209, 212, 213, 214-15, 217, 218, 219, 220, 221, 226, 227-8, 229, 231, 232, 234, 235, 236, 238, 240, 241, 243, 248, 252, 253, 254, 258n., 272, 274, 278, 279, 281, 285, 286, 287, 288, 289, 290, 292, 295-6, 297, 303, 304, 307-8
Yeats: the Man and the Masks, 12, 121n., 174n.
Yeo, Colonel, 9
York, Archbishop of, 191
Young Ireland, 22, 117, 151
Young Ireland movement, 117-18, 173, 289
Younger (brewer), 194n.
Yudkin, Dr. Simon, x
Ypres, 192

Zola, Emile, 33, 42, 47n., 54, 56, 61, 73, 254